Liana, the one who taught me unconditional love and non-judgement, this was the book I wrote for you... Your heart and spirit will always be my life's anchor, and if I were one-one-millionth as flawless in your eyes and heart as you will forever be in mine, I know I have lived a life worth living.

My deepest, most special thanks to my mother, father, brother, my daughter Yasemin and son Alkan for being the greatest gifts of my life; whatever I do has always been for all of you.

Eternally grateful to Nina and Tamaz, your daughter was the embodiment of an Angel on Earth; her brilliance, beauty and impeccable character were passed down and a reflection from both of you. I thank God every day for having blessed us all with her presence, and I know her legacy will live on forever.

EndGamers

Dominic V Knight

Clink
Street

Published by Clink Street Publishing 2023

Copyright © 2023

First edition

The author asserts the moral right under the Copyright, Designs and Patents Act 1988 to be identified as the author of this work.

All rights reserved. No part of this publication may be reproduced, stored in a retrieval system or transmitted, in any form or by any means without the prior consent of the author, nor be otherwise circulated in any form of binding or cover other than that with which it is published and without a similar condition being imposed on the subsequent purchaser.

ISBN: 978-1-913136-30-7 - paperback
978-1-913136-31-4 - ebook

Disclaimer

Nothing in this book is to be taken as medical or financial advice in any way whatsoever, it is exclusively for information purposes only, the author accepts no responsibility for any interpretation or misinterpretation of the text. The reader is solely responsible for their own interpretations and behaviours. The author clearly states that anything of medical or financial nature should always be conducted under the guise of a registered medical or financial professional.

Contents

Introduction

This book is for anyone who rejects the notion that their dreams must be immaterial. It distils nearly two decades of research and practice conducted in Harley Street, both as a Master NLP Practitioner and Business Consultant. I have worked with both people struggling with emotional problems and with clients and companies who went from the inception of an idea to reaching astronomical growth and even unicorn status. I developed and evolved methods, enabling them to unlock their true potential through cognitive restructuring. I created *EndGamers* based on a simple yet revolutionary theory: any problem or presumed limitation holding one back could be solved as quickly as it started – at the speed of thought.

Believe you cannot fail, and you never truly will. This is the core of *EndGamers*. The stories, messages and parables have been deliberately dramatised, loaded with suggestions, embedded commands and language designed to uplift, inspire and most of all evoke the requisite feelings to make things finally work. We learn through emotions as emotions are the building blocks that construct our reality; imagination produces a feeling that creates an activation in the essential part of the grey matter. Science now proves that our brains are designed to learn through narratives. As for the academic, when brains are scanned it becomes quite easy to observe that, in thinking out a solution, *the brain formulates and translates abstract imaginary numbers and equations into eloquent illustrations.*

An athlete visualising a championship is imagining an unknown; an architect, a musician – it's all imagination. The richer the imagination, the faster it appears that the universe renders the image into physical form. Mathematics began as a way to quantify our world, measure land, keep track of exchange and even calculate the distance of planets. As this field advanced it reached a point where specific calculations were impossible, birthing what was and is still known as 'imaginary numbers'. Go as far as you can and the only way to stretch further is to imagine more.

We only have one shot at life; you, reading this book, are one in a trillion (current scientific calculation) and knowingly or unknowingly are privileged and blessed; throw as many excuses as you want of the odds being against you and I can conclusively tell you that you are wrong. The odds of you being here have positioned you as royalty. No one is above or below you, and the same stream of life runs through us all. Those who appear to oppose you or that you perceive to stifle your progression are characters in life playing their chosen roles, providing resistance to strengthen both your will and resolve as well as forcing your brain into imagination mode, a compassionate act of the universe impelling you to realise that inherent within the problem is the image of a solution reflected right back at you. Though absent of instructions, the only route to reach the EndGame is in your own self-belief and nothing else...

This compendium will enable readers to overcome the power of their own preconceptions and ignite a passion through excellence and unleash the 'EndGamer' inside.

I have intentionally changed some of the chronological order of events to ensure a smoother flow and an easier read throughout the book. Each chapter builds upon the last, from the inception of a desire, right the way through to leadership and legacy. This is a book with no limits or restrictions, equipping you with the tools to design life on your terms and achieve the very things you had once considered impossible.

It was a regular Thursday afternoon, and I looked casually through my book collection as I awaited my next client. I picked-up a copy of *Teachings of Billionaire Yen Tzu* and thumbed through the pages. Metaphors, fables and stories are the language of change, not facts and figures. Perhaps the methods of ancient civilisations using language to equilibrate the mind were more effective than the profit-driven chemicals of today's advanced medics. Let us not forget the power of placebo; the stories, whether true or false, undeniably elicit healing. Words many times have the power to be loaded with more tranquillising substance than a full dose of valium. Don't get me wrong: drugs do have a time and place, yet just like anything else they need to be carefully monitored. In fact, most drugs serve the purpose of instructing the brain to release or restrict more of what it naturally produces. A drug will rarely introduce something into the mental software that isn't already there.

Religious texts are rich with deep metaphors. An adept scholar of any religion attempts to derive meaning from the narratives, or to deliver their accounts as life lessons, replete with wisdom; they may be likened to a trained art critic whose eyes attempt to derive meaning from the stories told by the combination of paints on the canvas. *Their colours, and even the rhythm of the brushstrokes, have a profound story to tell.*

The phone on my desk rings, and my receptionist informs me that my client has arrived. Helping a teenage boy who has been having uncontrollable bouts of anxiety at school is never an easy task. Every one of us has a safety system in place which attempts to extricate us from a situation we don't want to be in. In fact, the only time it is a problem is if the signal produced becomes so exaggerated by the body that it creates great discomfort, and then it is seen as a threat to our very survival.

I don't blame any teen for their chaotic behaviours and many internecine decisions. *Parents most often need greater direction and understanding than the teenager.* A parent's confusion over a teen's dysfunctional behaviour is no more bewildering than the confusion of why a drunk person struggles to put words together. *It's obvious: judgement is impaired by biology; a child will throw a tantrum because it's instinctive and part of development.* A teenager's ration has not yet fully formed and the natural rebellion occurs through the concoction of hormones playing havoc with both reason and sense to help break away from the nest.

Though these years appear to be joyous and free – a time to explore with curiosity – they undeniably have their fair share of torments, and no one makes it through their teens unscathed. From the unsuspecting popular kids to the shy reserved child in the corner of the room, and even to the bullies themselves, plagued with self-doubt and insecurities, it is my personal view there is no such thing as someone with a superiority complex. There is only an inferiority complex whereupon one attempts to belittle another. Of course, they are only doing so out of fear and an attempt to gain significance, something we all naturally crave by biological design.

The tragedy is the aggressor knows no other way, and ends up not only breaking down another person but breaking down themselves. True significance is a result of excellence of character and achievement in worthy ideals, yet those ideals are rarely reached in the teens. If they are, then they have a way of fizzling out far more quickly than the breakthroughs which can happen later in life.

The truth is that everyone suffers and some just conceal it better than others. Whether it be raging testosterone, hormones, temper, agitation, rebellion, yearning to break free from the nest – it is all a cocktail for countless battles. Although rarely taken to the concrete surface of the world, these battles are always waged within. With all that in mind, I open my office door and pause briefly before introducing myself. I could see he was fifteen years old with a twinkle in his eye, and that there was something special with this one. It could only be described as a strong presence, a soul beaming with potential. No, I am not peering into the future, but I recognised in his tone of voice, his body language and from his general demeanour that he projected a bright future. In that moment, having been informed by his parents about the myriad of issues he was struggling with, I knew immediately that he came pre-equipped with his own limitless supply of rocket fuel. I was only there to provide the spark necessary in hastening his journey to the top.

"So, what brings you here?" I ask.

"I just have a build-up of tension in class. It feels uncontrollable and I want to escape."

"You know, there were many classes I couldn't wait to get out of myself, so I am with you on that one. You get totally stressed? So would I if I were somewhere I didn't enjoy."

I was mirroring back every truism, and I knew he felt understood. I said, "It's not really an issue of an anxiety attack, it's more to do with learning to be patient. Remember, that time will pass and no sensation in the body lasts forever. Nerves habituate and what that means is, as uncomfortable as any feeling may appear, if you felt it constantly it would cancel itself out and neutralise. Your body needs to learn you are not under any threat, that you are in charge of the powerful stallion that will take you wherever you wish. But only if you take charge of the reins.

"What is it you are most passionate about?"

"Football! My mum said I even used to sleep in my football boots. I live it and breathe it."

"If anything were possible, what would you do?" I ask him.

"Play in front of the nation."

"You know, dreams have meaning. There was a painter called Van Gogh, who once said, *I dream my painting and then I paint my dream.* Of course, one must back this up with practice. Why don't we start recognising the things you like, and then get you to trust yourself? You are so preoccupied with how you think your body will react that you predictably bring it upon yourself. *Stop doing that!* Let's make a massive overhaul and redesign what's under the bonnet. I'm going to help you learn to think in a way that will propel you in any direction you wish to travel. This isn't anything I am doing – I am only suggesting things. It's you who are in the driver's seat. I say, *it's time for you to trust you!*"

A couple of years had passed, and one afternoon on my social media feed I saw a victory goal and I instantly recognised the face of the player who had made the winning kick. It was Kem Cetinay scoring the winning goal at a soccer event, playing along with a star-studded team which not only had an audience close to forty thousand but also raised over £38 million in aid for UNICEF!

Cetinay had gone on to become a celebrity in his own right, deciding to slay his demons by boldly throwing himself into the firing line of reality TV in the midst of peak emotional turmoil to finally gain control. This led to appearances on many popular TV shows, and even having his own successful line of clothing. Now an advocate for helping all who experience inevitable moments of a turbulent mind, Cetinay transformed his life by acting, in spite of how he felt. He had taken charge of his destiny, and this was far from a lucky break. Cetinay had planted the seeds for his future during some of his toughest times, and now he was reaping the harvest in the most unexpected ways.

It would be near-enough impossible for anyone to map out a blueprint for this journey. *The only clear agenda is to make the most of what you have while being your best in every moment.*

That evening, I headed to afternoon tea with my parents and their guests, who had just arrived from Turkey. My father's friend asked me what I do, and with Cetinay's moment still fresh in my head I paused, reflecting back over nearly two decades of research and work.

"Create EndGamers," I replied.

"And how do you do that?" he asked.

"I simply reduce any doubts they may have about their potential, and have them conclusively recognise that the qualities they wish to express already reside within them. This evokes a true sense of self which provides them with the tools to become an architect of their own destiny."

"You should write a book," he replies.

CHAPTER ONE

EndGamers: Architects of Destiny

There are some people who live in a dream world and there are some who face reality, and then there are those who turn one into the other. – Erasmus

This book is not designed for any person satisfied with the mediocre or the one who argues vehemently for limitation. It is for the freethinker, the one who, if thrown to the wolves, comes back with the pack; the person capable of extrapolating right from wrong and able to decipher the areas they need to work on for themselves en route to becoming their own greatest ideal, their own living hero.

When peering into the past, a common theme emerges about the people who seem to shape and steer our reality: when met with the illusion of unfavourable conditions they use the presented stimulus to redesign the world, on their terms. Circumstances have no place in their vocabulary because they create their own circumstances. Any outdated ideas, mistakes or behaviours, though acknowledged and reformed, have no basis for defining who they are as they recognise that even the noblest amongst us– the likes of Mandela, Jobs, Nightingale and even Gandhi – began with questionable pasts, moving forward as renegades to reshape the world.

This compendium for life has no real beginning and no real end. Your ideas will be challenged, your emotions charged, and your thinking will be improved. You may find yourself returning to some of these chapters many times throughout your life. I have attempted to fill this book with knowledge, along with timeless life principles. I have also incorporated some of the latest findings in neuroscience, psychology and quantum physics; in doing so, I have attempted to filter out pseudoscience to produce a piece of work that will stand the test of time.

My goal and ultimate vision for this manual of life is in affirming the wisdom of the past while paving the way for the future.

This book is a courageous attempt to ignite the EndGamer in You!

EndGamer

noun

One who is never constrained by reality, adept at turning imagination into tangible form by evoking requisite feelings, an architect of destiny.

I want you to imagine for a moment that you have no limitations whatsoever, that absolutely anything in life you desire can be yours. Because all the things you could need – all the knowledge, experience, qualifications, money, resources and connections necessary to make your dream a reality – are already in your possession right now, this very moment.

If you knew you could not fail, what would you be compelled to do?

You may find it hard to imagine such a scenario. Maybe you've long given up on ever realising the dreams you once had for your life. If that's your experience, then you'll want to pay attention to what I'm about to say…

This book was written for you.

You see, I know without a doubt you are designed for success. You are engineered for greatness. And you already possess everything you need to fulfil every desire of your heart. I don't expect you to agree with me yet. All I ask is that you evaluate the evidence I will share with you in every chapter of this book. Then – and only then – decide for yourself whether or not what I'm telling you is so.

To begin, allow me to share a true story…

At first glance, a skinny boy growing up in an inner-city borough of south London appeared to have very little going for him. He was generally unwell from birth and continually in and out of hospital during the first six years of his life. As a result, he consistently came last in all his school's sporting events. Even peers in class saw him as weak and without promise.

Primary school presented its own set of challenges. Chronic attention deficit disorder rendered him incapable of focusing on his studies or adhering to the demands of a standardised classroom environment. He was soon labelled a misfit and a troublemaker. However, despite his difficult beginnings, this young boy had a dream. For as early as he could remember, he dreamed of one day becoming a great fighter.

And because his dream was so vivid, the image he saw when he looked in the mirror was quite different from what everyone else saw. Instead of a sickly child, he envisioned an intimidating competitor capable of knocking out any adversary or opponent he faced. His dream was so absolute to him that when he was only six years old, barely tipping 43 pounds, he began learning karate under the watchful eye of his great-uncle, Eddie Emin.

All he could think about was preparing himself for the one thing he wanted more than anything else in the world.

Unsurprisingly, the famous actor and martial artist the Dragon Bruce Lee became his idol.

Lee believed in using martial arts only in actual circumstances for self-defence. As a result, he never fought in tournaments where rules and restrictions controlled the outcome. This philosophy resonated with the young boy, and following the untimely death of the iconoclast at the age of 32, the boy committed himself to pick up where the Dragon left off. On hearing an interview where the icon boldly claimed: "I am probably the greatest fighter in the world," he knew what he had to do.

In college, he continued to train with a vengeance, pushing himself beyond all reasonable physical limits.

Then, waking one dismal morning in excruciating pain, he realised his body was no longer responding. It had thrown in the towel. MRI scans confirmed multiple prolapses and spinal deterioration. The unavoidable addiction to painkillers came at a high price. After a couple of years of emotional turbulence, broken relationships and financial hardship, he found himself at the bottom of the food chain. But somehow, somewhere in the dark recesses of his mind, he never let go of his dream. He knew he would one day rise from the ashes, rebuild his body, and step into the ring again. He held firm to his belief – even while standing nervously in the doctor's practice awaiting the inevitable prognosis.

"You may as well come to terms with the fact that you'll never fight again. You'll be lucky to lift a tea kettle, much less another weight. You're wasting your time and money on rehabilitation. Your only hope is major surgery – spinal infusions – and, of course, you already know these come with no guarantee." He'd heard enough. He hobbled out of the room, slamming the door behind him. The X-rays and MRIs documented the surgeon's prognosis. But with everything in him, the fighter kept fighting, although now he fought to hold fast to his dream and not let it die.

He was certainly no stranger to difficulty. But always before, when he encountered problems, he found solace in his training. It had been his lifelong companion, helping him deal with and overcome life's many obstacles. Now that was gone too. In what seemed like an instant, he lost everything that mattered to him. Everything he lived for and had now hit rock bottom. Confined indoors, completely alone and alienated from the outside world, he was faced with a decision: to completely give up or commit to working on the only thing he had left – his MIND.

The fighter in him welcomed the challenge. He knew what he must do. Driven by the same obsession he'd always had for fighting, he began his quest for answers. He researched everything he could find on his condition. The medical literature had nothing to offer. Every documented case study he could see only confirmed his surgeon's dismal prognosis.

And although a few alternative health practitioners hinted at a more hopeful solution, they all fell short of producing any tangible and lasting results. So he dug deeper until he ran across some case studies that had been done on the mind–body connection, which proved to be quite an incredible discovery – a phenomenon known as 'spontaneous remissions'.

'Spontaneous remissions', by definition, are when something that is considered 'incurable' disappears – and though occurrences of this phenomenon are rare, the experiences are well documented in scientific literature. But what was even more startling was the fact that the only common denominator among those individuals who reported an incident of spontaneous remission was BELIEF!

In other words, in every one of the documented cases of spontaneous remission, the person with the 'incurable' diagnosis held firm to the belief that they would be cured – despite all the objective evidence to the contrary. He had found what he was looking for – a glimmer of hope for his complete recovery.

This discovery sparked an insatiable desire to learn everything he could about how the mind works. Could it be that our mind creates the body, or is it the body making the mind? He began devouring hundreds of books and scientific journals on the mind–body connection. Further topics were researched, relating to religion, psychology and philosophy. Distilling the wisdom and dissecting the knowledge of the world's leading thinkers, both past and present, was no easy task. Common themes kept re-emerging; if the mind were balanced, everything would naturally follow as dusk does till dawn. Thoughts are as tangible as the stars you see in the sky; thoughts create chemical reactions in the body and are the foundational building blocks of our existence.

He developed relationships with world-renowned philosophers and thinkers and attended seminars by the likes of Dr Richard Bandler (co-creator of Neuro-Linguistic Programming: NLP). Then the phase of attending lectures by intellectuals and academics like Stephen Hawking and Richard Dawkins. The final stage was learning from complementary thinkers and spiritualists like Deepak Chopra on the other side of the spectrum.

Fascinated by the mysteries of the subconscious mind, he began researching Freud's theories on both the subconscious and unconscious mind and then moved to learn the works of psychiatrist and medical hypnotherapist Dr Milton Erickson. After endless hours of trial and error, he was finally able to expose the missing piece of the puzzle – the secret to directly communicating with that part of you that controls your every heartbeat and breath.

… the subconscious mind.

At that moment – in what felt like the blink of an eye – his life went from darkest night to brightest day.

The dream held dormant for so long began to take shape once again. Visualisations crystallised. His body began to regenerate itself, almost miraculously, and the pain started to disappear.

Fast forward a few more years, and you'd hardly recognise this strapping specimen of a man as he bears only traces of resemblance to the bent, debilitated patient who lumbered out of the surgeon's practice years earlier.

His body is now completely healed, yet he is still suffering from years of residual financial duress. He hears of a business venture in Turkey that comes complete with a connected bloodline and a hint of superstition, so he feels this is a sign. Believing this could be the one that will turn everything around for him, he begins to prepare for his trip.

It is the beginning of May, and having just enough time before his meetings, he conducts his regular morning ritual – an Earl Grey in the Langham Hotel. Walking through the grand lobby, he heads to their Artisan bar. While awaiting the hostess to direct him to his table, he casually looks around, and his eyes are drawn to a girl perched on a seat by the window.

Luxuriant dark hair, neatly pulled back, is accentuated by perfectly shaped cheekbones. Distinct dark lashes ornament her inquisitive brown eyes. An impeccable appearance, wearing a long turquoise décolleté dress with a silk necktie – she exudes a presence that captivates his attention, an irresistible mixture of grace, innocence, and class. To him, she is a perfect throwback to the days of Audrey Hepburn.

She glances at him. Their eyes meet, briefly at first, and then instantly, they are the only two people in the world. Nothing is said – yet everything is communicated between them at that moment.

His mind goes into overdrive, attempting to formulate an opener. What does he say to her? He notices the name of the book she is reading, *The Man Who Planted Trees*, by the French author Jean Giono.

Walking over boldly to override the gut anxiety, he builds the nerve to ask about the book. They soon begin to engage in conversation. She is part Georgian, part Siberian, and ironically, has family living just minutes from his office. She is in the process of developing a bespoke wellness centre that will use the latest technologies from around the world to rejuvenate both body and mind. She hopes it will bring genuine healing for anyone who joins, in an environment that feels like a home away from home.

He listens attentively, and then there is a moment of silence as he processes his thoughts, which go something like this: you are building that for yourself. It is a place you were searching for but could never find, so you decided to create this yourself. This has nothing to do with making profits for you.

He decides to chance speaking his thoughts out loud.

She sits still, listening, and then pauses in astonishment. "Who are you, and how did you know that?"

"It was the sincerity in your eyes," he replies. "I'm currently working on a book. It has to do with pushing the boundaries of human potential, evoking latent resources to enable change at the speed of thought… be the change you wish to see in the world." He pauses and then smiles. "By the way, that was a quote from Gandhi…"

"And you are writing that for yourself?" she mirrors back his statement. "I shall read it."

He pauses, eyes dipping down to his gut and smoothly raising back up in one fluid motion and then locking on to hers. Pupil to pupil, her eyes dart left and right. The ceaseless dialogue continues in his mind. "Read it? You are living it."

The conversation continues – he mentions an upcoming trip to Istanbul, and she replies, "I am heading there myself for a friend's wedding later this year." He notices her response appeared spontaneous and orchestrated simultaneously, almost as if destiny was positioning and guiding their lives to collide artfully.

"Tequilas tonight?" he asks her.

"How did you know I like tequila?" she smiles.

At 7 p.m. sharp, she pulls up by his office in a customised G-Wagon, a stark contrast to the petite and delicately ornamented young woman he had observed earlier. Somehow, the vehicle symbolically honours both the feminine and masculine within, he muses to himself.

They head to Meraki Bar as Mediterranean cuisine would surely set the perfect stage. Greeted by renowned founder Alain Dona. Dona a serial entrepreneur and connector in the private circles of the worlds elite, had also been instrumental in mentoring the protagonist. He escorts the couple to an exclusive section and has them treated as royalty, it was as if the dreams of a lifetime where now falling into place.

He lies in bed at dawn, realising the time with her sped as fast as the blinking of an eye. He feels compelled to deliver a heartfelt prayer as he drifts off to sleep. "For the first time in my life, I hand my plans over to you," he says out loud. "If I am good for her, and she for me, then bring us together."

He is left feeling overcome by the powerful force of this newfound love. The blossoming energy serves as a catalyst which he soon finds propelling him to far greater heights than he has ever known before.

Several months pass, and during one late Sunday evening, he is watching the finals of Pride FC, Japan's most notorious and dangerous martial arts event, the one with the fewest rules. The thought flashes into his mind:

'What would it be like to compete and fight for real?'

The following day whilst boarding the Victoria Line underground on the way to work, he notices a billboard advertising a seminar; the headline reads:

What one great thing would you do if you knew you could not fail?

The answer is unconscious, instantaneous. "I'm going to fight again; it's time to prove to myself I'm unbeatable; there is no time like the present to slay my own dragons!"

By now, you may suspect that the skinny boy, the patient crippled by pain, the rehabilitated man, infatuated with someone from another world and the author of this book are one and the same. And you are right. This story is my story.

And I'm sharing it with you so that no matter wherever you are in your life right now, you know I have been there too, not only emotionally but physically, financially. And I may have just discovered the way to turn everything around.

Now back to the story…

Though I had been fully rehabilitated, the memory of it still haunted me. I had trained well, but I hadn't faced an opponent since before that injury took me out of the ring all those years ago, derailing my dream. Nevertheless,

I made up my mind. The desire to fight again, fuelled by my passion for fulfilling a childhood dream, gave me all the resolve I needed.

I knew what I had to do.

I searched for the next scheduled Pride FC event. As fate would have it, professional trials were to be held in Los Angeles in two months. Try-outs were open to anyone worldwide. My heart skipped a beat.

With only weeks to prepare and a medical certification to pass, it was an understatement to say I had the deck stacked against me. Besides, there were thousands of applicants – all highly skilled fighters, many of them professionals. What chance did I have? Though I wasn't sure how I would ever pull this off, I knew one thing for sure – I was determined not to live the rest of my life in regret. Regardless of the odds, I would apply, I would pass medicals, and I would compete.

Mid-November, seven days before my flight was scheduled to leave, I made my way to an old secluded training ground, a park in New Cross, South London. The grass was still wet from the morning dew. A fresh mist filled the air under an overcast sky. The silence was broken only by the chirping of birds and the occasional rustling leaf. I began with my standard routine – closing my eyes, focusing on breathing, emptying my mind of the usual chatter, centring myself into the silence and solitude of the moment. In that space, I summoned the resources of the universe to provide everything I needed to make my deepest desire a reality.

While in this state of heightened awareness, I sensed a familiar presence. Opening my eyes, I turned. "Dom!" Sia, the 280-pound martial arts trainer who'd worked with me since college, called out to me, arms open and beaming.

Sia was a different breed – ex-SAS, a combat veteran and former amateur boxer who trained with several of Bruce Lee's original students. I knew the routine. We made our way to Sia's training facility to begin the gruelling preparation. The semi-terraced house he occupied was void of the usual furnishings, having been converted into a hand-to-hand combat training compound, complete with all sorts of equipment sufficient to either confirm one's mortality or transform one into Superman himself.

If you think I'm exaggerating, you should take a closer look.

One of the more 'notable' pieces of equipment was a floor-to-ceiling punch ball adorned with taped army knives. To make friends with this one, you had to learn to not only punch with the precision of a master but also deftly avoid a potentially fatal return attack.

This exercise always reminded me of a game of Russian roulette – except here, your destiny lay squarely in your own hands.

Trials would consist of three, five-minute rounds per opponent, so I knew I needed to be 110% for a full five minutes. We planned to prepare for a solid twenty-minute match – essentially quadruple what would be required. As a fighter, you do what no one else is doing. You push yourself beyond reasonable limits, both physically and psychologically, until you reach a point where your mind is no longer calculating moves. Your body acts and responds on instinct. Sia and I were both well aware of this fact.

We were two long, gruelling hours into the session. Overcome with nausea, I was on the verge of collapse from the punching, kicking and grappling sequences. I had reached my threshold of pain. Sweating profusely, feeling like my heart was near exploding, I saw that look in Sia's eyes. I knew what it meant, like a sixth sense anticipating your opponent's next move. Suddenly – without warning – he wielded a switchblade from an inside pocket. Armed with a short stick in one hand and that glistening blade in the other, he swung at me with force sufficient to kill.

Sia's timing was calculated. He knew what he wanted, and he got it. My body had reached the tipping point and responded instinctively, moving without thought or deliberation. My pure fighting instincts had taken over, successfully evading the onslaught of his attack.

Sia stopped as abruptly as he'd begun. "Your training is now complete."

Morning of the Trials

Fear is a legitimate component of being alive. In the presence of real danger or risk, the level of fear naturally mirrors the degree of danger.

I was about to enter an arena where my fighting and survival acumen would be severely tested. I was voluntarily subjecting myself to one of the most dangerous environments in the world. I had pushed my body to extremes of human potential – well beyond acceptable limits – to prepare for this moment, a moment I had dreamed of and aspired to my whole life. But my mind was fighting tooth and nail against me. On the brink of caving in, fear had me locked in a stranglehold.

My inner voice told me I couldn't go through with it. The surgeon's prognosis, "You'll never fight again," rang incessantly in my ears. Flashbacks of my dad in tears as he watched my great-uncle attempt to straighten my body and help me walk.

"You can't do this; what do you think you're doing? One more injury and it's the nail in the coffin."

My inner dialogue was eating me alive, and with trembling knees, I gave in. I couldn't go through with it. I walked out of the arena to the parking lot to catch the first flight back. It wasn't worth it. I called my daughter to say I would be home soon, then spent some time speaking with my son. My heart gave a massive pang. In these moments, our true character is revealed.

My greatest aspiration as a father is to be a good role model for my children, to illustrate by my life that anything is possible and when you move in the direction of your heart – win or lose – the outcome will be for the greater good. I understood what victory would mean at that moment, and I knew I had to do it for them. Making it through these trials would be a breakthrough metaphor for anything else I would attempt in life.

Though the fear was still very much alive, my collected life experiences taught me the correct response to fear in this context is to see it as a green light to move ahead. Otherwise, you can never achieve any dream you aspire. I was aware of this logically, but of course, my body was still responding as if under threat of attack. However, with newfound resolve, my fear began to subside.

I became the adventurer I read about in novels, searching for my treasure, ready to conquer whatever obstacles came my way.

"I haven't come this far only to come this far!"

I leveraged my adrenaline and used it as a tool to make me sharper. I quieted my anxious dialogue and replaced it with empowering thoughts. Then I took a massive 180-degree turn and walked back into the arena.

Thomas Edison once said, "Nearly every man who develops an idea works it up to the point where it looks impossible, and then he gets discouraged. That's not the place to become discouraged."

Objectively, nothing had changed. The odds were still not in my favour. That was a fact, and I knew it. But I also knew it was time to create my own odds.

Moment of Truth

I had never felt more alone in all my life than I did at that moment. There would be no team effort, as every single person was there for themselves. Once this night was over, broken bones, spirits and dreams would undoubtedly be everywhere.

I signed an inch-thick document containing all the legal disclaimers. I raced through the medical questions, swallowing hard as I did so.

I grabbed a skipping rope and some cables to warm up, then hit the push-ups to pump myself up for the camera shots.

Following a couple of shadow-boxing moves, I felt a slight twinge in my spine. My eyes welled up involuntarily. I prayed my body would not quit on me.

My number was called. I stripped down to my bare briefs for the weigh-in and professional poses. My weight was on the number – a perfect 195 lbs.

I was pitted against a two-time MMA Champion with a string of victories – extensively more professional experience than me. In the bleak chance of winning, I would have several more fights to contend with and isolated testing rounds in each range of combat. I would need to prove competency to strike, wrestle, grapple and the ability to put the whole combination together.

The threat was real. The matches would be gruelling and dangerous. Some of the Pride FC management and Bas Rutten, a movie star/martial arts icon and former UFC Champion, would be judging (and scouting talent).

My heart pounded out of my chest.

My opponent and I took our positions, toe-to-toe. I heard the referee call out: "You know the rules: hit to hurt. Go for the knockout or submission [making your opponent say 'I quit'] and aim not to leave it up to the judges."

I slipped in my gum shield…

What happens next will be shared a bit later.

But for now, let's get back to the question I posed to you at the very beginning:

If you knew you could not fail, what one thing would you be compelled to do?

How did you answer that question?

Become a millionaire or billionaire? Develop an aesthetically flawless physique you've always dreamed of? Celebrity? Win over someone's heart, content, world peace, happiness?

So, what's holding you back?

Suppose all the information you need to accomplish any goal is readily available, which theoretically it is. Why is it that two people may target the same marketplace be in the same industry, use a near identical approach, and one triumphs, whilst the other makes nil?

Here's a statistic that will blow your mind. Eric Schmidt, former Chairman of Google, quoted at a tech conference: five exabytes (exa = one billion billion) of new information is discovered in the world every 48 hours! That's more information than was found from the dawn of time until 2003.

Now, think about this.

If there is a blueprint for just about anything you want to accomplish that is easily accessible and works almost every time with a few adjustments, why isn't everyone successful to their desired degree?

Why can't we apply the available information to achieve the goal we desire and move immediately into the realm of dreams fulfilled?

The reason may surprise you, but studies in psychology and physiology have shown that it's because our bodies are genetically hardwired to automatically pull us away from a sensation of discomfort or confusion and move us back to a state of comfort and equilibrium.

(It's the psychological equivalent of quickly removing your hand from something hot so you don't get burned.)

In all likelihood, you are where you are in life because it is 'comfortable' and familiar. Even if your relationships are dysfunctional, you don't have enough money to pay your bills, or you're not in the best of health, these are all familiar problems. They may be painful on one level, but it is a pain you're at least familiar with. In essence, you're in a 'comfort zone'. Further, the repetition and duration of being the way you are has sculpted your identity/self-concept, so you think and behave in predictable ways, which are based on past reference points; in doing so, your identity, your consciousness how you perceive yourself has been rigidly confined, there is a route out, and that's a complete overhaul of identity, and in doing so becoming the person, who can not only have and achieve the things they want on this planet but also leave their footprint in history and example for generations to come.

Let's look at the following example: in your current profession you already recognise there is room for so much growth. If you could have what you wanted, you'd take charge of your life and even 10x your income.

Why then – when there's more than enough information available to help you achieve those goals – do you still get up every day without total follow-through?

It's because, to do something different, you have to step out of your comfort zone, which is nothing other than a sensation in your body that feels risky, uncomfortable and scary as well as contradicts your current view of who you are. So even if you begin to move in the direction of change, your body senses the discomfort and fear then pulls you back to a level of equilibrium or what I like to refer to it as your 'setpoint' back to the familiar. You may on one level say you are not scared, but the reality is you are; procrastination is a biological response to fear.

When you must do something that makes you feel uncomfortable, have you noticed what great lengths you go to to create some form of distraction? For example, you may pick up the phone and call a friend, aimlessly browse social media, turn on the TV or do anything else that moves you back toward something more comfortable. Why does this matter?

Because until you learn how to interrupt this cycle and override your hardwired response, and develop the 'will' to follow through, you can never accomplish what you want to accomplish. You will never achieve what you aspire to and can never become the person you want to be.

In his classic *Think and Grow Rich*, Napoleon Hill wisely states:

"Whatever the mind of man can conceive and bring himself to believe he can achieve."

(In his private lectures, Hill commented on this universal truth, saying he used "can" – and not "will" – intentionally because to achieve it is up to you.)

After reading hundreds of books on the topics of personal achievement, psychology and philosophy and studying under some of the most illuminated minds in this field, I have discovered a rather simple technique that allows you to overrule the discomfort impulse and set yourself up with the potential to create anything in life you desire.

Using this technique, you can give yourself a command that overrides the uneasiness you feel when you decide to move in the direction of a new goal, allowing you to pursue that goal more freely and predictably.

The various methods and techniques I teach have been field-tested many times over, not only in my own life but also in the lives of my thousands of clients, some of whom you will meet in this book.

(In fact, I have logged 14,846 client hours using the very same methods I will be sharing with you in detail within the later chapters.)

We will now bring our attention to some foundational truths that must be established, explained and understood before proceeding; this is because our belief is directly linked to our very own biology Developing a sense of certainty in your potential literally unlocks your brains capacity to permit your body to follow through.

Let's begin with a basic understanding of the human potential.

Your body is made up of tissues and organs, which are made up of cells. Cells are made up of molecules; molecules are made up of atoms, atoms are made up of subatomic particles (protons, neutrons and electrons). And subatomic particles are made up of frozen light, which, explored deeper, is pure energy.

In other words, if you could examine yourself under a sufficiently powerful electron microscope, breaking every structural component in your body down to its most singular form, you would be left with nothing but pure, raw, potential energy.

And beyond that, you find nothing – apart from a pure potentiality amplitude, meaning anything can be created from it. That's the quantum 'soup' from which everything in the universe arises.

In short, you are a cluster of ever-changing pure energy – the same substance as the stars you see at night.

In other words, you are not in the universe; you are one with the universe .

And so is everyone and everything else around you. (I know this is mind-blowing, but these facts are well documented in the field of science known as quantum physics.)

Our universe began as a moment of pure potentiality seeking expression – manifesting all that is from the singular purest form of energy.

Humanity is an integral part of that pure potentiality. We all come to exist from that singular beginning and as such, are all interconnected – all part of this one essential matrix we refer to as 'the universe'.

So here is the first principle that must be understood:

Recognise you are an independent original idea of creation, energy in its purest form and you exist within and are an integral part of this universal matrix of pure potentiality that is 'the universe'. As such, by aligning with this realm of pure potentiality, recognising that this power flows through everything, you can set in motion every resource you need to come to your aid in the fulfilment of your desired goal.

The second principle that must be understood to achieve your desires is the significance of objective reality versus subjective reality, in order to extricate yourself from what your senses perceive. For our purposes, 'objective reality' will include the aspects of our physical world that appear to the naked eye to be factual, provable and documentable from a rational and reasonable perspective. Referencing my personal story, the MRIs and X-rays that the surgeon considered to offer a prognosis of my condition would be examples of objective evidence or objective reality.

And had I accepted this objective 'evidence' as my fait accompli, my body would have begun responding in sync with my belief.

I would have grown continually weaker until, eventually, I would've been bedridden from the pain of a debilitating condition.

Now, contrast with 'subjective reality' – the truth about me and my understanding of the universe that I choose to believe in my mind.

Please do not miss the point I am about to make.

If I had *chosen* to believe the objective reality that my surgeon was trying to get me to buy into, there would have been no distinction or difference between my subjective reality and my objective reality.

However, since I am pure potentiality – pure energy that is ever-changing, constantly creating and being created – I have the power to choose a more desirable (subjective) reality if, in fact, I do not like and therefore don't agree to accept whatever objective reality I am experiencing at any given moment.

This truth is what makes Einstein's insight so brilliant when he states: "Imagination is more important than knowledge. For knowledge is limited to all we now know and understand, while imagination embraces the entire world of possibility, and all there ever will be to know and understand."

Knowledge is the realm of objective reality. Imagination is the realm of subjective reality. So, since you are pure potentiality, whatever you can *imagine* in your 'subjective' mind, you have the potential power to *create* in your 'objective' or physical world.

You're no doubt familiar with the phrase: "I will believe it when I see it."

And though the masses of people think this is how life works, this statement is fundamentally flawed.

The truth is quite the opposite: *To see it, one must first believe it!*

Take a look around you. Everything... *everything*... you see began as a thought, an image, a construct in someone's imagination long before it ever existed in the physical world.

A prime example of this truth is demonstrated in the early pioneers of flight – Orville and Wilbur Wright. The fact that no *objective evidence* existed in the world when Orville and Wilbur chose to create a 'flying machine' never deterred them from their *subjective vision*.

This is a perfect demonstration of how imagination is more important than knowledge.

They had to first 'see' it in the world of their imagination before they could ever create it in the physical world.

Here's the underlying and unchanging principle behind that statement: whatever the mind dwells upon, the physical body will begin to act upon and express in some form. The subjective reality (imagination) was so vivid that even though the experiments necessary to develop such an incredible machine were expensive and potentially fatal, they never lost sight of their outcome.

And even after their mission was successful and the very first aeroplane was created and flight-proven, they were still ridiculed. The collective opinion of the entire world at that time was, "No one will use it… apart from daredevils!"

Illustrating the fallibility of the collective.

(By the way, similar opinions were proffered upon the invention of the first railway, telephone and then much later, the first computer.)

This brings us to a third principle:

When you employ your subjective reality, that is to say, your imagination, in the pursuit of your dreams, you must remain independent of the opinions of others.

If you study the life of any successful person, you'll find that without exception, they all possess this quality. It allows for an 'independent vision'… and with it comes the freedom to follow one's own truth, 'natural grain' and inspiration.

Taking this position also harnesses the power of the universe, though exactly how and why is almost impossible to conclude.

Let me explain…

Remember when you were four or five years old and believed you could be a superhero, an astronaut, royalty a president or a prime minister? You possessed an awareness of that 'magical' power of the universe even then, *using your imagination.* How else would you have believed you could ever accomplish such extraordinary feats?

This same invisible force is available to you now, ready to propel you forward toward your dream. It is the power that allows you to unlock your potential.

For example, a gold medal Olympian or Oscar winner didn't just 'get lucky'. They saw themselves winning in their mind's eye long before it became an objective reality. Not unlike what children do when they see themselves accomplishing great things in their imagination.

Then, as they continue to cultivate a solid belief that they will achieve their dream, their body responds by exerting the effort, practice and persistence necessary to make it happen. Thousands of hours naturally follow, through practice they become excellent, excellence leads to happiness, and the performance or delivery becomes so great, that they simply cannot be ignored by the rest of the world. It is here that endless opportunities follow.

All successful people tap into this hidden power that fuels their imagination, their unseen awareness that says: "What if I am right about my dream? I'm taking a chance. I'm taking my shot!"

An awareness of the existence of this power is the first step toward any goal.

So even if the entire world is against you, but you believe in your dream and see it vividly in your imagination, then align your subjective reality with the pure potentiality that is who you are and available to you at will in the universe, you cultivate that unborn dream on route to physical crystallisation.

When a desire becomes so compelling, it falls into the realms of obsession. Cravings emerge; these natural forces may have negative connotations within the very definition; however, if the energy is directed properly, one can move in the direction without discipline or external motivation. Action is almost always out of inspiration. It, in essence, becomes a choice that no one can hold you back from, even yourself; it takes on a life of its own. In the next chapter, we will be exploring how to tap into the power that will turn you into a force of nature.

CHAPTER TWO

Desire: The Secret Ingredient for Success

I have taken a floodlight of information and condensed it into a laser beam. Everything you are about to read will be all you ever need on your journey. This guide will become your companion manual for success.

Remember the first time you fell in love? I mean totally *'head-over-heels smitten'* in love?

I certainly do. The moment I saw her she took my breath away! Auburn hair perfectly framing those huge, luscious brown eyes and silky olive skin –

"Can I have a go of your game?" she asked, looking on as I played an addictive hand-held round of Las Vegas. I was so mesmerised that I could hardly answer and passed her the little bright red electronic device without uttering a single word.

It was the first night I ever lost sleep over a girl. Never mind, I was nine, she was eight, and our initial meeting was during lunchtime on the playground.

You know the feeling –

An initial encounter, some brief exchange, and then suddenly, this incredibly powerful, unmistakable force rushes over your body. You have fallen victim to love and are now under its spell. *Every part of your being* – thoughts, emotions and behaviour – *is controlled by this magical force of desire.* Your whole world now centres around that individual. You search for them in every crowd. You bring their name up in every conversation. They consume your every thought. You dream about them. You write their name a moment a pen is in hand. You lose sleep over them. You go to any lengths necessary to be with them.

Not surprising, this 'gift' of desire is the most potent intangible force in the universe .

It is so powerful that a person may risk everything good in their world and throw away their entire future, acting on an uncontrolled impulse of desire.

And there's a biological reason why this is so.

Strong feelings of love and desire release 'feel-good' neurochemicals in your brain, triggering euphoric states of intense happiness, excitement and preoccupation as well as physiological responses like rapid heartbeat and sweaty palms. One of these neurochemicals in particular – dopamine – is responsible for reward-driven and pleasure-seeking behaviour. To give you an idea of just how powerful it is, this is the same feeling produced by certain addictive drugs like cocaine.

Desire: The Language of Creation

Every man, woman and child you see is a product of creation born of desire or an act of passion so intense it transcends any other human experience. (There is a massive clue in that.)

Desire is the essential ingredient in all of creation – whether it's the desire of a man and woman in love to procreate, an inspired composer to create a musical masterpiece, or the desire of a talented architect to design a stupendous skyscraper.

Desire is the fuel that drives one to create, and it must be present before anything can be created.

Fall in Love with Your Dream

What if you could harness this kind of desire to create success?

What if the *desire to realise a lifelong dream* was so strong that it could produce the same dopamine effect (feelings of euphoria), resulting in a preoccupation that leads to an 'addiction' to seeing that dream become a reality?

This is not only possible, but it is also essential to creating massive success!

In much the same way that our body responds to a love/attraction impulse and an all-consuming desire to procreate, we can 'fall in love' with our dream – *the thing we want more than anything else.*

… and our body will naturally and automatically respond to that impulse, moving us toward behaviour that creates the thing we desire, making our dream a reality.

Forces of nature are unstoppable; you can't stop an avalanche in motion, a volcano after it has erupted or a tsunami in all its fury; the motion once created cannot be reversed. The intent and desire of nature see it all the way through to completion; there is a lesson to be learned in that nature is not a part, it is a whole, and every part is a part of the whole.

Cultivating a desire that triggers momentum sees the once perceived, illusionary obstacles melting like an ice cube thawing in the summer sun.

When one yearns for something that they are continually preoccupied with that desire, emotions (impulses of thought) are triggered that produce action (behaviour) toward the goal in sight, creating the desired outcome.

Bill Gates, the co-founder of Microsoft, is a prime example.

When Gates was in the eighth grade, the mothers in his class had a bake sale. With the proceeds, they bought a computer for the class.

Now to get the computer to work, holes were punched in a card and then the card was inserted into the computer.

Gates was intrigued, challenged and consumed with this process. He continually thought about how it worked and what he could do to create different outcomes. He continued to work with it over the next two years until he could go no further. By now, he's a sophomore in high school. As it turns out, the University of Washington was close by. There he could access the next level of computer technology, which he did on a regular basis. In fact, he was so preoccupied with desire and intrigue to learn everything he could about how it all worked that he would sneak out of his house at 2 a.m. just to get back to it.

He was a boy possessed with a dream, so overcome by the 'gift of desire' that he went to any lengths necessary to see his dream become a reality. I think the evidence is in – he succeeded.

The only asset Microsoft has is the human imagination. – Bill Gates

An additional aspect of truth lies behind Gates' success that is profoundly significant, though often overlooked. That is, when Gates began to gain momentum with Microsoft, his dream was a PC in every home in the world.

Now, you may think that comes from his desire to build wealth. But if so, you're missing the point.

You see, Gates *so believed* in the value of his product that he wanted every household to know the benefit of owning one. His desire was to provide value to humanity. The resultant wealth was a by-product. Think about it: when you are sharing an idea about something you like, with a friend, at that moment there is no agenda other than wanting the best for your friend; it's actually a selfless act, that's one of the reasons a great idea spreads like wildfire: there is no agenda or pitch.

Here's the essential truth in this story: the more value you bring to the world and the greater number of people you serve will directly correlate to what you will earn. You have no choice but to serve people if you want to create a great life for yourself.

Here's another example...

Steve Jobs co-founded Apple Computer at the age of 21. Just two years later, he's a millionaire. However, at age 30, his own company fires him because of conflicts over his leadership style and ensuing power struggles.

His response?

"You can fire me from my company, but you can't stop me from doing what I love!"

After a unique turn of events, however, in 1996, he returned to the company he helped create and led them to their greatest successes ever.

"I'm convinced the only thing that kept me going was that I loved what I did. You've got to find what you love."

He was under the 'spell of desire' – the essential ingredient to massive success.

When you genuinely love someone or something, you exert more energy, attention to detail and effort and want only the best. In today's day and age, with a bombardment of messages now pushing follow your passion, why is it only a few people who follow their passion succeed in doing or creating something extraordinary?

The answer is twofold: if the love is genuine, your effort towards creation will be so heightened that the quality of what you produce will be in a class of its own. If you follow what you tout as a passion without exerting the necessary efforts, it never was your true passion to begin with. Love requires no explanation.

"There is a stage after which language fails When you step into the zone of love you won't need language. – Elif Shafak

When great effort is put into an endeavour, that thing becomes excellent, and it is *The Excellence* that leads to happiness; you will recognise it really is the journey and not the destination, the melding refinement of character; the journey is the philosopher's stone, not the stone itself... When authentic passion begins to come to the surface, happiness and gratitude is real in each moment, not contrived falsely with fake repetitions; it doesn't need to be; it flows without words spoken. The creation of something remarkable is never by chance, rather deliberate design – the design results in excellence. We may be more accurate in saying pursue excellence over happiness; happiness cannot exist without excellence.

Excellence results in happiness; it is when you are in the present moment and paid your dues to reach a particular point that you enter states that produce behaviour without thought. It's that moment that you are writing or dancing or even communicating an idea with someone and catch yourself for a moment thinking: where did that even come from? It was produced with painstaking hours as an act of love.

The widespread phenomenon of business tycoons working their entire lives and never quitting is not so much to do with fear of losing wealth or greed; rather, it's to do with desire. They never stop, even if they are in a position that they can.

Why?

Because they have fallen in love with their dream, and that dream continues to evolve.

They are under that 'spell of desire' – the dopamine effect that leads to 'addiction'. Once hooked, it is almost impossible to break away.

They have an addiction… albeit a very healthy one… to success.

How to Condition Yourself For Success

Just like the example given above, you can *condition yourself for success* by creating desire-driven thought patterns that trigger behaviours conducive to success.

To illustrate how this works, I want you to imagine being in the depths of a forest, unable to find your way out. After wandering around in the thick brush for a while, you happen upon this well-formed path. You immediately and automatically (without any conscious thought) take that path because it's the easiest, quickest route out of the forest.

This example gives a clue into some of the workings of our brain – the three pounds of convoluted grey and white matter that controls all of our thoughts, feelings and behaviours.

One of the primary functions of a healthy brain is to receive, store and transmit information.

And the primary function of a healthy body is to respond to thought impulses or messages received from the brain and carry out the corresponding behaviour. The brain receives data from our environment through the five senses, categorises the data, and then tells our body what to do based on the information received.

This information falls into one of two categories:

1. New information that the conscious mind has to think about before acting upon.
2. Familiar information that the subconscious mind associates with similar data. In this case, the brain then transmits a message to the body to do the same thing it always does in that situation.

Some sources suggest that the average adult makes about 35,000 decisions throughout one day. Thankfully, you don't even have to consciously 'think' about most of those. That's because our mind is wired to look for shortcuts so efficiently that 95% of all behaviour is done 'without thinking' via impulses from the subconscious mind.

You know the phrase – and probably have even said it yourself – *"I did that without thinking."*

What you mean is that your body responded without you even consciously thinking about it because it was a habitual pattern. You had done a similar thing so many times before that your body just naturally kicked into autopilot. This is the equivalent of the well-formed path in the forest. Just like you would do if you found a well-formed track out of the forest, your brain chooses the easiest, quickest way to get the job done.

Now let's go back to the forest…

But this time, let's say you want to cut a new path through the stand of trees. Of course, initially, you encounter a lot of resistance. There's lots of brush and undergrowth to cut through. However, once that's done, if you go back to that same area and walk it again, it's a bit easier. Each time you walk that same path, it offers less resistance and becomes more prominent and more well-formed. That's how the neural pathways in our brain work. That is, the first time you introduce a new thought, you encounter a lot of mental or 'biochemical' resistance. But the continued repetition of that same thought over time wears down the resistance. The connections between the brain cells on that neural pathway become stronger. Given enough repetition, a new well-formed thought pattern or habit develops.

Further, the brain has a built-in servomechanism that serves as a goal-seeking feedback system, causing well-formed pathways or habits of generalised 'thought feelings' (thoughts associated with strong feelings) to develop over time *through repetition of similar thoughts* via a feedback loop.

In other words, when a new thought impulse is picked up, the brain automatically searches for similar thought patterns to associate it with and attach it to. Furthermore, thought patterns that are linked to strong feelings (both positive and negative) create more defined neural pathways and, as a result, formulate many of the beliefs we hold about our self and our world.

Take someone who has a history of unpleasant experiences. Maybe their father was physically abusive, or their mother was absent or cold. As a result, they developed specific 'thought feelings' or beliefs about themselves and their world... like "I'm no good" and "The world isn't a safe place" or, even worse, "I can't be loved." Their interpretation of these experiences has created well-formed pathways of negative thought patterns in their brain, resulting in an imbalance of negative energy. As a result of the feedback loops at work, they continually evaluate, judge and polarise towards those unpleasant events – only seeing them from one angle and giving them only one meaning. This process creates what I call 'mini-landmines' that must be defused to forge a clear path forward.

We will explore this concept in detail in a later chapter, but for now, just remember that the practice of non-judgment is not a luxury or some new-age nonsense. You must practise non-judgment of your past to break negative thought patterns and release the clutches of victimhood. If your perception of unpleasant events in the past polarises to one side, meaning you only recognise the negative, this creates an exaggeration in your perception as you are not seeing the whole; an exaggeration in the perceptions creates an exaggeration in the nervous system. Almost all illnesses have a psychological root; counselling sometimes more powerful than medication, some 75–90% of visits to the doctor are stress-related, and stress may be viewed as the foundational building block of all illnesses, both physical and psychological.

And because of the 'feedback loop' function of the brain, these negative messages and their associated negative emotions are revisited and rehearsed repeatedly, making their neural pathways much more prominent and even more well-formed over time. Also, the subconscious mind (which controls all of our learned functions like habits and attitudes) is impartial to the information stored in the brain. Questioning nothing, it accepts whatever is 'believed' as absolute truth. It simply takes the easiest, quickest route – the well-formed pathways that have been developed through repetitive or habitual thought patterns.

If these habitual thoughts are thoughts of failure, the body automatically responds and behaves consistently with 'failure' thoughts. This is why one who believes themselves to be a failure continues to fail.

In the same way, however, thought patterns of success and wellbeing create well-formed neural pathways of 'success' thoughts that lead to automatic and habitual 'success' behaviours.

Hopefully, you're beginning to understand how it's possible to *condition yourself for success.*

The fact that you can retrain the brain for success by creating new neural pathways in the subconscious mind that, in turn, produce behaviours consistent with any goal you desire to achieve may be the most important truth I can share with you.

Now maybe you believe you've had too many negative experiences in life, that by now your issues are too deeply ingrained and your adverse pathways of thought are too well-formed. As a result of having been this way all your life, you believe you simply cannot change. That sounds plausible enough, and I can see how that would appear to be true.

However, if I didn't know better, it would also appear plausible to say the earth is flat because it both looks and feels that way.

You can choose to believe the earth is flat, but you'd be unquestionably wrong.

And the same holds for believing you cannot change your thought patterns. Neural pathways are not static. They are not set in stone.

Just the opposite is true.

The brain has a neuroplasticity quality, which means it can reorganise itself by forming new neural pathways throughout a lifetime. Changes in neural pathways can occur in response to altering one's behaviour, environment, thought processes and emotion. Your brain is constantly morphing, evolving and regenerating, receiving and responding to the input you feed it.

It is important to note that any feeling in the body is nothing more than either a trained (habitual) response or an interpretation of sensory input that results in a hardwired natural reflex.

So, it follows that if we can control the impulses of thought, we can alter the body's corresponding automatic response – that is to say, our feelings and behaviour.

This is the process of conditioning yourself for success.

Here's a real-life experiment that exposes the fallacy of deeply ingrained and unchangeable behaviour or being.

A guy goes to a bike manufacturer. He asks them to construct a bike that operates exactly opposite to how a standard bike operates. In other words, if he pedals forward, the bike stops. To go, he must pedal backwards. If he turns to the right, the bike goes left. If he turns to the left, the bike goes right.

As you might imagine, the outcome was a disaster... *at first*.

But this was all part of the experiment.

Given enough trial and error – *with enough practice* – he was able to ride the 'backwards' bike as effortlessly... without thinking... just as he rode a standard bike before.

How is that possible?

With sufficient practice he retrained his brain – he formed new neural pathways that, once established, served him as efficiently and effectively in this new venture as the old, previous ones had done.

Now, pay attention to what happened next.

On his attempt at returning to ride a standard bike, he fell off! His brain had replaced the old thought patterns with new ones.

This real-life example has serious implications. If you decide you are the way you are because of your past, you are absolutely right. That is the truth. However, to say you can't change because of your past and those deeply ingrained habits and behaviour patterns, you are completely wrong.

If you want to truly move on with your life in a new, positive direction, you must let go of that limiting belief.

Live each day as if your life had just begun. – Johann Wolfgang von Goethe

Here's another quite fascinating experiment...

When the space program was still in its infancy, NASA designed an experiment to test how the weightless environment of space would affect the astronauts in training. They were concerned that there could be some unexpected negative consequences – like blacking out or an inability to function – that would endanger the astronauts or their mission. To perform the experiment, NASA scientists fitted each astronaut with convex goggles, which flipped everything in their field of vision 180 degrees. In other words, everything they saw through those goggles was completely upside down. They had to wear them 24 hours a day, seven days a week, even while they slept.

And although they suffered from some anxiety and stress initially (evidenced by elevated blood pressure, respiration and other vitals), they gradually adapted to their new reality.

Then something quite fascinating occurred for one of the astronauts on the 26th day of the experiment… everything turned right-side-up again, even though he continued to wear the goggles 24 hours a day. And over the next four days, between days 26 and 30, the exact same thing happened for the rest of the astronauts: their brains actually created neural pathways that 'rewired' their ability to see their world normally again.

What NASA scientists concluded from this experiment is that after 26–30 days of uninterrupted new input, the brain created new neural pathways that synced with the new information. Then they repeated the experiment with a slight change. This time some of the astronauts took off their goggles for a short while partway through the 30-day period, then put them back on. On the 30th day, their world was still upside down. But after leaving them on for an additional consecutive 30-day span, the same thing happened. Everything was right side up again.

So, what's the conclusion?

It takes about 30 days of continual conscious, intentional thought practice to form new neural pathways of habitual thought patterns; current research from UCL now suggests it may even be up to 67 days. Irrespective of duration, the key is uninterrupted consistency, creating a natural compounding effect.

Persistence is the main component in the process, but that's where the fuel of desire will keep you preoccupied with your goal, producing deliberate action in the right direction.

Desire Must Be Authentic

As a young child, I spent every moment I could with my grandfather – a magnificent carpenter and sculptor – who created priceless works of art right before my eyes. Over the summer holidays, I would learn by watching him magically infuse life into otherwise inanimate pieces of wood. My training was both observational and practical; the craftsmanship was not a matter of acquiring information; it was about producing something real. He would take a rough, unformed piece of wood – one with no observable qualities – and, as I stared in wonder, create the most beautiful musical instrument, table or chair.

I learned a great deal from my grandfather, but one fundamental lesson in particular that never left me was this: when working with the wood and filing it down, all wood has a natural visible direction to its grain. *You never go against its natural grain, or you will destroy it and render it useless.*

Here's the life principle that experience taught me...

Just like each piece of wood is unique, so are we. We are as individual as our fingerprints. We all have our own 'natural grain'. A unique mission that we alone can complete. A dream that is ours only.

As long as you follow your heart, doing what you love – which is your natural grain – you can be, do or have anything you want. And when there is congruence between who you are and what you want, everything in the universe races to your assistance. However, if you try to go against your natural grain to follow someone else's path for you – someone who wants to inject their own values into you – your inner guidance system will baulk and resist.

Insurmountable obstacles begin to appear, and you end up on a treadmill, exhausted... *and getting nowhere.*

And you know what else happens?

You eventually resent the people or community you were attempting to appease, blaming them for your lack of success, fulfilment and happiness, when YOU are the one responsible. You are where you are because YOU didn't have the courage to honour your own dream and make your own way and follow through with whatever activity you were doing in an excellent fashion.

But your story won't end there.

If you continue to live in opposition to your natural grain – inconsistent with who you really are – in time, you will experience increased stress and eventual illness and disease. Here's a bit of research that proves my point. Studies have been done that show a spike in stress hormones, such as cortisol and adrenaline, *in working people on Mondays.* In fact, these findings suggest that human beings are the only species in existence that predictably die on a specific day and a specific time – 9 a.m. Monday morning. Also, more heart attacks and other cardiovascular events occur on Mondays than on any other day of the week. There's even a name for it – 'Monday cardiac phenomenon' – and it has long been believed to be related to work stress!

Want to know why?

It's because the body isn't designed to behave in opposition to who you are and what you want. Without congruency, the body will eventually cry out in pain. Using MRIs scientists observed and documented that when people are chronically depressed and anxious, blood flow in the brain is directed toward the amygdala, or primitive (early) brain – the area responsible for 'fight or flight,' our survival instinct.

What's interesting, however, is that when this same group of people were instructed to focus on thoughts of love and gratitude, blood flow shifted to the frontal cortex – the most developed part of the brain.

Why is this significant?

Because it shows that when you are doing *what you love*, fulfilling your desire and mission in life, you are operating out of your higher mind where executive decisions are made. In other words – *you are smarter.*

The point I'm making is this...

Your body is beautifully engineered to come to your aid when you are following your own natural grain.

Keeping all this in mind, let's revisit the question I posed at the beginning of Chapter One: if you knew you could not fail, what one thing would you be compelled to do?

In other words, what do you want more than anything else in the world? I want you to think very carefully now about your answer. Is this something *you* genuinely want... something that speaks to *your* core values... *your* individuality... congruent with who *you* are and what *you* really want out of life? Now let's suppose for a minute that this claim – *that you can be, do or have anything you want in life* – just sounds too good to be true. Like it's too big, too out of reach, to take on.

As opposed to what?

Would you rather live with self-imposed limitations and the injected beliefs of others? Are you willing to just blindly accept what someone else wants for you or thinks is best for you? Why not, instead, summon the courage to look inside and determine to honour your uniqueness, to be true to *who you are* and what *you* want.

If you don't yet know exactly what you want, then it is paramount that whatever you are doing is to be done in an excellent fashion, to higher standards than you had previously set for yourself. Become better today than you were yesterday. The presence of awareness and going the extra mile will pay dividends in your future. Never underestimate what you are currently engaged in, no matter how mundane it may appear on the surface. Look for the correlation and benefits of what you are currently engaged in and the link it has to the future.

A soccer player doesn't drop in the middle of the pitch and do a plank or sit-ups but these seemingly unrelated exercises are instrumental in that athlete's success. So are your own activities you are engaged in each day. The missing pieces of the puzzle magically appear when the time is right. Use everything to your aid.

Standards and progression are everything. In the words of my good friend Derek Mills, author of *The 10-Second Philosophy*:

"DailyStandards™ are your daily, real-world guideposts of how to be the best you, where to come back to when you lose your way and where your greatest talents operate from. They are chosen by YOU, and when they come from YOU, they allow you to play life at a higher level."

Think of someone who has achieved great success in life that you admire. Did you know their success would not have been possible if they had kept themselves confined by the chains of imaginary limitations? Don't sell yourself short! I'm giving you the key that unlocks the chains of your ridiculous, intangible, 'imagined' limitations.

It's time to stop defending your self-limiting beliefs and commit to living a life worthy of who you are and what you desire.

You may be wondering how you can know if your desire is truly authentic. Here's how. Put it to the test…

Ask yourself what you are willing to risk for your dream to become a reality? Pain?

Disappointment? Temporary defeat?

Take Anderson da Silva, for instance.

Born into an impoverished family in Sao Paulo, Brazil, Silva wanted to learn the martial art of Jiu-Jitsu. But his family couldn't afford to pay for lessons. Besides, Jiu-Jitsu was considered a sport reserved for the upper class. However, this didn't stop Silva. He figured out how he could learn the desired skill from others – friends whose families could afford to pay for lessons. He learned it in the streets. Notice that no one had to motivate Silva to study Jiu-Jitsu. No one forced him to spend thousands of gruelling hours mastering his craft.

Why? Because he was following his own natural grain… his desire, and his inner inspiration. And he pursued other martial art forms like Thai boxing with the same intensity.

So, did he ever realise his dream of becoming a champion fighter?

Absolutely. At the time of this writing, he holds the longest title defence streak in UFC history, with 16 consecutive wins and 10 title defences. You see, his dream was authentic. It was his alone… and the desire to see his dream become a reality was the fuel that kept driving him toward his goal, even when his opportunities for success looked bleak. A little later in this chapter, I will begin to outline methods you can use to reprogram your subconscious mind for success.

But first, let's dig deeper into the topic of thoughts, as they are a key component in this process – to condition yourself for success, you must learn to control your thoughts.

And the first step in controlling your thoughts is this:

You must be able to separate who you are from what you think.

Here's what I mean: You are the thinker. You are not the thought.

To successfully manage your thoughts, you must first recognise them as being *separate from who you are*.

You must be able to witness your thoughts and thought patterns much like a third-party observer – objectively – before you can have power over them. The significance of this is that by doing so you have suddenly become pure awareness, and in a realm of no limits, you are now the observer.

The second step in managing your thoughts is:

Realise that thoughts must be evaluated by your conscious mind to determine if they *are* true before they are accepted and believed *as* truth. In other words, just because a thought *feels* true doesn't mean it *is* true. The earth to us feels still, though we all know conclusively that it is not. Furthermore dwelling and questioning a negative thought only serves to carry you in a current that you will not want to go, so shrug it off and move on; it has no power over you unless you consent to it.

And further… you *choose* what you want to believe.

Remember the example from my personal story that I shared in Chapter One… when my objective reality (my surgeon's diagnosis) didn't match my subjective reality (what I chose to believe about my future)? I made the conscious choice to believe a different reality, and by doing so I eventually created my preferred, chosen reality. My *chosen* reality became my objective reality in time.

And the third step in managing your thoughts is:

Believe that you CAN.

The majority of people allow their thought patterns (habits, attitudes and beliefs) to control them. This is a prescription for failure.

Allow me to demonstrate just how simple it is to re-direct your thoughts.

I want you to think about your favourite pastime. Why do you enjoy it so?

Now I want you to think about what you had for dinner last night. Was it a pleasant meal?

Now I want you to think about your closest friend. What do you find rewarding about your relationship?

Using these three simple 'commands', you have just shaped the direction of your thoughts and changed what you were presently thinking about.

Granted, once you start thinking about something else, those thoughts are gone. But that's not the point. The fact remains that you can command your brain to think about anything you choose and move in the direction of good.

Remember the forest?

If your well-formed paths (your dominant thought patterns) are negative, that's only because new trails have not yet been cut.

You are the only one who can change that. But the important point is this: you *can* change your old thought patterns (thanks to the brain's neuroplasticity) from failure to success, and the more you *desire* this change, the easier and more quickly you will *experience* success.

You see, thoughts are charged electrical impulses. They emit frequencies that influence the very fabric of our universe.

When you concentrate on a particular thought, you emit a vibration. The stronger the emotion associated with that thought and the longer you hold it in your mind, the stronger the frequency and the more powerful the impact. (This is the process of cutting a new mental pathway through the forest.) The more you replay those thoughts over time (think of re-walking the pathway again and again), the more automatic they become.

Once a new well-formed neural pathway is established, your subconscious mind will automatically and habitually default to taking that thought pattern and sending the corresponding message to your body to act on those thoughts.

If you build success pathways, your body has no choice but to respond in kind with feelings and behaviours that create success. This process of creating your new reality is born out of desire. Inducing a state of intense desire starts to create change in the neural pathways of the brain. This is the mind–body connection, the science behind success. This is exactly how every successful person has created success – whether knowingly or unknowingly.

This also explains why others continue to experience failure.

If you had the ability to examine the thought patterns of any individual, you would find that their life circumstances mirror the sum total of their thought patterns and self-perception. Positive and balanced thought patterns create success, happiness, fulfilment. Negative thought patterns lead to unrealised dreams, restrictions, discontent and misery.

This is a universal law.

Stop trying to orchestrate events and reorganise the universe through willpower and effort that is out of your hands. *You cannot control all the variables.* If you are to be, do or have anything you want, then you have no choice but to see yourself as the person you want to be and then act *as if it is so* until it becomes your reality, all the while having faith in the benevolence of an impartial and infinite universe backing you.

When you find yourself compelled to do this and you begin to take what I call 'inspired action', you are well on your way to success. You will soon capture a current that moves you almost effortlessly to your destination. Act on the truths I share with you in this book. Begin to use these formulas to direct your thoughts – *the one thing you can control* – and you will create whatever you desire. In doing so, you will cultivate the natural energy resource required for your creations. It's more about energy management than time management.

Mastering Time

The duration of an hour should be a period of play. It should be a celebration for that one specific hour in life, and so you have something on your watch, something exciting, thrilling and engaging to represent it – Urwerk

Relinquish time management and embrace energy management, and make the most of every moment. Lists and structure are important, but the question is when you know what to do, how do you predictably work through to completion?

Its energy and having a potency sufficient enough to keep going past the finish line. The brain instructs energy production throughout the body, which loops us back to the function of inspiration; when inspired, we naturally activate the cells in the brain to improve neurotransmission; in essence, we think faster, better and more precise when doing something with meaning.

Schedule in your calendar precise times and dates that specific tasks are to be done, chunk down completely. Prior to beginning a task, prime yourself by remembering your why or biggest reason; next, begin by paying attention to your very presence, then imagine an ever-increasing supply of energy circulating through your body; doing this will bring even greater presence. Finally, as you work through the task, no matter how insignificant it may appear, link it to your higher objectives, recognise, in some small or large way it contributes to your plans and at the very least it is training your discipline muscles.

The world is awestruck by the individual with inexhaustible amounts of self-discipline, therefore be known for that.

When you step outside your home, become ferocious in pursuing and fulfilling your never-ending journey of dreams. Do the best you can with every moment of your life, and when you return home, look at your front door and think about the people that are on the inside and how to enjoy every special moment with them; by doing this, you are scripting a living Oscar-winning performance for your life.

Your Treasure Trail

Did you know that your brain naturally produces neurochemicals that create feelings of happiness and pleasure – much like that of a runner's high – when you set goals and achieve them?

Even simple, positive lifestyle changes can improve your brain chemistry, causing you to feel better and providing the motivation you need to maximise your full potential. Once you begin creating positive thought habits and programming your mind for success, your subconscious mind takes over and automatically starts to shine a spotlight in the direction of your goal, unravelling for you the path to your destination – one step at a time.

Let's look at the science behind this. Consider the magnificent function of the part of the network of neurons located in the brain stem known as the Reticular Activating System, or RAS. Your RAS plays a vital role in helping you achieve your goals.

Here's how.

Imagine you're in a busy airport terminal. It's very noisy, bustling… various sounds come and go… terminal shuttles whizzing past, dishes clanking at the corner restaurant, people talking, planes taking off, voices over the intercom announcing flight changes… but you're not paying attention to anything in particular. It's all just background noise.

That is until you hear *your name* called over the public address system. In an instant, your attention is full-on…

… thanks to your RAS!

This wonderful function of our brain acts as a filter between your conscious and subconscious mind, sifting through all the data being picked up by your five senses, filtering out the unimportant and bringing to your attention only what's relevant. This can be particularly useful in achieving your desired goals because you can deliberately program your RAS to draw to your attention specific information that relates to the goals you seek.

And one very effective way to program your RAS is through visualisation techniques which we will explore a little later on.

(In fact, the visualisation methods I will share with you are so powerful that they come with a warning: only use them wisely with full knowledge of their power. As the adage says, "Be careful what you wish for.")

Another advantage to your RAS is that it does not distinguish between objective reality and imagined reality. In other words, it will believe and look out for whatever message you give it. As long as you deliberately and effectively create a precise picture of your desired goal in your conscious mind, your RAS will pass that image on to your subconscious without questioning its validity. Your subconscious mind (RAS) then goes to work for you, bringing to your attention any and all relevant information that might have otherwise been overlooked as just background noise.

One last but very significant point remains.

If the life you are living is not congruent and in harmony with your authentic self (who you are and what you want), *then your RAS will block the transfer of messages to your subconscious.* In other words, your RAS recognises any incongruence and only works in support of the authentic self, which is another reason why you must follow your own path as well as guard against erroneous ideas if you desire to be happy, at peace, and wildly successful.

Seeing the Invisible

Every great work of art is an immersion of desire. And what is not readily visible to the masses is patently clear when viewed through the eyes of the master.

In the dark halls of the church of Santa Maria del Fiore, Florence in 1502, a marble figure gathered dust. Once a magnificent piece of raw stone, an unskilful sculptor had mistakenly bored a hole where the figure's legs should have been. Master sculptors made attempts to restore it, but everyone agreed the stone was ruined. None the less it had been put up for auction and undoubtedly was continually rejected… One evening a wise and gifted master attended the auction, his eyes immediately drawn to the amorphous lump of marble. Observing the rejected piece, he saw in his mind's eye something that everyone else had missed entirely. Without hesitation he bought the hidden treasure, realising what he had just discovered would serve to echo his work through the centuries.

I saw the angel inside of the marble, and all I had to do was chip away and set him free. – Michelangelo, referring to David.

You get to write the script of your life. You decide what you make of it.

You are the master of your destiny. And to that end, you must become your own visionary. A cultivated desire and attention to detail bring a near clairvoyance-like ability. Perhaps extrasensory perception is not a sixth sense, after all; maybe it's mastering your craft and, most of all, learning to pay attention to the present moment. Each day chip away at the parts that have been holding you back and release your magnificence.

Create a vision of who you want to be and live into that picture as if it were already true. – Arnold Schwarzenegger

Dream big. Think great thoughts and act relentlessly in pursuit of what you want to achieve. Believe in the unseen, become the instrument – that conduit – responsible for creating the world on your terms. Ride on the light of your desires and turn your dreams into reality.

The Science of Happiness

Whether or not you are aware of it, there is a consistent internal dialogue going on in your mind. You are continually communicating with yourself. In fact, 95% of what you feel flows directly from inner conversations. This steady never-ending stream, many times, is in contrast; we think one thing to ourselves whilst saying something different out aloud to the world. This mismatch of communication creates what psychologists call cognitive dissonance; it's like attempting to swim against a current so strong you end up nowhere or ushered into unknown and unwelcome waters. Later on, we will be learning how to develop coherence in both internal and external dialogue. And as we've already established, you have the innate ability to direct your thoughts. You can learn to take charge of your internal dialogue and manipulate these conversations to your advantage so that they align with your goals. Because we think in pictures and not words, we use visualisation techniques to communicate with our subconscious. The images are what evokes feelings, these feelings are the language that gives instruction to the mind.

In fact, Socrates himself said: "We never learn without a picture."

The mind doesn't distinguish between real and imagined images – the same part of the brain is utilised for both. This is a beautiful truth and one you can use to your advantage *because it allows you to create pictures in your mind of your desired outcome, regardless of what that might be.* Now, if you think you have a hard time visualising something, consider this. Do you ever worry? If so, what you're really doing is projecting a negative image in your mind and experiencing all the negative emotions that are attached to it. In other words, *you are visualising.*

Everyone can visualise… even young children. That's what they're doing when pretending to be Superman or Cinderella.

So, to begin gently training your mind to visualise effectively and take control, let's start with this simple exercise:

Find a comfortable sitting position in a room where you won't be disturbed. Close your eyes and imagine a beautiful, expansive scene with you in the middle of the picture. Maybe it's a vast field of wildflowers, a secluded beach that goes on for miles or perhaps a place that holds some of your most treasured memories. Visualise the scene in colour. Add in sounds, the scents… vivify the image to the point where you can actually feel, hear, see everything going on around you, imagine depth, textures to make the image more vivid and look through your own eyes, gently bring your awareness to what feelings are being evoked. Now for a thought experiment: imagine the outcome for something you presently want but don't have yet… the bridge between where you are and receiving what you want has obstacles on the journey. Let's imagine the obstacles become opportunities or stepping stones, to help you reach the goal sooner. The preconceived limitations in your character that held you back are withering away; just suppose for a moment that was true, now the person that can achieve the result you want is merging through you. Now project your mind to a time after your outcome has been achieved, next imagine the conversations you'll be having with friends, as well as how others perceive you and what they say about your great fortune.

Now, if that were true, what would you be thinking? How would you be feeling? How would you act?

Repeat this technique daily over the next thirty days before retiring to sleep… and your mind will begin to search for ways to justify the premise in your mind.

On awakening grab a pen and write out this question;

"How would it feel in my body were I the person that had all the necessary qualities at my disposal to make my most desired outcome real?"

Close your eyes and notice the feelings that come up, carry yourself like this throughout the day, become cognisant of any contradictory thoughts, behaviours or actions and immediately correct.

Generalise Your Good Feelings

To cultivate a strong, positive emotion that you can use as a bridge toward your desired goals, we must first get you to feel both a sense of poise and 'feeling good' most of the time; this is a state I will refer to as grounded with an expansive awareness; feel your feet on the ground and simultaneously bring your attention to the vastness of the universe and feel connected.

Now to capture a good feeling; this is one of the simplest and most effective techniques I have come across, the revisiting of pleasant memories, those that stand out as some of your happiest times.

Once you have one of those memories firmly fixed in your mind, allow yourself to replay that scene, use surround sound, make the image the size of a big cinema screen and the pixels even clearer, remember the time of day even the very aroma in the air as if you were replaying a movie in the memory right now, feeling once again the happiness you experienced then imagine the sensation of doubling the good feeling and bask in the memory. When a notion of the good feeling appears, imagine a time in the future and feeling even better, have a sense of gratitude for what you have just experienced.

Now, see yourself as the person you want to be, living the life you want to live. See yourself moving about, taking action toward your goal, and fully participating in the process as if it were already your reality.

This technique, utilising 'emotionalised thought', is one of the most efficient ways to create new neural pathways in the brain.

During the course of this book, I will have you do specific exercises on a regular basis to create automatic feelings of wellbeing, as well as spontaneous sensations of joy which are independent of life experiences; it's important to feel good for no reason; you will begin to recognise this more and your body will learn to produce effective and happy states on a regular basis.

Like attracts like… so as you begin to *feel* good, not only are you using the higher faculties of the brain, your mind will begin to scan for happiness more, you will observe what works and make it better and obstacles become opportunities and instructions on what to do next, progressively moving you more smoothly through the arrow of time on the way to your target.

… The Match Begins

I move toward my opponent, his sharp jab lands on my nose, and my eyes begin to water… a hidden right cross stuns me, I try to cover up, my head is grasped and guided into a grazing knee. It's happened all too quick; could this be the end? I fear the fight is over before it's even begun.

I feel like I've been hit by a freight train, an instant migraine, flashes appear in my vision, we are *only two seconds off the clock.*

I start back-pedalling. I need a brief respite, just enough for my head to clear.

Operating off sheer instinct and reflex. My opponent senses my vulnerability and races in. A further flurry of shots, my timing is off, and I am unable to avoid the barrage of punches; incessant ringing begins in my ears with these legs bucking from underneath me. There is no time to regroup and too much at stake. For a brief moment, I wish he'd hit harder and put me out of my misery.

As I gain some composure covering up and recklessly bridge the distance in my attempt to clinch and remove myself from the line of fire, contact is made as I pummel through his arms and fight to clasp my own hands behind his lower back. As I look for an inside trip, he snubs my attempt for the takedown and the referee breaks us up.

Calculating the situation my opponent wants to remain on his feet, countering his attacks will be my only option. I continue to circle away from his strikes, giving me a further moment to regroup and capture a rhythm.

I emotionally detach.

My inner dialogue begins to coach me, a reminder that he can break my body but not my spirit; he can't compete with my heart.

He becomes overconfident and throws wild shots. I control my breathing and begin to cover and evade well as the round progresses. I am now reading the patterns of attack; I notice a predictable sequence forming, a jab, a rear cross followed by a low kick. Exhaustion is seeping through his body. Resuming his first moments of success would have been enough to put me out, he now attempts to repeat the same combination. I continue to move around evasively as the haze begins to clear.

Broadening my vision and observing him peripherally enables a greater interpretation of his intended movements and attacks.

I slow him down in my mind (a technique used by Muhammad Ali). My reflexes quicken. With each attack, I use my footwork to evade his attempted onslaught and keep him just out of range of landing shots. Time to defang the snake by ensuring every punch fired at me is answered immediately. I go after the limbs; if his fist or foot is hurt, his weapons are rendered useless. I begin intercepting everything he throws with an attack of my own; my opponent starts to second guess himself, a look of uncertainty develops on his face. I maintain a high guard to protect my face; each punch is parried and skilfully guided to my elbow.

Now it is time to start chopping away at his base, to slow down his attacks further; I begin swiftly throwing low line hook kicks to his legs, targeting pressure points on the lower calf to numb his legs; my opponent starts to retaliate aggressively, attempting to return the same kicks only to be introduced to my outwardly pointed knee in defence; the expression of confidence has now flipped. I look overly defensive to an outside observer though the trained eye would see how I was tenderising him for the next round, making him hesitant before every strike.

I catch my second wind; my lungs are now warmed up.

The bell sounds, and I go to my corner to regroup. A doctor attends to my wounds, wiping the blood and smothering the damaged areas of my face with Vaseline to cease the flow of thick crimson. I sense another twinge in my spine. I suspect I may have lost the first round as damage, in the beginning, was clearly in his favour, and I look like an unholy mess; further, the defensive work would put me at a disadvantage on the scoreboards.

I regroup, recalling what Gary Lineker (who scored more World Cup final goals than any other Englishman in history) once said…

When I am about to take a penalty shootout, even though the whole world is watching me and millions rely on me, I take the pressure off of myself – at that moment, I reflect on how lucky I am and how this isn't hit and miss. It is not a game of chance. It's a skill at the highest level.

My frame of reference shifts. "Let's go and have some fun!"

I remembered watching my heroes in WWE when I was a child growing up. They were so entertaining and larger than life; the simple shift in my internal reference produced a sense of excitement that became very difficult to explain.

I have this opportunity now. My fear melds into gratitude, and I move out with only one objective – **TO WIN.**

A great psychologist once said that WIN is an acronym for What (matters) Is Now. There is power in the present moment.

I come out for round two. I am ultra-observant, using the entire periphery of my field of vision. I watch the minuscule changes in his face, the positioning of his feet, though he is attempting to hide his intention. I catch him amid thought with a perfectly timed jab and an overhand right followed by a liver shot. He is now reluctant to exchange as with each attack he receives a flurry of shots in return.

There is a moment in the battle where everything around you disappears – the crowds… the judges… the sounds… even the pain. Your brain kicks into a different gear, a higher mode. Once you capture your rhythm, it's as if the performance is playing through you. And it's flawless.

In the middle of throwing his right cross, I bob under his arm and come up with a right hook that clips the edge of his chin; I see his eyes glaze over. There's truth in the statement that it's the shots you don't see coming that knock you out. My opponent is on his way down. In the middle of his plight I launch towards his legs; in wrestling, we call it a double leg take-down. I do this to secure my position and ensure I remain in control of my fallen adversary. I am now mounted on his chest, knees pinching the upper torso, becoming near enough impossible to shake off; he attempts to bridge to buckle me off, all to no avail.

Without hesitation, I drop strikes toward his face, baiting him in to defend. He predictably covers his face, my right hand traps his left tricep, and in one smooth movement I swing my hips around, locking his arm in an arm-bar submission.

My opponent has no choice but to tap.

The bell rings. The referee grabs both our wrists. I say a silent prayer of gratitude, and my hand is raised.

The doctors rush over to wipe my face and begin working on my wound: one down, and no idea how many more opponents to go.

Chaos may be the only way to bring order... My mind goes back into onslaught mode as the adrenaline settles down; it was a fluke; I'm hurt the next bout will be worse for me, my opponent will be fresh... My heart starts to palpitate as I am losing control...

The doctor looks me square in the; you may have a concussion; the team will decide if we let you continue.

It's a bittersweet moment.

A star has to explode into a supernova to create gold; in fact, gold is not produced on our planet; it results from a universal cataclysm of a frightening magnitude. Chaos creates order; mother nature is ruthless, perhaps light can only be birthed through darkness. It's the struggle, the failure and the perceived things that we feel are missing that propel industries to grow and build and for our species to evolve and rise; as we lead into the next chapter, you'll discover how to utilise both good and the bad to pave the path to your destination. If you utilise everything on your journey, you are sure to accelerate and arrive even sooner than you thought.

CHAPTER THREE

You... An Alchemist?

Inherent in any adversity are the seeds of an equal, or greater, benefit. –
Napoleon Hill

French scribe and bookseller Nicolas Flamel resided in Paris in the 14th century. According to historical accounts, the educated Flamel was interested in ancient spiritual, philosophical and magical traditions, spending much of his life studying the art of transmutation and alchemy (transmuting a base substance into a thing of great value).

Shortly after his death in 1418, reports of Flamel's purported alchemical achievements spread rapidly throughout Paris. Over the next 300 years, it was reported all over Europe that he had indeed discovered the Philosopher's Stone, a legendary alchemical substance thought to be able to turn base metals into gold. Flamel was also said to have found the Elixir of Life, the key to curing all disease and achieving immortality. Although historians thoroughly documented Flamel's life, his story was, of course, densely layered with legend and lore. As time passed, he seemed destined to be an obscure footnote in the story of a discredited protoscience. But history was not yet finished with Nicolas Flamel. Powerful truths lay buried in his legend – facts that may have contributed to how we see the world today.

In 1936, more than 500 years after his death, Flamel dramatically resurfaced on the world stage, showing you should never underestimate the impact of your life's work and how it may contribute to the story of the universe.

The Last Magician

Precisely at 1 p.m., just after luncheon on July 1936, bidding opened at Sotheby's auction house in London. The object of bidders' attention was a metal chest which held private, handwritten papers and lab books almost 300 years old, most never before seen. They were the thoughts and ideas of a man known as 'the last magician', over a million words on the structure of magic by one of the most brilliant scientific minds of all time.

In Woolsthorpe Manor, Lincolnshire, this genius had penned his innermost thoughts, revealing an obsession with alchemy that had consumed years of his life. The papers auctioned on that fateful July day in 1936 showed that one alchemist's name was most prominent in his thoughts: Nicolas Flamel. Studying Flamel and investigating the ideas of other renowned alchemists had overshadowed just about everything during that time.

Absorbed by an unquenchable thirst for discovery, this intellectual giant never enjoyed a relationship and only took a very rare evening out. He was known to have attended just one theatrical performance in his life, only to leave a few minutes into the show, deeming it an absurdity and waste of time. The savant had kept close account of every precious moment of life graced to him. A mission to unravel the mysteries of the universe and glimmer into just fragments of the unseen would take lifetimes. Engulfed in his world, he went where his brilliant mind led him in pursuit of the Philosopher's Stone and the Elixir of Life while simultaneously unveiling the fabric of our very existence.

Human beings tend to gravitate toward the occult, to believe in fate, superstition and magic. However rational one deems oneself to be, we are open to the idea of the supernatural, of forces beyond our discernment or control. Once locked into a worldview, we naturally search for evidence supporting the accepted premise, irrespective of how absurd. Psychologists refer to this phenomenon as 'cognitive bias. It explains why some people believe in a flat Earth, or how a coldly rational scientist can accept an unscientific religious doctrine, allowing that the universe was literally created in six days, for example. A person's belief becomes their accepted truth. Since the birth of the scientific method, however, scientists have always made every effort to base their conclusions on empirical evidence proven by experimentation, supporting their findings by observational truths, independent of what one inherited by belief or feeling. By the 20th century, scientists realised that perhaps some things could not be measured – things that reside outside time and space. Some ideas may remain in the realm of the abstract and philosophy, such as the idea that human beings are the only thing in the universe with consciousness.

The long-hidden papers revealed that near the end of this savant's life, though celebrated globally for sheer brilliance, he felt he was no closer to his objective than when he had begun as a young man.

But was he wrong?

Today's scientific world is highly critical of the so-called supernatural or unscientific side of his research, even though he invested more time in that realm than in mathematics and physics. A closer reading of his life's work showed how many of the ideas indirectly served to unveil further secrets of the universe.

Sir Isaac Newton (for he was the author of the manuscripts up for auction) had immortalised himself.

Developing a more comprehensive vision and openness to all possibilities, Newton changed the game of life itself. Newton's collaboration with other alchemists likely influenced his work on optics, the physics of light. Alchemical teachings may have inspired another Newtonian discovery: that white light is a mixture of the colours of the rainbow. Alchemists were the first to realise that they could break complex compounds into their constituent parts and recombine them. Newton applied this principle to white light, which he deconstructed and recombined with prisms. The gruelling workload and personal sacrifice were not in vain. The exhaustive hours in pursuit of decoding symbols and even inventing entire systems of mathematics in support of his pursuit all correlated and connected to the discoveries that have now illuminated humanity. Although no alchemist or scientist ever succeeded in turning lead into gold, Newton's openness to alchemical processes informed his science, which is still part of the foundation of our understanding of the cosmos today.

Unlocking Your Alchemical Powers

Suppose someone had just given you a bucketful of lead, that ordinary, everyday base metal that most people find of no value. And suppose you also had the Philosopher's Stone, that magical alchemical substance that turns lead into gold. What would you do? Unless I am terribly mistaken, you would immediately begin using your alchemical powers to transform that bucket of lead into your own bucket of gold – and well, you should. But do you realise that people around you are doing this every day? Like Flamel and Newton, you and I possess alchemical powers. That is, we can choose to convert the base, the ordinary and the bad experiences in our lives into something of tremendous value. Humans tend to blame external circumstances – such as skin colour, gender, race, religion, government, class, upbringing – for our problems. But such an attitude leads to surrender – it assumes you have no control over your life, that you are a victim of uncontrollable circumstance.

It is time to rise above that. An empowered individual cannot be overpowered.

Take Floyd Mayweather Jr, for example. This professional boxer, by many accounts, is the wealthiest athlete in the world. The money he made in just one recent fight worked out to almost $1 million for every minute he was in the ring! Mayweather boasts an unbelievable record of 50 fights and 50 wins – 27 by knockout. He holds ten world titles in five divisions. By any measure, he is arguably one of the best in history. I met Floyd in 2020 at an event organised by my good friend James Taylor who is one of the world's leading event organisers. Floyd was courteous, a real gentleman and immediately opened a conversation with my son; both being fathers of teenage boys, unspoken mutual respect formed.

But life for Mayweather was not always so amazing. Baby Floyd was born into a home filled with chaos and terror. His father sold drugs to feed the family, even selling them to his mother, an addict. His dad missed Floyd's first pro fight because he was serving a three-and-a-half-year prison sentence for cocaine trafficking. Instead of the typical toys that most kids grow up with, young Floyd found himself surrounded by evidence of his mother's addiction. Needles littered their one-room apartment, and he often witnessed his father's angry outbursts, during which he frequently received brutal beatings. By his admission, had it not been for his father's mother, his grandmother Bernice, he probably never would have survived to adulthood.

Not only did his grandmother save his life, but she also kept telling young Floyd that he was going to be a great fighter, like his dad, and would be the best in the world. And somehow, miraculously, she instilled that belief in him. For amid all the chaos, horror, and even near-death experiences, Mayweather figured out the truth about life. He learned that life is not determined by your circumstances but by what you do with them.

Unknowingly, Mayweather had learned the art of alchemy: how to take his negative, traumatic experiences and turn them into pure gold. Floyd became an architect of his destiny and out of the darkness brought new life and prosperity to his entire family, community and generations to come.

Mayweather admits, "I do believe God has given me a special gift and being a great fighter was my destiny. But trust me, if I had not committed to the years, months, days and hours I have spent developing my destiny, I would never have gotten as far as I have in the sport."

Mayweather's philosophy? "I take every negative in my life and turn it into a positive." The very definition of alchemy.

Now let's look at another famous alchemist. 'Oprah' is a household word. Oprah Winfrey's accolades include ranking as the wealthiest African-American in the 20th century and the most outstanding black philanthropist in American history. Some regard her as the most influential woman in the world. Those accomplishments are nothing short of miraculous when you consider her beginnings. Oprah was born to a teenage single mother in poverty-ridden rural Mississippi. As one would expect from such harsh beginnings, her early childhood was precarious and otherwise burdensome. Oprah suffered the trauma of sexual abuse at the tender age of nine. She was raped and molested multiple times, assaults resulting in pregnancy when she was barely a teenager. "Mother was going to put me out of the house, so I was taken to a detention home. While waiting to be processed, a woman comes out and says to my mother and me, 'I'm sorry, but there's not enough room on our docket for your daughter. You'll have to come back in two weeks.'" Oprah went to live with her father in Nashville, Tennessee. She recalls, "That was my saving grace. From that moment forward, I felt like I had been saved. When that baby died [shortly after birth], my father said, 'This is your second chance. Seize this moment and make something of your life.'"

That was the turning point. She exercised her alchemical power of choice to transform traumatic, negative life experiences into a grand success. Oprah is widely praised for using her adversity to become a benefactor for others, evidenced by the more than $50 million she has given to charity.

Oprah's alchemic philosophy: "It's not your circumstances, but your heart that determines how far you go in this world."

Now allow me to introduce you to yet another renowned alchemist, a basketball superstar whose name I am sure you will recognise: Michael Jordan. If I listed all of Jordan's career achievements, they would fill the rest of this book. But what you might find most interesting is that when he was inducted into the Basketball Hall of Fame, the people he thanked were not the obvious ones whom one would assume had helped him succeed. Quite the opposite. Jordan went down the list of all the people who made him confront failure head-on and thanked them for his success. He thanked the players who were chosen to be on teams ahead of him. He thanked bigger-name players who many once believed were better than him. He thanked journalists who doubted his abilities and documented his failures. Jordan said these individuals, along with other instances of failure, were responsible for his astronomical success. He took every piece of negative criticism and transformed it into fuel for the fire of his desire to become the greatest basketball player in the world.

Jordan's philosophy: "I've lost almost 300 games. Twenty-six times I've been trusted to take the game-winning shot and missed. I've failed over and over and over again in my life. And that is why I succeed."

The words of a true alchemist.

You have no doubt heard of the very popular *Chicken Soup for the Soul* book series, co-authored by Jack Canfield and Mark Victor Hansen. But were you aware that 141 publishers rejected the initial manuscript? One hundred and forty-one publishers turned their offer down, repeatedly reminding the ambitious authors that "anthologies don't sell". So what did Canfield and Hansen do? Did they quit? Give up? Take their manuscript and go home? Not on your life. On the contrary. They turned up the heat. They worked tirelessly, coming up with hundreds of creative ways to market their book.

The result? *Chicken Soup for the Soul* books have been translated into 43 languages, published in more than 100 countries, and have sold more than 500 million copies worldwide. This is a perfect illustration of alchemy – turning rejection into gold. A LOT of gold. Just as crucial about his amazing story is that if the manuscript had been accepted early on, Canfield and Hansen would never have begun the arduous task of marketing it themselves, and *Chicken Soup for the Soul* would not have evolved into the success it has become today. God's delays are not necessarily God's denials.

Notable figures from history also demonstrated an understanding of the alchemy philosophy. Abraham Lincoln, the 16th president of the United States, guided Americans through the Civil War with a steady hand, issued the Emancipation Proclamation and championed the Thirteenth Amendment, abolishing slavery in the United States. Lincoln set a standard of success that only a handful in history can match, but he was a constant target for ridicule, criticism and outright vitriol. It was always open season on Lincoln the man – his ancestry, his lack of formal education, his appearance, and even his morality were subjects of scorn.

So how did Lincoln manage slander, criticism and hatred? He showed a deep understanding of the transformative power of the alchemic philosophy:

"I destroy my enemies when I make them my friends," he said. He appointed some of his strongest political opponents to positions of leadership. These men, after working alongside him during times of immense struggle, reportedly came to love and support him.

Winston Churchill – Britain's greatest leader – also faced strong opposition and slander from his contemporaries. E. D. Morel, the man who defeated him in a 1922 race for Parliament, once said, "I look upon Churchill as such a personal force for evil that I would take up the fight against him with a whole heart." MP Sir Henry Channon noted in his diary on the day Churchill was appointed Prime Minister that it was "perhaps the darkest day in English history." Did such stinging comments derail the great Churchill? Absolutely not. He remained focused and committed to his mission of defeating Hitler and saving England, a triumph still celebrated today.

This is only a brief list of champions who turned adverse circumstances in their favour. There are many more. All demonstrate a common theme: deliberately using one's innate alchemical power of choice to transform bad experiences – personal attacks, negative opinions of others, disappointments, failures, horrific childhood experiences and rejection – into victory. By so doing, these persons became impenetrable to defeat. They gave themselves no choices but success, and the very obstacles they faced became the tools they needed to become architects of destiny.

Now that you understand what alchemy is, and you have plenty of examples to support its validity, I will now show you the steps to transform your own difficulties, failures, disappointments and bad memories into experiences of great value.

The first step in mastering the art of alchemy is to realise that problems are opportunities in disguise. Hidden within every obstacle are instructions on how you are to move forward. Virgin Airlines founder Sir Richard Branson provides an excellent example. Branson was planning to fly from Puerto Rico to the British Virgin Islands, where a beautiful woman was waiting to meet him. At the last minute, his flight was cancelled due to insufficient bookings. Problem? Not to Branson. He saw an opportunity. He hired a plane on the spot, borrowed a blackboard on which he wrote "Virgin Airlines – $39 to BVI." His fellow 'bumped' passengers were delighted and voilà! Branson filled up his first plane. Thus Virgin Atlantic Airlines was born.

Stories like Branson's are not unusual. The best entrepreneurs view frustrations and adversity as an opportunity. Seventy per cent of Fortune 500 companies emerged during the worst economies in history. Why? Because a bad economy is ripe with problems to solve, and problems are always – always – seeded with opportunity. The more problems you solve, the more value you bring to the world and the more money you make.

Now, let's talk about YOU. Is there something in your past that is holding you back? A dark cloud that seems to hover over you, following you around like a looming shadow? An overwhelming fear of rejection, failure or ridicule that makes the world seem hostile and unwelcoming, keeping you from pursuing your dream?

Stop for a minute and let your mind roam free. Imagine what could happen if you were able to transcend that darkness? What if this negativity you perceive as worthless or even a roadblock to a prosperous future suddenly becomes your most valuable possession – a treasure trove of gold? What if you could use your innate alchemical power of choice to transmute what appears to be an utter failure into astronomical success?

This is not only possible; it may just be a law of the universe.

Nature has provided you with every tool you need to design your destiny. If you use them wisely, you will be rewarded beyond measure. The universe inexplicably nudges you toward improving your life, the world, and everyone in it – it may penalise you if you do not move forward. It does so first by urging you to improve yourself, to become the vehicle that will carry you to your dreams, bringing them to life.

You can be the alchemist transforming what seems worthless in your life into your most significant treasure.

This brings us to the second step toward mastering the art of alchemy: the concept of complementary opposites.

The universe naturally seeks balance and equilibrium.

Here are some examples:

- Water seeks its own level.
- Your body sweats to cool you when you get too hot and shivers to generate heat when you are too cold, bringing you back to homeostasis.
- If you are down and out, those around you will encourage you and lift you up. And if you are prideful, you will likely be eventually 'reduced to size' by universal laws.

Likewise, from a psychological perspective, if you experience trauma and label it as disastrous, never look for the balancing opposite truth; the universe will penalise you in some way. That is just life's way of seeking equilibrium, to compensate for the imbalance. You see, life is about contrast. There is no light without darkness. No hot without cold. No soft without rough. No wet without dry. As a result, everything serves a purpose, and it is clear that unpleasant experiences may have the potential to produce incredible blessings when you make the process of alchemy work for you.

After all, it is not what has happened to you but what you do with it that matters.

Remember the mention of mini-landmines in Chapter Two? To learn the lessons from your past failures and negative experiences, you must become a bomb disposal expert. You must learn to balance the perception of negative experiences by seeing their opposing latent benefit.

So the next time you ponder your worst experiences or are confronted with a new challenge, instead of seeing them as setbacks and roadblocks, ask yourself:

- What good can come from this?
- What was the benefit of going through this?
- What would be the drawback had I not gone through this experience?

This attitude not only primes you to learn valuable lessons and gain insights, but may help lessen the negative emotional charge that surrounds those experiences, releasing you from their negative grip and allowing you to move forward. Maybe you think that you have tried, but finding some level of balance for your situation seems impossible. If so, this may help.

Though this is an extreme example it may help adjust ones perspective and create the space necessary to move forward, once the dust settles. The devastating effect of the earthquakes and ensuing tsunami which swept through northern Japan in 2011 brought a nation to a standstill and a world to shock. It would be impossible for anyone to give meaning to disasters of this magnitude. Though we see time and time again the survivors are the ones who search for their own personal meanings and reasons to continue, Viktor E Frankl psychiatrist who survived the Holocaust, used the richness of imagination and a compelling feeling of love as a reason to share his story and continue on, which provided a form of counsel to the negative, needed to carry his body through such an ordeal, as well as help thousands of others in later years through his teachings.

While no one would ever wish for such a catastrophe to occur, the resulting events caused millions to open their hearts like never before to help others – entire new charitable organisations sprang up. Nations from around the world turned their attention from power struggles and war to help people in great need – proving, however temporarily, that differences can be put aside and the world can unite. Survivors move to safer areas, and authorities strengthen building codes so that new homes are more resilient and much more. This is an example of observing a situation and looking for the balancing opposite – the blessings and benefits that can emerge. Why not rise above the trauma and utilise your worst experiences as a source of your empowerment, rising above the wrath of nature itself? By following the instructions in the previous chapter about forming new success pathways in the brain, conditioning your subconscious to create the reality you desire – and deactivating all those mini-landmines in the process – you will be performing the very act of alchemy.

You see, no matter how much you may resist, the universal energy will eventually force you to focus on the hard truth about yourself. It is time to acknowledge the situation as it is and build an image of a new brighter future from the present dilemma, consent to it and believe in it. Resistance only leads to more pain and hardship if you try to defy this universal law of balancing opposites. You will have no more success than if you decided to challenge the law of gravity.

The emotional suffering you may be experiencing is a natural feedback mechanism that pushes you toward equilibrium – continually reminds you that you must do work to achieve balance and that the tools are right there. Once emotions are neutralised a method of revising past memories and imaging happier outcomes from your personal history, becomes a potent method of teaching your body that the past cycles are over. Though to many this may appear controversial, the techniques have been proven to assist in reducing negative memories from remerging as well as potential problems. It will however provide a new foundation for your mind to work from.

Consider all the examples of alchemy I have shared with you: Mayweather, Oprah, Jordan, Canfield and Hansen, Lincoln and Churchill. How would their lives (and the history of the world) be different had they chosen to surrender to victimhood? Had they chosen to merely exist, eventually disappearing from the world as an insignificant speck of dust?

They would have never achieved the heights, never have changed the world for the better. What a waste!

Be careful of revelling in failure and pain, shining a spotlight on bad experiences. You just set yourself up for more of the same. You are creating the future every second, and ruminating over past failures means you are taking them with you, further imprisoning your mind. If you fail to act on the rule of complementary opposites, you do nothing but accumulate further emotional damage. Your perceived trauma must be equilibrated, and you can do so only by observing the positive.

Interestingly, focusing on what you do not want produces the same effect. By continually seeking to avoid, your mind sees nothing but danger, everything that can go wrong. For example, if I say, "Don't think about a blue elephant," you automatically conjure a blue elephant. It does not matter that I said "Don't."

To be successful, you must switch your thoughts to only what you want and to exclude all else. Awareness of what may go wrong has a place, of course. Once you have prudently positioned caution in its proper place, most of your energy and focus can stay on the goal. To reach it requires that you be better than you were yesterday – better than you were before you even read this sentence. Begin by raising your standards – not for others, but for yourself – and remaining consistent committed to those standards. Don't distract yourself by focusing on the shortcomings of others, even though placing blame is so much easier than accepting responsibility. Choose to take responsibility because when you do, you have no choice but to change and improve. The truth is the change you avoid may be the very change that you must embrace to create the world you want.

I would like you to consider the following. Hundreds of years ago if you had a problem or wished for an improvement in your circumstances, you would have been at the mercy of your monarch or tribal leader. That person would have had the information, resources and access at that time for your solution. Today we are nearing an even playing ground for all. You now have access to almost any information at the touch of a button; the restriction to wealth is no longer there. We are in an age of angel investors, lending institutions even crowdfunding from around the world; the money is there at your disposal. Relinquish the concern of gender, government, race or religion; the only colour that influences access to wealth is green. Recognise that you not only have access to power you are the power.

We live in a benevolent universe. These universal laws work in our favour if we comply with their principles. If we grasp that the universe is on our side, our minds look for supporting evidence, and everything begins to race to your aid. Thinking the opposite only produces supporting evidence for failure and inertia.

The most important decision we make is whether we believe we live in a friendly or hostile universe. – Albert Einstein

Once you set your dream in motion, never quit. Remember, persistence is the key.

Before we conclude this chapter, here is an exercise to familiarise yourself with this method:

Find a quiet place where you can sit comfortably undisturbed. Close your eyes, focus on your breathing and quiet your mind. Then, choose to revisit an experience from your past that still carries an emotional charge, one you would describe as hurtful. Evaluate the meaning you have taken from that experience. Then, make the deliberate choice to look at that experience from an entirely different angle by answering the following four questions:

1. How can I profit from this experience?
2. What good has come about because of this happening?
3. How can this experience serve me for the greater good?
4. How may I help others from my own experience because of this?

Napoleon Hill, in reflecting on the hundreds of successful people he studied on his journey to success at age 70, said, "The biggest breakthroughs came directly after what appeared to be the biggest heartbreaks." The breakthrough you seek is yours if you are willing to find the balancing opposite to your dark shadow. Diffuse the negative energy by bringing the latent benefit to light. Neutralise the bomb. In that process, you will experience your own personal transformation of base metal into gold. In the words of one of my mentors, Dr John Demartini, "Don't be a victim of your history. Be a master of your destiny."

Give yourself the freedom to observe the opposite interpretation of any emotionally charged experience. Be creative in your thinking and identify some benefit you can derive from that time and reposition it in your mind in a positive light. If you do this effectively, you will neutralise the negative energy of that memory and bring yourself back into balance Having now learned to become deliberately observant of the light that is found in the darkness, you will develop a greater awareness of opportunity, and your mental barriers will begin to loosen their grip.

In our next chapter, I will provide you with the key that opens the gateway to the subconscious mind, revealing to you the tightly guarded secrets of the encrypted language used to influence your mind and create the change you are after.

CHAPTER FOUR

The Gateway to the Subconscious

It is the repetition of affirmations that leads to belief, and once that belief becomes a deep conviction, things begin to happen. – Muhammad Ali

Staring at the diamond-studded night sky, Napoleon Hill took a deep breath, re-entered his apartment and strode directly to the bathroom mirror. He looked squarely into his own eyes and spoke aloud his mentor's prescribed affirmation:

"Andrew Carnegie, not only am I going to equal your achievements in this lifetime, I am going to challenge you at the post and pass you at the grandstand."

Hill was now two weeks into his 30-day prescription, uttering this statement first thing in the morning and again before retiring to sleep. The young journalist had received this instruction from perhaps the richest man who ever lived, guidelines designed to change his self-image profoundly and to instil an idea which, carried to its logical conclusion, would revolutionise his life.

The affirmation was so farfetched, so seemingly impossible, he made sure no other human being could hear him utter those challenging words. In recent days he had noticed progress in his battles against self-doubt. 'There must be some truth behind those words,' he thought. He became aware of an emerging sensation as if a missing puzzle piece had clicked into place, connecting his jumbled life into a coherent whole. The self-programming had so saturated his thoughts and emotions his subconscious had no choice but to submit, the gates of its fortress succumbing to the power of affirmation. Now alive in the deepest part of his psyche, this seemingly simple idea was free to subconsciously direct his behaviour while simultaneously attenuating his emotions as he strode, on course at last, to his destination.

What happened next would seem the stuff of fantasy, but for one thing. It happened.

You have to find that place inside where nothing is impossible. –
Deepak Chopra

We are all aware that our subconscious exists, but ask yourself:

- Do you know how it works?
- Did you know it is the only determining factor in achieving success?
- Did you know you can harness its power to create your reality?

If not, you're in for a treat.

This chapter explores the subconscious – that hidden, compelling, often mysterious aspect of the mind that essentially defines the reality we experience and the reality we can create. We'll break down the Law of Attraction – what it means, how it works, and how our understanding of this universal law has evolved.

But first, back to our story…

American author Napoleon Hill was born in a two-room log cabin nestled in the primitive hill country of Wise County, Virginia, in 1883, a place defined by poverty, illiteracy and superstition. With the love and support of his wise stepmother Martha, at age 15 the ambitious Hill landed a position as a freelance reporter for a group of rural newspapers. A few years later, he secured a job with *Bob Taylor's Magazine,* a successful periodical offering advice on business and wealth.

In 1908 came an assignment that would change his life forever: an interview with the 73-year-old Pittsburgh steel magnate and philanthropist Andrew Carnegie – arguably the richest man who ever lived.

"What the world needs," Carnegie explained to a mesmerised Hill, "is a philosophy of personal achievement; a system of success principles from not only the country's leading businessmen and thinkers, but also the greatest minds in history, a system that will demonstrate the commonality behind their stories."

Carnegie's own rags-to-astronomical-riches story had convinced him that he could organise the principles of success into a formula anyone could understand and apply. His lack of formal education also motivated him; it was a sharp personal pain nudging him toward creating a framework for success that anyone with intelligence, drive and perseverance could copy – and thus build a life of achievement and success.

Three hours into the interview, Carnegie was so enthused by the discussion he invited Hill to dinner – the beginning of what would become a three-day conversation between the obscure young reporter and the world-famous mogul. And at the end of the third day, Carnegie concluded, "I've told you everything I know about this new philosophy. I've explained how 'thoughts are things' and how one can use the power of emotionalised thought to create the circumstances and conditions of life they so desire. I've shared with you all the possibilities and potential I see for this new philosophy on personal achievement." He then startled Hill with a question which, Carnegie said, required a simple yes or no: would Hill accept Carnegie's commission to become the author of this new approach to a life of success and achievement? Before answering, Carnegie cautioned, Hill should know that he would have to devote 20 years of research to truly understand what Carnegie was imparting, with no expectation of assistance from the great man, financial or otherwise, other than introductions to people who could assist Hill in understanding.

Hill would later write:

"I had just finished telling Mr Carnegie that I feared he had picked the wrong person to give the world its first practical philosophy of personal success… because of my youth, lack of education, and lack of finances when he delivered a lecture that I will never forget.

"'Let me point you to a great power which is under your control,' said Mr Carnegie. 'A power that is greater than poverty, than the lack of education, than all of your fears and superstitions combined. This power can take the station of your own mind and direct it to whatever ends you may desire.'"

Hill was convinced on the spot.

"Sir," Hill replied, "Not only will I accept the challenge, but you can depend on me to complete it!"

By 1933, Napoleon Hill was a successful man of considerable influence. Sitting opposite Franklin D. Roosevelt in the White House as an advisor to the president, he was an integral part of the fight to rescue Americans from one of its darkest periods – the Great Depression. He made a bold proposal to put to the test all he had learned about success and the power of the mind. He told Roosevelt he wanted to use the Mastermind Principle – the fruit of his two decades of research into Carnegie's ideas – to save the country. Roosevelt was captivated by the prospect of transforming the psychological perspective of the American people. With the president's blessing, Hill began a massive campaign to convince an entire nation that the economy was recovering and times were getting better. He gathered what today we might call 'influencers', religious figures of all denominations, radio personalities, newspaper and magazine editors, famous characters from both political parties – and influenced them to share the message of dawning prosperity and a bright future.

And it worked! Once convinced by their leaders that the economy was indeed on the rise, hope replaced fear, confidence replaced hesitation, action replaced fearful waiting – and the county began a full, final recovery from its greatest economic catastrophe.

Hill proved that the principles he learned from Carnegie, supplemented by his interviews with over 500 successful people, could be applied on a nationwide scale. He had met Carnegie's challenge, and in the end, his achievements may have surpassed those of Carnegie himself, just as his affirmations had declared.

Hill later wrote:

"Mr Carnegie made not over 20–25 millionaires at most. The millionaires I have had the privilege of making are legions. They are all over the world. But this is what I am most thankful for. I have brought men and women together in a spirit of harmony and understanding that didn't exist before. I have rescued men and women from financial devastation by helping them find themselves. I have been able to do for the world things that Mr Carnegie never did do."

Do you see how Hill's message was able to surpass the accomplishments of Carnegie?

He did it by bringing to light the power available to every person when they harness the natural laws of the universe.

The catalyst responsible for Hill's astounding success lies in those three days he spent with Carnegie and the challenge Carnegie put before him at that moment.

The mental-conditioning exercise Carnegie shared with Hill – which Hill practised daily – equipped Hill with an emotionally-charged mind that refused to quit. Nineteen years later, just a year short of the time Carnegie predicted he would need, Hill produced his premier work on the science of personal achievement, *Think and Grow Rich*. By the time he died in 1970, his book had sold 20 million copies and continues to hold a place among top sellers today.

And now I give you – in one sentence – the scientific formula for success for which Napoleon Hill is rightly credited:

"Whatever the mind can conceive and believe it can achieve."

It may surprise you to know that similar theories about the science of personal achievement predated Napoleon Hill. A generation earlier, Serbian-American physicist and inventor Nikola Tesla was making history with little more than his 'miraculous' mind and uncanny powers of visualisation. Even as a boy, Tesla said he could merely imagine an object and cause it to become so real and vivid in his mind that he found it difficult to tell the difference between the imagined thing and material reality. Mathematically inclined, Tesla's genius enabled him to 'see' solutions to mathematical and algebraic problems as soon as the equation was stated, having worked through the necessary operations mentally more quickly than if he had worked them out by hand.

Tesla was so gifted it is said that Albert Einstein, when asked how it felt to be the most intelligent man alive, replied, "I don't know. You'll have to ask Nikola Tesla."

Strange as it may sound, I'm not convinced Tesla was that different from you and me, except that he recognised – and used – the power of his imagination much more effectively than most of us. He honed his creative skills so exquisitely, whatever he imagined had moving, three-dimensional life in his mind. Tesla described the experience this way:

"I started taking mental journeys beyond the world of my acquired knowledge. I continually imagined places I had never been to. I created colourful, precise images in my mind of these places. I imagined living in countries I had never seen and making imaginary friends. These people were very close to me and seemed real.

"This I constantly did until I was seventeen, when my thoughts turned seriously to invention. Then, to my delight, I found I could visualise with the greatest facility. By that faculty of visualising, I have evolved what is, I believe, a new method of materialising inventive ideas and conceptions. It is a method that may be of great usefulness to any imaginative man, whether he is an inventor, businessman or artist."

Tesla is credited with dozens of inventions, all conceived, constructed and 'tested' in his mind.

"Without ever drawing a sketch, I can give the measurements of all parts to workers, and when completed, all these parts will fit, just as certainly as though I had made the actual drawings. It is immaterial to me whether I run my machine in my mind or test it in my shop.

"The inventions I have conceived in this way have always worked. In thirty years, there has not been a single exception."

How can this be?

The answer is simple.

The subconscious mind does not – cannot – distinguish between what is real and what is imagined. Tesla understood that. He harnessed the power of imagination and visualisation to create objects that had never before existed except in the mental realm of potential possibility.

Tesla did not wake up one morning with these superpowers. He developed them through continual psychological conditioning, which for him was both natural and enjoyable, much like an athlete works to improve physical strength, a habit Tesla shared with Napoleon Hill. Tesla and Hill intuited what is now clinically proven: every time you imagine, learn new things, memorise or undertake similar mental exertions, your brain adds neural connections. Just as an athlete who works against resistance builds new muscle tissue, our minds make stronger and further links when engaged in imaginative, creative thought.

Later in this chapter, I will give you Tesla's formula and specific steps for creating your subconscious power, perhaps one of the most powerful things you'll ever learn. For now, merely recognising you have this fantastic potential within you is itself very valuable. You must learn how to practise the mental training that will produce subconscious mastery – and turn you into an EndGamer.

What has changed in nearly a century since Nikola Tesla demonstrated the power of the mind to transform imagery into reality and Napoleon Hill wrote his success philosophy? Thanks to our ability to measure brain waves, electrical impulses and energy fields, a world of fascinating data now document much of what Hill, Tesla and many others believed.

The 'placebo effect' is a well-known example, a positive physical response to a 'fake' treatment. A patient with a documented condition such as high blood pressure or depression receives a sugar pill or a simple saline injection instead of medicine. Numerous double-blind studies show that in most cases, the overwhelming majority of patients who unknowingly received the 'fake' treatment improved only because their minds expected to improve.

What causes this phenomenon, and, more importantly, what does it prove?

The explanation is as follows. When patients *believe* they are receiving the appropriate treatment, they subconsciously signal their autonomic nervous system to produce the body's natural pharmacy of chemicals that mirror the chemicals they believe they are taking. These naturally-produced chemicals, in turn, heal the body. In one particular study conducted with patients suffering from depression, a full 81% of those 'treated with placebo reported improvement, a result confirmed by brain scans.

When informed they had been treated with a placebo, the most typical response was, "You must be mistaken. I am certain I got the real drug."

This is a powerful point that bears repeating: their minds believed their bodies were receiving medicines needed to get better. Because of this mental state, their bodies automatically went to work to produce natural antidepressants, based solely on the patients' subconscious belief that they would improve.

This is precisely the mechanism that made Hill's affirmations so powerful.

Here's the process:

The conscious mind believes it is receiving the drug necessary to heal the condition. The conscious mind then transfers this belief to the subconscious mind, which creates change at the cellular level and then manifests that change in the body, a physical reality that is verified by medical examination.

In other words, what they believed in their mind changed their physical reality.

What does the placebo effect show?

The answer can be found in the mind–body connection.

But first, let's do a quick review of fundamental physics.

You know what happens when you drop a glass; it falls to the floor (and usually breaks!). If you push a wheel, it rolls along until the resistance force is greater than the strength of motion. If you try to walk through a wall, well, the wall wins, and you get bruised. These things are consistently true because of the fundamental laws of classical physics. Classical physics was once believed to apply to everything in nature. But at the turn of the 20th century, scientists discovered something astonishing. They found that tiny particles of matter – atoms, electrons and light waves, for example – don't follow the standard 'classical' rules. Fundamental particles exist in a state of perpetual flux, only 'deciding' their state when they are observed, measured or experience an interaction of some kind.

The field of quantum physics was born.

Here's why that's important.

The 'classical' model of cause and effect says that for you to be happy, your external circumstances have to improve, which causes you to react positively.

In the view of classical physics, you are powerless to effect any positive change in your life.

Quantum physics says this is not true.

Remember our discussion on human potentiality in Chapter One? Our bodies are made up of tissues and organs, which are in turn made up of cells. Cells are made up of molecules; molecules are made up of atoms; atoms are made up of subatomic particles such as protons, neutrons and electrons; and subatomic particles are made up of exotic elements such as quarks and muons – 'frozen light' which, when explored more in-depth, are found to be pure energy in constant flux, winking in and out of physical existence.

If you could examine yourself under a sufficiently powerful electron microscope, breaking every component in your body down to its most singular form, you would be left with nothing but pure, raw, potential energy. In short, you are a cluster of ever-changing pure energy. This is your quantum reality. You are pure energy, and you exist within and are part of the matrix of potentiality that is 'the universe'. As such, by aligning with this realm of potentiality, you can set in motion every resource you need to fulfil your desired goal.

Thoughts or beliefs may seem ephemeral but are measurable as electrical impulses in the brain, and these 'thought impulses' impact the quantum field of invisible energy that surrounds you. In other words, your habits of thought determine the state these energetic subatomic particles 'choose' to become. Your thought energy shifts the universe on a particle-by-particle basis to create your physical reality – what you refer to as your 'circumstances'.

Everything you see in your physical world began as an idea – a product of the imagination.

This idea (thought impulse) organised the energy around it, which is in a quantum state until it is affected (physicists say until it is 'observed' or 'measured') by this idea, this outside agency. It then assume a form that reflects the image of the idea held in your mind, a physical object observable in the world of matter. Remember, Tesla could imagine reality so precisely machined parts in the real world did not deviate from the way he imagined them – they were identical.

This theory is easier to understand when you see it at work in your own life. Put simply: you become what you think about most of the time. Who are you as a person? What are the circumstances of your life? Can you see that the answers to these questions are alive in the world because you have imagined and believed that they are correct? You unconsciously seek supporting evidence for your beliefs, and your mind seizes that evidence like a hungry pit-bull terrier on a bone, refusing to let go. The world begins to appear as you expect it to look, and other potential realities never materialise, unless you make room for them by consenting to the desire that appears and then believing in its possibility.

Mental flexibility is critical to let go of an idea once you discover it is wrong and free your mind to create a new reality from new expectations and desires. Quantum physics show us that our world – just like our minds – is not fixed and unchangeable, even though it may appear to be. Instead, it is a fluid environment, continually reorganising itself based on its immediate quantum-level encounters. Even our mental habits – what we believe or do not believe – affect this material reality.

Whether you know it or not, you are continually creating your own circumstances by how and what you think! In other words, what you think about all day long is constantly rendering your reality. Quantum theory, now widely accepted, could be the basis for Napoleon Hill's formula for success and the power behind the truths you learn in this book. Once you grasp this, you can see that your habitual thought patterns, your inertial tendency to behave in a relatively consistent manner with the same emotional state and worldview, define the actual world you inhabit.

The key is this: habits are just that – a settled tendency, a familiar pattern of thought, feeling and behaviour. They are not your destiny. Why are habits so hard to change? Because ceasing old habits means stepping into the realm of the unfamiliar, the unknown, the uncomfortable and making different choices while thinking, feeling and behaving differently. But a little discomfort or dissatisfaction is often the mother of creation. When you begin to reorganise your energy field through new and different ways of thinking, you harness the power of your imagination and subconscious – exemplified in the lives of Hill and Tesla – and you create the new reality you wish to see all around you.

But harnessing the power of thought is just the beginning.

You also *feel* at a subconscious level. Have you noticed the way we describe meeting someone we are attracted to?

"I was *attracted* to them."

"I *felt drawn* to them."

"We just *connected.*"

These are terms associated with a subconscious charge we sometimes call 'personal magnetism', a charge that genuinely exists and which we feel strongly, if unconsciously.

It is essential to recognise that *feelings* are involved in breaking old thought habits and creating new ones. For example, many people describe a feeling of loss when they stop smoking as if they had lost a companion or a feeling of fear when they start something new, such as a challenging course of study. You can involve your feelings – your heart centre – in creating new and positive changes in your life. You will experience it as the magnetic feeling that unconsciously draws you to your new way of thinking. When you emotionally embrace a new future reality, you have both an electrical impulse of *thought* and a magnetic impulse of *feeling* that creates a much more significant impact.

The story I am about to share with you below serves to introduce you to an idea about influencing others even in the absence of words and how our own perception of 'self' can serve as a determinant factor how others interact with us at the most fundamental level, if we let it. It is important to note that throughout history, there have been figures that irrespective of colour, race, religion, gender, social standing etc have been an attractive force that could disarm any form of social prejudice with only their presence.

See Yourself as Royalty and the Rest of the World will Conform to Your Image

Abdullah the Ethiopian rabbi was living on 72nd Street, Manhattan, in one of the most desirable homes in New York City, once owned by the then US treasurer Henry Morgenthau. The mystic was a sight to behold, a presence that illuminated Time Square even more than its bright lights; his rich ebony glow was accentuated by the contrast of his bright white turban rapped boldly around his head; it could just as easily be mistaken for a crown rather than a cloth. Though very little has been written on Abdullah we do know he was a figure who offered counsel to many prominent figures in the world of politics and entertainment with two notable students, Neville Goddard and Joseph Murphy who would become instrumental in laying the foundation for the now multi-billion personal development industry.

This was during the 1920s, when America was at its pinnacle of prejudice, with segregation in transportation, theatres, districts and even schools, all based on keeping colours apart and accepted as the norm of society.

Heading to the ticket stand, Abdullah reserved two seats in the very centre of the theatre, the attendant nervously passed over his tickets. The apprehension was not that she was about to commit a crime by providing seats for a man of colour, but instead his sheer presence commanded respect and the attendant was instinctively looking to appease the request of such nobility. The rabbi's personal acceptance and recognition that he was an idea of God, coupled with his majestic appearance, reaffirmed his conviction that he was indeed a prince of power. Abdullah was not attempting to make a statement or fight discrimination; his frame of the world was so definitive, in seeing no divisions, boundaries or colour and even filtering all contradictory sounds and opinions of society. He was adept at creating the world he wanted and living within it. Abdullah believed that everything you experience, including how people respond to you, results from your feelings and assumptions of yourself. The masses have no choice but to yield and confirm to your view of self.

We are here to acknowledge and accept ourselves as architects of destiny and stabilise the identity; in doing so you become a magnetising power. As oppose to racing for one thing after another, let's build you into a position where the things you desire and want as well as the experiences you dwell upon are drawn to you becomes the norm. Barren images and whimsical desires have no effect on reality; emotion does. Emotion broadcasts louder than words and imprint our perceptions of self on those we interact with, which they then reflect right back to us, reaffirming our identity.

Feelings are the medium used to instruct the subconscious what we would like to have happen as well as how we would like to be perceived. The subconscious interprets this symbolic language of feelings and images, then goes on to transmit right back to us instructions via flashes of insights or instinctively compel us to make the right decision with no thought whatsoever, guiding us to the results we are after.

Developing clearer internal pictures works as a tool to elicit the feelings we would experience within the desired outcome. We then turn our awareness inward, asking the question:

How would I feel if this were true?

In doing so we can begin to familiarise ourselves with the requisite feelings to construct our reality.

Feelings are transmissions that set the wheels of creation into motion and are a complete language in and of themselves. Learning to decipher sensations and evoke the necessary emotion is key to ensuring the desires of your heart come true. In creating new and positive changes in your life, you will experience it as the magnetic feeling that unconsciously develops and brings to the surface a more accurate and automated way of doing things. When you emotionally embrace a new future reality (living in the assumption that you are already there) the electrical impulse of *thought* is activated and a *magnetic* impulse of feeling is created producing a significant impact on behaviour in return creating the potential and inevitable event appearing to you.

It is also important to note once again that the subconscious cannot differentiate between what is real and what is imagined. By adding the power of visualisation to create a three-dimensional working image of the desire, your subconscious is primed to set in motion the process of making that new reality.

Direct instruction to your inner mind results in it transmitting to you the correct feelings, behaviour and actions to take:

- Script the person you are to be that would easily create the outcomes you want – that is, your intention and become the embodiment of that
- Ask yourself, how would I feel were this desire real? This allows your inner mind to provide you with an accurate feeling to work with.
- Ensure all your internal dialogue and what you dwell upon matches the target outcome.
- Build a clear experience in your minds eye of already owning or having the outcome you desire
- Allow your mind to provide you with the emotions and feeling states you would experience were the desired result an everyday part of your life.

Thus you transform the elements of the universe both within you and without to fulfil your intention. Your emotional commitment signals the subconscious to go on high alert in searching for opportunities that were once invisible to you. People pick up on these unspoken communications – your new magnetism – and will be drawn to you, even if they cannot articulate why.

It is only logical that the more strongly you inculcate emotion into your commitment to change, the more frequently you will use conscious thoughts to adjust your subconscious views, and the more clearly you can define the images you want to create. Ultimately, you will bring more influence to bear on the universe to rearrange itself to manifest your desired reality. It is often said: success breeds success. As you begin to notice a positive change, you will naturally invest the sweat equity needed to become world-class in your field of endeavour.

In Chapter Two we discussed how the brain has a neuroplastic quality; it is always morphing, evolving and regenerating in response to the input you feed it. It follows that you can change the physiology of your brain based on how you consciously and deliberately think and feel. A new, exciting field of study known as epigenetics is documenting physiologic changes in the body's DNA response to sustained electromagnetic impulses of thought and emotion. This development may help further explain the placebo effect. Remember, people who experience the placebo effect are not faking it or fooling themselves – their conditions are undoubtedly improved. Medical testing proves it.

Epigenetics shows that what you think and feel stimulates an electromagnetic charge that impacts every atom in your physiology as well as in your material reality.

In sum, the scientific models of quantum physics, neuroendocrinology and epigenetics point to a magnificent mind–body connection, demonstrating that the mind is always influencing the body through impulses generated by conscious and subconscious thought and that the body, in turn, is always influencing the mind in the same way.

Which do you think your brain perceives as lasting longer: 30 seconds of a good massage or 30 seconds of holding your hand over a flame?

It follows that if you live today by the same thoughts, emotions and behaviours as you did yesterday, your mental and physical reality will stay the same. There isn't a person in the world excluded from this equation. There is a good reason we say, "Old habits die hard." Change takes sustained effort. Reprogramming your mind and body in the direction you seek is a process of breaking old habits.

But we all come preloaded with the biological/neurological machinery to effect change and create the reality we want. The outdated idea that 'biography determines destiny' still runs rampant despite new scientific evidence to the contrary. The fact is we just too easily allow ourselves to follow like sheep, believing what we have been told is true, denying ourselves the freedom to take complete responsibility for our lives and our destinies. Through inertia, conscious choice or ignorance about our capacity for change, we too often fail to fulfil our ability to be as content and accomplished as we wish to be. Old habits do indeed die hard, but the change is well worth it!

As should now be clear, it is you, the EndGamer reading this book, who must shoulder the responsibility for breaking this paradigm.

Most of our heroes in life are not those who talk but those who act and accomplish – people whose behaviours and achievements do the talking for them. I believe we select these heroes because we unconsciously know this is precisely what we want to emulate – conduct and accomplishments, not talk. Thus we are drawn to heroes who fulfil a life we desire for ourselves – we subconsciously feel that magnetic attraction we have discussed.

But there are many steps between admiring a champion and acting like one. And that leads us to the concept of 'setpoints'.

Equilibrium – the sense of balance in our inner lives – is maintained by setpoints, a concept with the power to change everything.

Changing your setpoints resets the fulcrum upon which you balance your life and is the surest way to improve your current results.

For example, if we took all the money from the top 5% and distributed it evenly among the 95%, it won't be long before the money is again in the hands of the 5%. This is because those who have earned a great deal of wealth have a different equilibrium – a different setpoint – than those who have not. They become restless, uncomfortable and dissatisfied if they feel they are not achieving highly and will do anything to recapture that success.

There are undeniably basic structural advantages and disadvantages built into each society, which are part of what keeps people organised consistent and maintaining their setpoints. This helps explain why those who have much less, if presented with a sudden windfall, soon return to their familiar setpoint of having little money and back into society's pre-built framework. Breaking through is only possible by stepping out of that structure, changing self-perception by seizing control of your own power and recognising yourself as your own architect of destiny, embodying the consciousness of wealth and unlimited possibility.

We are all programmed to be consistent, with our own self-perception and identity.

Later in the book we will be taking a deep dive into powerful methods used to change setpoints, living deliberately and not leaving your future to chance.

The Gateway Into Your Subconscious

Think of the most powerful supercomputer in the world. It is really only a collection of circuit boards and wires sitting mutely in a room. Its extensive capabilities exist only as pure potential until you upload software that enables it to do the fantastic things computers do.

Your mind is like that computer. The power of the subconscious is only pure potential until your conscious mind (via thought patterns) uploads your software (beliefs). But once that's done, the output is automatic – and astonishing. Your mind, like the computer, does what it is made to do based on the software you upload.

The question is: what software will you upload to your computer? By using your tools of thought, feeling and the power of imagination to define your desired future reality every day, you can change the physiology of your brain and body and bring about your new reality. This is a phenomenal truth!

Once you penetrate the subconscious in this way, you are tapping into the same energy field that fills the interspaces of the universe. Its power is virtually unlimited, and like Tesla, Carnegie and so many others, you can claim control over your inert resources and lead yourself to do something great.

When your desired reality becomes part of your subconscious physiology, your behaviour automatically follows, carrying out the 'orders' of the subconscious control centre.

Now, let's put this all together.

Let's take that raw impulse of thought and start to create something out of it.

Whatever you are dreaming about or dwelling upon in your mind is real. It exists in the quantum field of potentiality.

As you continue to think about it, you transmit electrical impulses into the universe – frequencies and images of the imagined thing. The universe is continually reorganising on the subatomic quantum level, subtly reacting to the feedback it experiences, which scientists call 'observing' or 'measuring'. By just writing down the thing you most desire, you are taking the first step in making the intangible tangible.

By speaking your desire aloud to yourself, you project a frequency of sound into the universe – another step in affecting the cosmic structure around you. As that emotion of desire grows and combines with the repetition of thought and intention, you project an intense particle flow of electromagnetic energy into the quantum field. With time and consistency, your body and mind will blend in a state of belief that what you desire is already yours. With your inner world coherent and synchronised, you can relax because the reality you seek is imminent.

This is the essence of actual change. This is how you can deliberately create your own reality. This is what greatness is all about.

Communicating with Infinite Intelligence

Consider how your life began; scientists now estimate one-in-a-trillion achievement, a single cell that won the competitive struggle for life. What was the intelligence that informed your development in your mother's womb from that single cell into a fully-formed human being? How did you know when it was time to be born? How did you know you should no longer take fluid into your lungs but breathe air instead? How did you know when it was time to sit up, crawl and walk?

There is a robust innate intelligence within every cell of your being that controls the beating of your heart, your every breath and your autonomic responses. It tells your body to heal when you cut yourself. It is your very life force. That same intelligence programs the movements of the planets in our solar system. It controls the ebb and flow of the tides and our circadian rhythm.

If you had a way to communicate with this intelligence, to plug into the matrix of the universe, would it change the way you think and feel about your life?

Of course it would.

I believe the Almighty is revealed in the mysterious, powerful, undeniable interactions between our minds, bodies and the external universe . This is the power that intended and initiated the creation of everything – along with an eternal, unwavering persistence that brings it all to fruition. Everything we perceive begins with an idea; nothing just appears. A thought or 'intention' is nurtured into life with 'attention', the emotion, visualisation and expectation that creates reality.

When you recognise this Infinite Intelligence and put your trust in the higher power that gifted life and awareness, you no longer have to rely solely on your limited perceptions of how to bring about the reality you desire. You begin to build the framework and lay a foundation for change based on your *intention*. Combine your commitment with the conviction that Infinite Intelligence has transmitted you the desire to either consent to or reject the outcome that you want. The desire contains within it the potential for its realisation, yet to set the wheels of creation in motion the logical or rational mind is to find its own way to believe and have faith in the outcomes possibility. It is only then the innate potential activated and you are then granted the right to achieve your potential and live your best life.

You don't have to know *how* this occurs, just as you don't need to be a mechanical engineer to drive a car. With intention, visualisation and emotion, you plug into the system that allows you to control your direction, and the universal mechanism then delivers you to your destination. If you doubt that you can direct the raw data of the universe and model it into your own heart's desire, consider: you are already doing it! The result is your current set of circumstances. Now it's time to assert *intentional* control over the subconscious mechanism and make your dreamed-of reality happen within your mind and in the universe .

You don't need to understand quantum physics to create your desired reality. Quantum mechanics has existed for billions of years, with very few humans even being aware of it, let alone understanding it. Your task is to trust in the formidable intelligence that created the universe and created you, literally from stardust. Believe that if you follow the 'formula for success' we have discussed, well-established in history and documented in science, you will be swept in the direction of your dreams as if by an invisible current.

Often the mind appears on a conscious level to be two – that is, how we process information and formulate actions. Who are you speaking with when you talk to yourself? With whom are you angry when you are mad at yourself? Occasionally, 'you' will argue with 'you' that any changes you achieve with the tools you are using are 'just a coincidence' or even an illusion. When that happens, recognise that is inertia talking, a powerful force that resists change of any kind, and which, if heeded, can poison your dream, perpetuate the status quo, and result in your ideas being delivered stillborn.

Our doubts are traitors – William Shakespeare

Take George, for example.

George wants to own a supercar; from the very beginning he would play with toy cars gradually progressing onto building Lego models; as a teen, hours were spent on racing video game simulations. On family holidays George would travel to watch the Monaco Grand Prix. His desire is authentic. In maturity, an avid car enthusiast, he continually thinks about how it would feel in the driver's seat, experiencing the rush of excitement and power as he speeds down the motorway.

George is visualising, moving in the direction of his dream. He is engaging his thoughts, emotions, and his imagination. Because of the intensity and frequency with which he transmits his desire through his physiology, his subconscious mind is beginning to formulate a plan.

Maybe he can generate the income to buy the car of his dreams.

Or he may win it.

He could begin a business that pays for it.

Or establish a car rental company that would pay for the car, ultimately making both ownership and a financial return possible.

See how flexible George's thinking has become? He has a mature perspective, considering many different ways to get what he wants.

Now, let's say George's circle of friends are car collectors and enthusiasts. Suddenly George feels a subtle pressure to fit in. But, even more motivating, each time he travels in a friend's car he is living in the assumption and feelings that he too has ownership, and the images become so real that he dreams at night of awakening and seeing one in the driveway. George now wants to build a lifestyle for himself and his fiancé that demonstrates to her and her well-to-do family that he is a go-getter who can provide whatever luxury no matter how far a reach; the vehicle also serves as an unconscious status signal.

Now, what was before merely a dream has turned into an obsession, triggering his brain to bring to his attention the opportunities, people and events that will have the vehicle in his possession. George knows what he focusing on, and as he continues to behave in ways that move him in the direction of his goal, he is adding value to the world. As he improves, he has a positive impact on others, motivating them to improve.

Let's look at another example.

We began with the story of Napoleon Hill and how, through a chance meeting with the richest man in the world at that time, Andrew Carnegie, the direction of Hill's life was forever changed.

But what of Andrew Carnegie? The man who went from $1.20 a week to $309 billion and then gave it all away.

How did he come to be so sure that success could be reduced to a formulaic science?

No doubt, it was a result of his personal journey.

Carnegie was born into a modest home in Dunfermline, Scotland, in 1835. For generations, his family had been master handloom weavers. But the Industrial Revolution replaced manpower with steam-power, and the family business collapsed. Carnegie states, "It was burnt into my heart that my father had to beg (for work). And then and there came the resolve that I would cure that when I got to be a man."

When Carnegie was 12, he and his family emigrated to the United States and moved in with his two aunts in Pittsburgh. They all slept in a single room. Carnegie's first job was in the boiler room of a textile factory when he was 13, though not long after that he took a job as a messenger at a telegraph office. During the next several years, young Carnegie made a special effort to know the influential people around town. By the age of 17, he worked as a telegrapher and assistant to a local railroad man for the impressive salary of $35 a month. Over the next decade, the railroad proved immensely profitable, thanks largely to Carnegie's participation in the business.

About the same time, Carnegie began investing. A $217 investment in a sleeping car company soon paid out $5000 a year. He then helped organise a pig iron company to build railroad bridges. His investments became so profitable that it wasn't long before his $2400-a-year salary from the railroad accounted for only 5% of his income.

In 1873, Carnegie organised the first of his steelworks, and over the next few decades, Carnegie Steel grew into an empire. By 1900, Carnegie Steel produced more steel than all of Great Britain. Just one year later, Carnegie, now 66, sold Carnegie Steel to JP Morgan for $480 million, making him the richest man in the world at that time.

Remember the point at which Carnegie 'resolved to cure' the poverty his family endured? I believe that was the moment he set in motion the direction of his life. And with clear intention, emotional resolve and ability to 'see' in his mind exactly what he wanted in life, and his determination to take action, the universe had no choice but to yield.

Acting on Your Destiny

As you're reading this book, please make sure you take the necessary time to digest these concepts before you begin implementing them in your life. This book is a training manual that encourages you to think imaginatively, freely and effectively. But it is only beneficial if you apply what you learn.

Imagine memorising a workbook on driving. You still couldn't drive until you got behind the wheel of a car and applied what you learned. Only through the implementation and practice of these techniques will you learn to redirect your thoughts, feelings and imaginative powers to create the life you want.

On the power of thinking, here is what Tesla said of himself: "I am credited as one of the hardest workers in the world if thought is the equivalent of labour!"

He continued, "I have devoted almost all of my waking hours to it. I have thrived on my thoughts. The impressions I have received from my undisciplined imagination were instrumental in my inventions."

Tesla remains one of history's most inspiring models for the Power of Thought. Notice that in Tesla's seven steps for inventing, all but one takes place outside the mind.

Tesla's Seven Advanced Steps for Inventions

1. Build up the idea in your imagination
2. Construct the image in your mind
3. Reconstruct and improve the image until it is vividly clear
4. Operate the device in your mind
5. Run it through and note any deficiencies
6. Make every improvement you can conceive of
7. Put it into concrete form

As you organise your thought patterns and create the image you desire in your imagination, you will be increasingly able to vividly and precisely picture your goal. Your powers of perception will become more significant. In other words, the more clearly you see your destination, the more likely you are to spot opportunities to make your dreams happen. Seizing opportunities, in turn, allows you to refine your plan continually.

Just writing out your clearly-defined goal is one of the most powerful secrets to accelerate your results.

Thomas Edison is an excellent example of this practice.

Scientists and engineers had been trying for more than fifty years to bring the concept of the electric light bulb into reality when Edison took up the challenge. Edison, a man with only three months of formal education, did it in less than three years. How? By writing down his findings, ideas and discoveries.

I suggest you not only write out your dream in explicit detail, I urge you to carry it with you at all times. The presence of this note on your person is the first manifestation of your determination to bring your dream into the physical realm, and it can be a powerful and steady inspiration as you break old habits and form new ones in concert with the universe.

The Nine Universal Principles that Lead to Predictable Success

1. Before you begin to journey down any path, ask this question (taken from Carlos Castaneda's *The Teachings of Don Juan*) Does this path have a heart?

If the answer is no, you will know it, and you must choose another path. The problem arises when you don't ask the question. At some point, you realise you've chosen a path without a heart, and you are miserable. Very few stop to deliberate; they just leave the path. On the other hand, a path with a heart is easy; it does not make you work at liking it, it is neither contrived or forced and most importantly authentic. If you follow the 'desire of your heart', the attainment of your goal will be in alignment with who you are – the natural grain of your personality – and there, you will find true happiness and peace. It is the pursuit of excellence in that endeavour that inevitably yields the greatest results. Infuse whatever work you are doing with love to access and activate the higher and more evolved faculties of the brain. As understanding grows of how our thoughts affect our physical reality, it becomes more apparent that as you do things in a spirit of love, people respond in kind. We can all feel the tone of a message we receive; we sense emotion.

2. Connect the dots and learn the lessons

Recognise complementary opposites: all your perceived wrongs had seeds of good, and by 'connecting the dots' of all the good that lives in your past regrets, fears and failures, you transform the energy into the rocket fuel needed to transport you to any destination you choose.

Joseph Campbell professor of literature expanded upon Nietzsche's idea of 'the love of your fate.

"Whatever your fate is, whatever the hell happens, you say, 'This is what I need.' It may look like a wreck but go at it as though it were an opportunity, a challenge," Nietzsche wrote. He went on: "If you bring love to that moment – not discouragement – you will find the strength is there. Any disaster you can survive is an improvement in your character, your stature, and your life. What a privilege! This is when the spontaneity of your nature will have a chance to flow.

"Then, when looking back at your life, you will see that the moments which seemed to be great failures followed by wreckage were the incidents that shaped the life you have now. You will see that this is true. Nothing can happen to you that is not positive. Even though it looks and feels at the moment like a negative crisis, it is not. The crisis throws you back, and when you are required to exhibit strength, it comes."

3. Let go of guilt

Whatever you do to another person is reflected right back at you, though not always directly from that individual.

In the Tibetan language, there is no word for 'guilt'. In its place is a word that expresses 'learning from experience'.

Make amends with others and, most of all, with yourself. Neutralise the guilt. Otherwise, it becomes a cyclical experience leading to unnecessary suffering. If you have wronged another, recognise how it may have served them; this is not to justify the wrong rather to neutralise the negative.

4. Rehearse the habits you desire

Rehearse behaviour over and over to the point that it becomes automatic.

When you are driving a car for the first time, there are massive spikes in neural activity. However, as many of the actions become automatic, brain activity diminishes. Our brain looks for shortcuts. It's built into our physiology. Once you internalise how to operate a car, the knowledge recedes from the centre of your consciousness. This is good news! It means you can create 'success grooves' in your brain so that successful attitudes and behaviours become as automatic as breathing.

5. Clarify what you want, but don't get caught up with the how

Micromanaging detail interferes with the process of creating the reality you desire. If you are baking a cake and open the oven every two seconds to change its position, you won't get the final product you expected and prepared for. There is a difference between desire and desperation. Trusting the process means not trying to control every detail. Micromanaging is the surest route to having the circumstances of life working *against* you.

Investing any anxiety and negative emotions in worrying about what you don't want will lead to *failure* becoming a self-fulfilling prophecy. Doubt may in fact be the biggest enemy. Most successful companies have business plans, but they rarely follow the route that they initially laid out. The act of crafting a plan stimulates the mind and draws out your ingenuity, and from there, you grow, expand and create. The focus is on the outcome not on the process of getting; the process is to be flexible, while the ideal concrete.

6. Build a network of winners

I will go through this in detail in later chapters, but I want to introduce the point now: we learn from 'mirror neurones', a phenomenon in which our brain chemistry and brainwave frequencies begin to match those we associate with. A study conducted in India placed non-meditators with holy men trained in meditation, adept at controlling their brainwave frequencies. Just by sitting in the presence of these master meditators, the brainwaves of the non-meditators began to match the masters. This discovery may explain something we see all around us – similar groups band together, be they futurists, musicians, people on welfare, religious groups, certain political affiliations to billionaires, or royalty. What we think about and feel in the presence of others evokes feelings within them and ourselves, and it is the power of feeling that constructs reality.

When Carnegie was asked what he owed his mass fortune, he cited his Mastermind without hesitation. Who we collaborate with, we become.

Mark Victor Hansen, the co-author of *Chicken Soup for the Soul*, relays the story of asking Tony Robbins how he built such an empire.

Tony responded, "Tell me about your Mastermind."

Mark replied proudly, "Everyone in there is a millionaire!"

Tony, very wisely, responded, "That's exactly why you are not where you want to be."

Mark was dumbfounded!

Tony's explanation? "My Mastermind is full of people with net worths of $100 million and beyond!"

That is not by accident.

7. Practise non-judgment

The time you spend hating on someone robs you of your own time. You literally hate on yourself, and you don't even realise it. – Joe Rogan

By practising non-judgment, the conflicts of your life will naturally dissipate, as dispute can only ever arise through judgment. If you are no longer judgmental, you will deprive the enemy of the artillery they need for battle. Never accommodate self-pity and never be self-righteous. Stop all comparisons and learn to be emotionally independent of both the good – and bad – opinions. In doing so, you unleash an authentic power. Within conversations, we almost always hear our own reaction to what people say, and usually that reaction is a judgment. It is time to take a step back in order to fully accept and honour each person as they are. Sometimes the best way we can help others is not so much in words we say, but instead in the behaviours and actions we take. If we must emphasise a point, we need to create an environment that will help deliver that message.

If someone carries prejudice and you treat them with the utmost respect, never once compromising who you are or belittling your own values, this will have a far deeper reach and potential for that person to improve. It will cause them to question their own ideas and then elicit personal changes. It also provides the necessary spotlight to exercise your own compassion and tolerance.

For one to be that critical of another, surely there must be some intense internal anguish. If, however, you violently oppose their worldview, it will only serve to strengthen their justifications, creating a stronger bond between the like-minded and furthering division. Everyone has a history ridden with guilt and regret! By welcoming change and respecting reform, we encourage a better world, and this itself provides more confidence for everyone to improve as best they can. As well, it will better illustrate that who we were yesterday has no relevance to who we choose to be today.

Within this book, I have intentionally mentioned people who had both turbulent and dark pasts yet who then found it within themselves to rise above all of that and reform. Changing the world in front of them and becoming even stronger than most thought they could. This provides points of reference and encouragement to those who see no way out. By letting go of another's past, you indirectly let go of your own. Positioning you to take every new moment as a fresh start, a unique point in which to begin. Harness true creativity and position yourself to mould new and fantastic realities from the substance of your own thoughts. The problems that we see that have yet to be resolved cannot be solved using old ideas; otherwise, they would have been figured out already. Further, they cannot be solved by contrived, stringent conditions and rules. Rather conditions change when one changes and shifts consciousness itself, and the ultimate shift comes about through the exercise of non-judgment.

Here's my challenge to you:

To formulate the reality you intend to manifest, know that the impulse of desire is God's gift to you and consent to it with gratitude. Have faith that inherent in the desire is the action plan or road map that leads to its accomplishment; access to the plan is only obtainable via faith, and that's faith in yourself!

Begin right now to sharpen your powers of thought and imagination and tap into the deepest desire of your heart. Create a living, breathing fourth-dimensional image in your mind and become obsessed with it, recognise you have everything within you to make this happen, enter that awareness. By doing so, you will ignite the Law of Attraction to work for you. Write everything in detail on a piece of paper that you carry with you wherever you go. Speak it out loud daily, as often as possible, but keep it quiet from others as it is a sacred and personal commitment only to yourself. When it feels as natural as the light of day, and this dream feels an indistinguishable part of your reality, you have entered the space that makes it happen; no more rehearsal is required.

Design a plan of action and begin to work on your project immediately. Do what is possible today, and don't worry about the particulars. Live in a spirit of expectation and hope, enveloped in love and knowingness.

Follow these steps, and you will be equipped with a foundation for the next chapter – the opportunity to re-create yourself!

CHAPTER FIVE

Re-Creating Yourself

Your personality creates your personal reality. – Dr Joe Dispenza

This chapter is perhaps the most important. Here I will show you how to develop the traits necessary to create, produce and direct your life as a personal masterpiece.

A quantum computer requires a deliberate operator to program its functions to test and ultimately uncover previously unknown realities.

You must develop similar mind-directing tools that perform automatically, as musicians do under the direction of a great maestro. What you are about to learn will change the dynamics in your life – and you will discover the world which once appeared to oppose you is ready to respond to your every need.

We begin with the 'will'. When sufficiently developed, the will unlocks abilities that allow us to break through the stratosphere and, in time, reach the edges of the galaxy. Take the example of an entrepreneur, Elon Musk; Musk proved that one man's 'will' can send rockets into space. Musk did not need to invent the rocket; instead, he influenced enough people and had the discipline to follow through until his vision became fact.

What is 'will'?

Will is your ability to manifest thought into your chosen reality. You will achieve what you want in life to the degree you can operate your will effectively.

Intent precedes will. Consider a building. It began as an idea – an image in one person's mind. With enough strength of intent, the person can interest an architect, bring contractors together, raise money, organise construction – convince the necessary people of the determination behind the intent, the feasibility of turning intent into reality. That's will.

What you are about to learn in this chapter develops and strengthens your will; a magnetic personality evolves as a result, and charisma comes forth.

People will be drawn to you, perhaps without knowing why find you so compelling; they will enthusiastically assist you on your quest.

Please take the following example of a child who recreated her life and personal destiny; looking at life's circumstances as malleable with the raw ingredients supplied from birth, she began sculpting the world by her very imagination.

"The universe begins to look more like a great thought than like a great machine.
– Sir James Jeans

Gabrielle was born August 1883, in Saumur, France, to an unwed mother employed as a laundrywoman at the local charity hospital. Her father, a rambling street vendor, made a meagre living peddling work clothes and undergarments.

As if poverty and an unstable family weren't challenging enough, at the age of 12 she lost her mother to bronchitis. Her father, unable to support the family, sent her and her sisters to the convent of Aubazine in central France. Aubazine was demanding, and Gabrielle was depressed there, so unhappy she fled to a Catholic boarding house for girls in Moulins. There too, the strict rigidity triggered a desire to break free. She spent hours fantasising about touring the wonders of the world as a royal.

Despite the drudgery and repression, she learned a valuable skill during her six years at Aubazine, the ability to sew – which later earned her a job as a seamstress. Though she didn't know it at the time, this skill would eventually become the key to her success and global reputation. Gabrielle also sang in a cabaret and made her debut singing in a Moulins pavilion, La Rotonde. Her stage name was 'Coco', which stayed with her for life. Escaping the dull routine of Aubazine, she pursued a career on stage, moving to the resort town of Vichy in 1906.

But something about her new life did not ring true, and she returned to Moulins and her job as a seamstress, still dreaming of luxury and living like royalty. Soon after, Coco fell in love with a dashing captain, Arthur Edward Capel, who encouraged her and helped finance a boutique dress shop where Coco showcased her work, which became quite popular. Her pieces were strikingly original, feminine but with an air of masculinity, expressing defiance of cultural norms born of the repressed atmosphere of her upbringing. But moving in the opposite direction to the crowd unexpectedly brought Coco to the very front.

Observe the masses do the opposite. – James Caan

By 1919, she was so successful she was a registered couturier and established her 'Maison de couture' in one of the most fashionable districts of Paris. Constantly challenging herself, she created highly influential signature women's suits and black dresses and soon developed a personal fragrance line. By 1935, at the height of her business empire, she employed as many as 4000 people.

Coco Chanel is still a household name. Her products continue to be popular in high-end department stores and exquisite boutiques worldwide, decades after her demise. How did that all happen to an anonymous girl named Gabrielle, born into poverty and raised in a strict boarding school?

In the words of Coco herself, "My life didn't please me, so I created my life."

Whether she was conscious of this fact doesn't matter; Coco followed natural, universal laws of intent and will, drawing people into her life that helped bring her childhood image of opulence and royalty into reality. The pictures in her mind naturally informed the choices she made and propelled her to success. From Coco, we learn that whatever is at the front of our mind has a way of dictating our behaviours. What we display is an output of what we think and rarely about what we say.

In the same way that you can't escape the law of gravity, you can't avoid these universal laws of natural creation. And just as attempting to defy gravity can produce disaster, the natural laws of personal creation are almost guaranteed to work against you if you try to challenge them.

What I am saying is this: you create your reality. Every day. Whether you realise it or not.

Your personality, character, attitude, demeanour, mindset and outlook are the ingredients that go into creating your life as you know it. Habitual thought patterns determine your feelings which will dictate your behaviour; this affects your choices and serves as an attracting or repelling force that results in the outcomes you may experience.

This is a universal truth: your life may not be moulded by chance or fate; an attitude of being the captain of your ship gives you a level of control that appeared to have always eluded you. It is an outward expression of who you are inside and the images you carry in your mind, consciously and unconsciously.

Even if you don't like what you see, you must understand great HOPE in stating this aloud. Because if, like Coco Chanel, you say, "I don't like my life," YOU have the power to change it. Regardless of your present situation, you have the opportunity – and the ability – to tap into universal laws and shape your life into any form you desire, as long as you develop the tools and do the work necessary to make it happen. Look at it this way. If you want to be a world-class football player or a national chess champion, but you refuse to put in the hours of practice such an achievement requires, you have zero chance of reaching those heights.

It is only through thousands of hours of practising fundamentals and fine-tuning the necessary skills that you can perform to such an extraordinary level. To break from your past requires an act of applied faith, a conviction that you can do something that no human has done before. Achievements come through adhering to the image in your mind, believing it as a statement of absolute fact. Everything around you at one time did not exist. It resided only in the imagination of a being bold enough to believe in the unseen and insist that image become a tangible reality.

That is the game of life. Succeeding at the level of an EndGamer requires that you become the person that achieves the results you imagine.

Take responsibility for becoming the person you want to be; we need to build things in ourselves that exceed the scope of what came before. Dismantle the old self. Transport yourself to your core strength: the recognition of your inner power. Then reconstruct your personality based on how you define your new self. Think magnanimously; act as if you were royalty and be ultra-observant of people's needs, treating them with the utmost respect. Then watch what happens. Don't let the simplicity of these universal principles fool you – they are magnificently powerful. They are at the foundation of your transformation into an EndGamer. They are the personality traits and behavioural qualities that unlock your true mastery while simultaneously building a strong internal support structure that is with you always.

With years liaising amongst the socially savvy and entrepreneurially elite, researching and dissecting many ancient spiritual teachings from Ayurvedic to Toltec as well as the contemporary discoveries in modern-day psychology, and observing first-hand the psychology of hundreds of my clients from all over the planet, I have come to recognise the keys to emotional intelligence and the unspoken rules of engagement. I have experienced first-hand how powerful these traits can be and how failing to cultivate them leads to failure and frustration.

Based on my research and personal experience, I can confidently say you are not yet where you want to be. You cannot achieve your goals with your present behaviours. How do I know this?

Because you would already be there if you evoked and brought forth the character traits necessary to make it happen, the next question will turn your existing paradigm upside down, so take a moment to reflect on this:

How did you become the person who doesn't have the things they want?

Whatever your answer was to the above question will begin to shed some light on the power you already possess and the awareness that if you can produce and maintain results that you are unhappy with, the opposite is also true. You do have in your possession dormant resources at hand ready to awaken within you once recognised. When the feelings are stabilised and maintained the qualities request to achieve what you want will assist you on your quest.

Humans, by nature, always yearn for an increase. Even a monk who renounces the world desires greater enlightenment. This is good and natural, as the whole universe is steadily growing and expanding. Your current reality is merely the outward expression of your current patterns of thinking, which in turn are the results of your conscious decisions that have programmed your subconscious responses – which now run 95% of your life choices on autopilot.

Today you are a bundle of predictable reactions. You must consciously deconstruct and reformat these reactions by continually choosing new behaviour patterns that will be installed in your subconscious, overriding your old responses and bringing forth new patterns of behaviour. Growth and advancement will be a by-product. By committing to the work based on the tools I provide in this chapter, you will lay the foundation for adopting new ways of thinking and being that will support astronomical growth in your life. Once you uncover the personality traits and behaviours that inhibit you and neutralise them using the techniques I will describe, you will experience smoother sailing en route to your destination.

Think of yourself now as one who utilises universal laws as leverage to reach any destination of choice. It is never too late to be the person you want to be. Be the author – and the hero – of your own story by asking yourself this question:

"What is the greatest ideal of myself that I can be today?"

Evolving into your Higher Self

Now that you have a basic understanding of the significant role your personality plays in creating your reality, the next step is to understand the unspoken codes and principles that will cultivate extreme power within and project a magnetic force around you. The journey of self-improvement involves struggle, but never fear: the size of the hero is always dependent on the opponent's size.

Let's begin.

Code #1: Authenticity

You were born an original, don't become a copy! – Coco Chanel

When Elvis Presley left this world in 1977, statisticians predicted that by the early 1980s one in three men would be an Elvis impersonator. Likewise, millions began emulating martial art icon Bruce Lee after his passing. Marilyn Monroe, James Dean, the list goes on. What is it about icons that cause others to want to be like them?

I believe it is because these legendary figures mirror to us the dormant potential we sense inside ourselves. Yet, at the first sign of adversity in achieving this potential, we tend to shrink back rather than grow. The people cited above faced obstacles too, yet used their resilience to break through.

When someone's authentic self shines through, it inspires us to do the same. So it's natural to admire and gravitate toward someone living their legend.

After all, who do you remember? The authentic original or the impersonators?

Questions to think about: How will others respond to you when you allow your true, authentic self to come forward?

What is the highest expression of YOU?

Code #2: Utilise both good and bad conditions to move forward

Observe reality as it is. Honestly, observe both positive and negative. Should something appear negative, immediately look for the complementary opposite and utilise it for good.

One of the best models of this truth was the insurance magnate, philanthropist and pioneer in personal development W. Clement Stone. Stone's father died when he was just three years old, leaving nothing but gambling debts and a widow and son in the throes of poverty. When Stone was six, living with his mother and relatives in an apartment on Chicago's rough South Side, he began selling newspapers to help support the family. Competition with older boys for the prime street-corner location was fierce, but the young Stone was amazingly resourceful. This challenge, in his mind, was an opportunity. He decided restaurants would be better places to sell papers.

In what he later recalled as his first experience "turning a disadvantage into an advantage" he repeatedly returned to one restaurant to try to sell papers, only to be thrown out each time by the owner. Finally, due to his sheer tenacity, the owner agreed to let Stone set up shop. Not long after, the owner became a great friend and supporter. Stone kept working his newspaper enterprise until, at 13, he owned his newsstand. He dropped out of high school at 16 to work for his mother at an insurance agency in Detroit. Already an accomplished salesman and positive thinker, Stone quickly took to the insurance business. As he matured and refined his skills as a salesman, he sold huge volumes of small, inexpensive policies, at one point more than 100 in a single day, becoming one of the company's top performers.

One Monday morning, while Stone was vacationing in Miami, the agency called him out of the blue and told him not to return. He was fired. Now, the average person would have responded with: "How can they do this to me? I will sue, and they will be sorry." But the ever-positive Stone took a different approach: "How can this serve me? How can I profit from this? Perhaps this is God's way of knocking on my door."

Stone had, for some time, dreamed of starting his own insurance company. So in 1922, with an investment of just $100, he returned to Chicago to establish what would become the Combined Insurance Company of America, a company valued at $2.56 billion.

This is a prime example of what you may accomplish when you choose to rise above victimhood to the level of excellence and refuse to let life's circumstances hold you back.

Code #3: Impeccability in speech

Never say anything about yourself that you don't wish to be true. – Brian Tracy

Early research by the Stevens Institute and many studies since then have conclusively proven that a large vocabulary is the most recognisable performance characteristic shared by successful professionals.

Not physical size, not appearance, not financial backing, not family connections.

Vocabulary.

Someone with an extensive vocabulary can expect to earn three times the annual income of someone with only an average command of the English language. One twenty-year longitudinal study of college students shows that those who had the highest vocabulary test scores were in the highest income bracket twenty years later. And those who scored the lowest earned the least.

Here's why.

Words have the power to create and destroy. They can be used in the service of truth and love or lies and destruction. They can build you up or tear you down. They are the bridges between hearts. They begin and end relationships. They can ignite a war and bring peace and resolution.

Words can create an instantaneous change in your biochemistry, which then metabolises in your body. For example, when you hear something sad, your body responds chemically, emotionally and physically. The same is true when someone says, "I love you." It is the same process, just a different experience.

The mind processes words at a fundamental level. Even when one does not understand the content of what is being communicated, the subconscious searches for meaning and evokes emotion. This is why we instinctively understand how toxic it is to watch the news or read the newspaper; for every positive story, there are, on average, seventeen catastrophes delivered. The messages of negativity have the potential to evoke states in your body that result in fear, worry, doubt, depression and other debilitating thoughts and behaviour patterns.

On a caveat, anger over current circumstances serves a purpose only if one is prepared to do something about it! Most charity organisations and movements were created from a person distraught with the way things were; the difference is they utilised the unpleasant circumstance to create change. The change would begin using the Endgame Imagination of the ideal, then putting together a framework to improve the situation. This is a book of movement and action tilted toward the creator more than just the consumer. When an idea, thought or desire enters and is allowed to remain in your mind eventually you incorporate it as part of your worldview, speaking about it, reflecting on it, breathing life into it.

The physical aspect of creation begins with speech. You may remember times when something you spoke about came true. That's because words express your thoughts – your inner reality – which has the energy to attract forces in the universe that create the physical reality.

This truth is most relevant to the topic of this chapter for this reason:

The most powerful words are those you speak to yourself.

The messages you continually repeat to yourself about yourself – such as "I'm just so forgetful" or "I can't help but worry" or "I can't do anything right" – forge your identity and your personality. In other words, YOU determine who you are because you become the person you tell yourself you are. That's how these universal principles operate within us.

Every time you agree to an appointment and turn up late, you are going against your word. Internally you perceive this as a 'lie', even though you may make an excuse. These 'lies' accumulate over time and will eventually destroy your faith in yourself and even your health because mind and body must not be incongruent. If you fail to keep your word, your body will begin to fail to follow your intentions. Why do you think so many people talk yet fail to act? You must commit to the small things first – small actions congruent with speech – before you can move mountains.

These are the patterns that need to be cleared in the process of deconstructing your 'old self', and we will work through exercises later to change these destructive patterns.

Takeaway: Begin immediately to affirm what you wish to be true and live by those ideals. Build your vocabulary; there are many great courses available; additional words will illuminate your path, create clarity of mind as well as give others faith in you, providing an air of sophistication to your choice of words; there is no substitute for precision in language. Be impeccable with your words. Speak with integrity. Say what you mean.

Never use the power of words to speak against yourself or others. Commit to using the power of your words for 'good', always in the direction of truth and love.

Code #4: Never take anything personally

Piero Soderini, Florence's mayor studying the near finished sculpture of David told Michelangelo while it was superb, the nose was too large in proportion to the face. Michelangelo knew changing the shape of the nose would ruin the entire dimension of the sculpture. But he was astute enough to realise that addressing this to Soderini – who recognised himself as artistic in judgment – would likely put any future projects. Michelangelo, a master of his craft had no reason to take things personally, as he was well aware that what he had created was a masterpiece.

Michelangelo immediately took the initiative making his way up the scaffolding. On reaching the centre of the face, pretended to sculpt away the excess. Soderini's eyes glued just a few feet away, Michelangelo continued to tap lightly on his chisel, and drizzled some accumulated dust. Michelangelo did nothing to change the nose, though he gave every appearance of altering it per Soderini's suggestion. After a few minutes of this pretence, he confidently gestured to the finished piece, positioning Soderini at a slightly different angle.

Soderini nodded in approval. "You've made it come alive."

Michelangelo did change something, but it was not David's nose. He altered Soderini's perspective. By bringing him closer to the nose and appearing to make minor adjustments, Michelangelo satisfied Soderini without making him realise that he was the problem all along. He kept the perfection of the statue intact while making Soderini believe he had improved it.

It is essential to keep in mind that what others say about you or attempt to action you to do is not necessarily because of you. It is merely a projection of their reality, their perspective and many times their ego.

In the worst cases, they may be trying to tear you down to gain significance for themselves, a sad reality of too many human interactions. Since you cannot control what others say or do, when you make yourself immune to others' opinions and actions you save yourself a lot of needless suffering. Generally speaking, people do the best they can with what they know. They don't think; they merely react based on their conditioning. There are very few people who genuinely listen and pause to think before they reply.

When you take the time to consider what someone has said before you respond, you are honouring them. You are demonstrating a rare quality of character and a level of class. Besides, there may be grains of truth in the criticism of others, no matter their intention. Listening without reacting gives you an opportunity to step outside yourself and consider whatever truth may reside in what seems to be negative comments. Criticism also affords a great chance to rise above victimhood to a level of empowerment. By valuing criticism and not reacting to it as a personal attack, you permit yourself the liberty to consider how it could serve you and how you could profit from it.

Code #5: Be independent of the good and bad opinions of others

But under the sky, under the heavens, there is but one family. – Bruce Lee

A thousand people equate to a thousand opinions. Trying to be agreeable with everyone is not just impossible; it's a recipe for disaster. Even pleasing a small group of friends can be extraordinarily complicated.

Do you recall what we discussed about the laws of equilibrium in Chapter Three?

The people with an outsized impact on human history – Abraham, Jesus, Muhammad, Buddha, Jobs, Carnegie, Tesla, Mother Teresa – experienced fierce opposition while riding a tide of tremendous support.

The late queen of hearts, Princess Diana, was a constant target for the hate-filled media who sang her praises only after her death. Governments worldwide strongly opposed even her humanitarian campaign to abolish landmines and save the lives of millions of innocents, calling her campaign 'an unnecessary distraction'.

If the best among us can't even get everyone on their side, what chance do we have?

Conversely, the most twisted and sinister figures in history somehow incurred support from the unquestioning masses. The harsh reality is that 95% of the time their motive is to pillage other nations under the banner of freeing their people. Hitler used seemingly rational arguments to justify himself, raising armies of millions of mindless supporters for a campaign of ruthless mass murder.

Our responsibility is to find creative alternatives that allow us to live in harmony, not in power-obsessed destruction.

We live in an expanding, abundant universe, and the idea of scarcity or limitation is fundamentally flawed. Some minor asteroids have higher amounts of gold than the entire planet, for example. History proves that if a resource appears to be running out, our focus shifts to identifying alternatives. After all, it was not long ago that the most valued fuel for home lighting was whale oil.

We don't create abundance; abundance is always present. We create limitation. – Arnold Patent

The world has always been and will always be a composite of complementary opposites – positive and negative. But here's the remarkable truth behind that fact: You can bring both forces to your aid.

Takeaway: Do not be swayed by the opinions of others. Learn to think independently. Think creatively. Make good choices. Real power and strength of character come from a relentless pursuit of your dreams, independent and unswayed by the opinion or opposition of others. Both support and challenge are necessary for growth; embrace it.

Never forget *your* choices – not the choices of others – determine who you are and create your reality.

Code #6: Always do your best

I was invited by brothers Mahesh and Kunal Tulsiani to speak to a private group of highly successful entrepreneurs. Even members of the YPO attended. These are the minds redesigning London's skyline, providing jobs for generations to come and helping shape not only the local but the global economy.

I knew I could share ideas, tools and concepts to powerfully impact such an influential group, and that the materials I prepared were not a week in advance but years in development. Whichever individual or groups seminars were delivered for, I had always kept in my mind to far exceed my previous efforts; in doing so I placed just as much emphasis on the presentations delivered to underperforming schools as the groups at LSE or Google and the like. By seeing all as equal and giving my best each time I honour what makes them unique and improve myself simultaneously, so when an opportunity arises, my skills are finely tuned and in doing so have the self-reliance and ability to get the desired result.

So when someone in a seminar or private Mastermind is ready to make a change, I have an ever-improving set of tools to profoundly affect that individual.

When a client talks about not reaching a particular goal, I always ask, "Did you give it all you have? Were you operating at 110%?" The answer will almost always be no. Helping people realise that they can operate at higher levels and remove excuses will always be a fundamental characteristic of my lifes work.

Every morning, on awakening, ask yourself: "What is the greatest idea of myself I can be today?" Then decide to live by that.

Keep in mind that your best is going to change from moment to moment. It will be different when you are healthy as opposed to when you are ill. Though by continually refining the character, maintaining focus on always making the best of what you have, habits of mind and body develop, raising performance in every area.

Never tire of giving your best. Never give up. It is the only way to gain mastery of your life.

Anyone who masters their craft spends thousands of hours behind locked doors learning fundamentals, honing and refining. They become obsessed with mastery and persevere until they achieve it, then they push a little further.

There is only one real shortcut – giving your very best in each moment.

Code #7: Boldness

In order to understand how reality works, one must step back and observe things as they are, without any immediate judgment and without holding biased conclusions. *This is far more difficult than one may think.*

Each problem that arises is much more valuable than you may currently realise. A particular issue may be a goldmine in disguise. The more people that the problem's solution helps, the greater and bigger the bounty. When using innate ingenuity – *as each answer is revealed, it is stored as equity in your arsenal of experience* – remember, this has the potential to compound forever. As your experience is catalogued in your own personal database, the next time something similar appears, you have an immediate reference point to work from.

Dutch-British tech entrepreneur David de Min exemplifies this approach excellently, moving forward without the need to ask for permission. Though originally given many labels from ADD to dyslexia, David joins the ranks of the Bransons and Einsteins who also had these prescribed labels. Rather than something which would somehow cap their potentials, if anything, they served as a powerful driving force.

Dyslexics have led us to improve pattern recognition and thus have enhanced our ability to see how complex things connect. David's inability to concentrate in class produced the circumstances to birth his entrepreneurship. At the age of nine, David's parents were called into school by his headmaster, as an expulsion was looming. David had been caught selling cap guns to several students after acquiring them at a discounted price whilst on a family holiday in France. In this instance, the headmaster said he would not expel David. Though he disapproved of his actions, the headmaster thought that David had displayed the ingenuity and ingredients necessary to build a business. This sparked a flame of confidence in the young boy, which still blazes to this very day.

Fast forward to the future David, now accomplished in the fields of property and tech, came across a derelict fort in Dover. This was not any ordinary fort; it had once been used to keep the might of the Napoleonic forces at bay, and it had served to barricade the United Kingdom, protecting it from the enemy. Centuries ago, the structure was celebrated as cutting-edge – pure sophistication for that era. It now lay lifeless and motionless.

David felt destined to do something significant in the world of technology. He devised an ingenious idea to resurrect the fortress and convert it into a tech hub. His vision was replete with an environment to nurture and develop visionaries, welcoming forces of technology that would work together for the greater good. Before procuring the fort, David had already put the wheels in motion, establishing friendships and relationships with contractors, entrepreneurs and even government bodies to help pave the way to its acquisition and realisation.

David, being quite active within a multitude of seminars and networking events in the world of tech, had heard that Steve Wozniak (Apple's co-founder) was to present on a particular evening. With no time to lose, David formulated a plan to kidnap this industry icon and present the ideas to him first hand. His hope was not in terms of getting anything from the Wizard, or even collaborating for that matter, but rather exposing Wozniak to the potential of this hub by planting the seeds for future opportunities. Through a sheer flash of insight, David immediately contacted the organisers of the event and said to them he would arrange transportation via Rolls-Royce for the Wizard, courtesy of the most prestigious car company in the world. Of course, the organisers consented. Now, David neither owned a Rolls-Royce, nor for that matter, knew anyone in their dealerships. Nevertheless, the intent and desire to do this was so strong that he personally went to the showroom and convinced them to loan him a car. This would give both him and the dealership great exposure and the privilege of having one of the founding fathers of the technology generation in their vehicle. It worked like a well-oiled machine, and everything fell right into place.

This isn't luck: this is seizing the opportunity with everything you've got the moment it presents itself. **The world rewards the bold!**

Where there is no reference point or foundation, you construct a new one. Who doesn't love a game? Of course, the uncertainty may keep you on edge for a while. And yet, the more formidable the challenge, *the anticipated victory becomes even sweeter.*

You are in a position of knowing what to either avoid or what to do more of that is working. With this base of understanding, you can never lose, as each experience becomes a clearer illustration of the correct path to take, as well as providing you with even greater guidance for the future. Each step forward, much like an advancing video game, gets progressively more complicated; however, your reflexes and recognition of what may or may not come next enable intuition to kick in. *You are then viewed as having a sixth sense.* The layers of reality gradually become clearer as you become more familiar with visualising what you want to create. These guiding mechanisms are what keep the machine of reality running, and they now start to work in your favour.

Your thoughts are independent, and as an original thinker, no one stands in the way. *They can't!* **When your certainty becomes greater than the planet's doubt, your certainty will triumph over an infinite number of doubters.** In the case of JFK, one man's vision to land humans on the moon rose above the doubts of an entire planet.

The resilience and desire for completion become the predominant driving force, belying the inevitable pains of the process until they almost always become unnoticed. If any is even felt, the pain itself is just further instruction of how to create more effectively.

Any resistance which may appear along the way is used to strengthen and refine the will to follow through. Smarter cuts to the top erase unnecessary roadblocks found along the way. An ever-expanding vision that sees lifetimes into the future, whilst fastidious to detail, metrics and feedback, proves every bit of data as valuable.

Code #8: Highlighting elephants

What I am about to take you through is pure gold; I have had the honour of sharing platforms with Carlos Espinal, co-founder of Seedcamp and one of the sharpest people I have ever met. At the time of writing this book, Carlos now has over 350+ investments, seasoned to the core and with an uncanny ability to qualify within seconds if an investment may grow exponentially or disappear as quickly as an ice cube in the summer sun. Carlos explains in his own words that his processes of decision-making at times will be a hyper gut feel, and other times hyper structured and rigid.

In order to present an idea and rally investment support, one must always address the elephant in the room and never ignore it. The elephant in the room is a metaphorical idiom in English for an enormous yet overlooked topic in a confined space. Now here is the thing: *it is impossible to sweep under the carpet, and unless addressed, it will build in the prospect's mind until it grows to a magnitude that overshadows and eclipses the product or service you are presenting.*

This brings us back to the two most important principles I have emphasised throughout this book: ***authenticity and honesty***. If you have no problem with the elephant, you are leveraging it. In this way, it can serve to strengthen whatever you present. Let me give you an example.

If one is to open a coffee shop, it would be easy to presume fierce competition in the form of Starbucks. However, the angle that may be presented is that the juggernaut has created a coffee shop culture, thus paving the way for smooth profits for new and innovative coffee brands.

Code #9: Constructing your own beliefs

If one were able to position their hopes in the same location in which the inevitable future is stored in the mind, very quickly the mind would develop a conviction that the outcome is inevitable and as discussed throughout the book, our beliefs unlock the requisite potential to succeed. I will now guide you through this powerful process of how you locate the direction and feeling in the mind.

Close your eyes and think of something inevitable, like the rising of the morning sun. Now physically point to the direction in your mind's eye (it may be to the left, right, the middle of your chest or in front of you). Next, think of something that is not true –such as Mario and Luigi are in your living room – and physically point to it. You will notice it is located peripherally in a completely different location in space.

This leads us to the method of strengthening our belief: think of how you would like to be or what you would like to have happen and position the image in the location of the sun rising in doing so your brain begins to perceive the inevitability of the result. This is a gentle way to prep your mind, before you build to the assumption of your desired outcome.

Code #10: Commitment to mastery

Only one who devotes himself to a cause with his whole strength and soul can be a true master. For this reason, mastery demands all of a person. – Albert Einstein

Always do your best, yet stay wary of perfection; most perfectionists are immobilised by the fear of not getting it just right. A wise man once said a good plan executed today is better than a perfect plan tomorrow. 'Perfection' can be considered the lowest human standard simply because it is unreachable.

Having the intent to reach mastery, irrespective of how long it takes, sets you on the path to greatness – giving it all you've got under any circumstance will allow you to avoid negative self-judgment and regret.

Martial arts is a way of life, a commitment to self-improvement; this is because techniques can only be effectively delivered when ones emotions are managed and in doing so the correct response triggered; if one attempts to force a manoeuvre prematurely or aggressively impose an outcome it will predictably backfire. In the midst adversity, control is still maintained if anger is in the equation it not only exhausts the practitioner but impairs their accuracy of technique, leaving them susceptible to defeat. Therefore martial arts serves as one of the most powerful and practical models for self-development.

Observing some of the UFC's greatest champions throughout the years like Royce Gracie, Khabib Nurmagomedov, Jon Jones and George St-Pierre these are martial artists of the highest ilk, practising their respective arts continually with no off season; even during periods of injury or even retirement the practice continues. These not athletes competing for recognition and an inflated paycheque, rather for legacy, and the results self-evident.

Code #11: Never make assumptions

The great magician and escape artist Harry Houdini drew crowds to his performances by standing outside police stations and inciting fights. When the police came to arrest him, he would amaze and delight the crowd with his ability to escape the handcuffs while promoting his shows.

But Houdini had a bigger dream. He wanted to perform in Europe. Using Houdini's savings, his management company arranged for him to perform in Cologne, Germany. Using his tried and true tactics for drawing a crowd, he made his way to a high-security police station. But this time, the local police arrested him, rushed him off to a cell and then hurriedly slammed it shut. The escape artist quickly removed his cuffs and began working on the cell door, a type of lock he had not previously seen. He felt his whole career and reputation was riding on the effort. If he failed, he would be labelled a charlatan. After 45 minutes he gave up in despair. Then he slipped, hitting his head on the cell door. It flew open! The officers had been in such a rush to secure him they had forgotten to lock the door. The lesson? Never make assumptions. It was his belief in the cell door being locked that trapped him; the reality was it was open all along.

How often do you make single-minded assumptions about the way the world works, or how people will respond to you, or what outcome you should expect?

That is the problem with making assumptions about the future – we simply have no way to know what will happen. The universe operates as it will. Since there are so many things we don't yet understand, it is unwise to make assumptions about the world, about life and your individual results.

Be as flexible as the wind. Find the courage to ask questions and to express what you want.

Communicate with others clearly to avoid misunderstandings, sadness and drama. Being in accord with just one understanding person can completely transform your life. Coming to conclusions, making judgments, assuming you are correct all lead to self-righteousness, a risky position. For when you elevate yourself above others, you inevitably fall. This is a universal principle. Keep an open mind. Do not judge. Refrain from assuming you can predict outcomes or that you know more (or better) than others. Always be flexible enough to change.

Takeaway: Assuming you know how people will act or respond to you is delusional. People behave based on their intrinsic values and beliefs, not yours. Rather than make assumptions, communicate your wants and needs as effectively as possible in a language everyone can understand.

Code #12: Carry a million dollars in your wallet at all times

A business executive sat on a park bench, head buried in his hands. His company was in trouble financially, and he could see no way out. Creditors were breathing down his neck. Suppliers demanded payment. Bankruptcy loomed.

He looked up to find an old man standing in front of him.

"Something must be troubling you," he said.

After hearing the businessman's plight, the old man responded, "I believe I can help you."

After asking his name, the mysterious visitor filled out a cheque and insisted the businessman take it, saying, "Use it as you need. Meet me back here exactly one year from today, and you can pay me back." He turned and disappeared as quickly as he had come.

When the business executive looked, he held a cheque for $500,000, bearing the signature of business tycoon John D Rockefeller.

"This is unbelievable! My money worries have been erased in an instant," he thought.

But instead of using the money, he put the uncashed cheque in his safe. The executive had a sense that just knowing it was there might give him the courage to find a way to save his business. With a new spirit of optimism, he negotiated arrangements with his creditors. He closed several large deals. Within a few months, he had turned things around and was making money once again.

Exactly one year later, he returned to the park with the uncashed cheque. Right on time, the old man showed up. But just as the executive was about to hand back the cheque and share his success story, a nurse ran up, and taking hold of the old man, said, "I'm so glad I caught him!"

"I hope he hasn't been bothering you," she explained to the astonished executive. "He's always escaping from the rest home and telling people he's John D Rockefeller." She lovingly led the old man away.

The executive stood speechless. For the entire year, he had been confidently closing deals right and left, convinced he had half a million dollars to fall back on. It dawned on him that it wasn't the money, real or imagined, that had turned his business around. It was his newfound self-confidence empowering him to achieve whatever he wanted. Belief triumphs doubt.

This fable tells a compelling truth: realise that the cavalry you are waiting for is within you. The knight in shining armour is reflecting at you each time you look in the mirror. It is time to become the hero in your own life. Bringing that hero to the surface means cultivating self-reliance.

Code #13: Belief triumphs over biology

After former middle-distance athlete Sir Roger Bannister ran the first sub-four-minute mile, making history, this once deemed impossible goal had 37 other athletes follow suit just months after. Once the 'impossible' was possible, many athletes who previously fell short miraculously improved their performance. The only thing that had changed was their solidified faith in observing that it could be done. But the only one etched in the journals of history is Bannister, the one who didn't need to see the goal tangibly accomplished to know it could be done.

You may read many books and attend many seminars on self-improvement. Study dozens of techniques for building self-confidence. But until you can fully apply these truths, the odds will work against you. Learn to have faith in the unseen and artfully believe in something before it has come to pass, and you may just start to see your own miracles. It's now time to become your own hero. Rewards for faith and belief are immeasurable; the early investors in Apple, Disney, Rolls-Royce, Google, Nestlé and now Bitcoin generated fortunes for what would appear to be minimal amounts of money invested.

The astronomical yields came from having enough faith in the future of one persons dream. Never, ever underestimate the power of belief; the rewards are almost always certain to be immeasurable.

Code #14: Never elevate or minimise anyone
Work until your idols become your rivals.

If you elevate someone, you are not on par with them. You are a fan. In lifting them, you minimise yourself. The other person senses that and will treat you that way.

When you meet someone you admire, recognise they are an expert in their field and that you are an expert in yours. You can show respect without elevating.

For example, I was invited to a private screening of *American Hustle* at the Soho Hotel in London a few years ago. After the screening, I approached director David Russell to compliment him on a brilliant film.

In response, David replied, "You are doing drinks with us!"

Had I approached David as a fan and set him up on a pedestal, he would have sensed that. Instead, I came across as a genuine person who appreciated his work and acknowledged his efforts; he then treated me as a respected friend.

Let's now look at a man whose incredible self-confidence is propelling his life well beyond what would be considered 'reasonable' limits.

This man is Elon Musk – Canadian-American business magnate, engineer, inventor and investor.

You would think that after playing a significant role in the founding of Zip2, PayPal and Tesla Motors, Musk would be satisfied with his achievements and bank account.

Not so.

Musk has turned his attention to space travel, testing technologies that will one day permit the colonisation of Mars. Musk is developing his own space program because he is passionate about exploring the possibilities of humans living beyond earth.

Imagine taking on the likes of NASA. What an impossible challenge. But Musk did not seek permission or ask for approval. He acted on what his internal reality was telling him.

Sylvester Stallone experienced over 1200 rejections before *Rocky* made it to the screen. By failing to recognise someone's actual value, every one of those companies missed out on tens, if not hundreds, of millions of dollars.

The people who are crazy enough to think they can change the world are the ones who do. – Steve Jobs

Takeaway: Stop elevating, minimising, categorising and classifying people. See the potential in everyone –most of all in yourself.

Code #15: Fearless in the face of battle

What do you do when your army of just 100 men is trapped in a fortress, and you know an army of 150,000 is charging, bent on your destruction?

Here's what the great general Zhuge Liang did.

During China's War of the Three Kingdoms (AD 207–265), while leading the forces of the Shu Kingdom, he dispatched his vast army to a remote camp while resting in a small town with a handful of soldiers. Suddenly messengers hurried in with alarming news. Sima Yi's enemy force of 150,000 was approaching. With only 100 men, Liang's situation was hopeless. The end was near.

However, Liang wasted no time. He ordered the troops to take down their flags, throw open the city gates, and hide. He then seated himself on the most visible part of the city wall, donned in a Taoist robe. With incense smoking around him, he strummed his lute and began to chant. He watched the vast army approach what looked like an endless number of soldiers. Pretending not to notice, he continued to play and chant. The enemy army was soon at the city gates. Sima Yi instantly recognised Liang, the famed 'Crouching Tiger' and 'Sleeping Dragon'. He had fought against Liang dozens of times. When he came upon Liang praying on the wall, he was stunned. Liang's behaviour – relaxed, serene and focused, out in the open – seemed to Yi to be intimidation. Liang was daring him to walk into a trap. Yi could not convince himself that Liang was genuinely alone and desperate. His fear of Liang was so great that he dared not risk finding out. He ordered his men to withdraw. This is the power of reputation in action – forcing a vast army to retreat without firing a single arrow.

We are not likely to find ourselves in such a dire predicament. However, when experiencing fear, it is essential to control your thoughts and your feelings, so your mind can find bold solutions and present a controlled outward appearance, instead of the automated, panicky response most produce when faced with fear.

Animals under attack exhibit the same fight or flight response as we do. However, once the situation passes, they quickly return to their homeostatic state. Our response is very different. We anticipate more danger and can remain in this heightened fear state for an extended time. Eventually, we can even adopt a low-level, subconscious fear state as our 'normal' mode.

Living in fear – playing out worst-case scenarios in our mind – results in subconscious body language, thought vibrations and emotional energy that may draw those dire situations to you. Use those moments as a catalyst to imagine the ideal outcome.

Fear is simply focusing on what you don't want, thereby broadcasting the thoughts and emotions and triggering a natural process that draws these unwanted events into your life. The only way to break the cycle of fear – to banish your focus on the negative – is to make a conscious effort to focus on what you DO want until this positive thinking becomes as deeply embedded in your mind as your previously negative thoughts. Here is a simple process that you can use to neutralise fear:

- Pivot the thought. As soon as you recognise you are focused on something you don't want, do a 180 in your mind. Pivot in the opposite direction – think of something you DO want.
- Stop attaching importance to repetitive thoughts of fear. Stop taking these thoughts seriously.
- If fear attempts to impose itself regularly, in those moments interrupt the process by firmly saying inside your mind STOP, next engage in some game or mental arithmetic to force the brain back into logic, finally when settled dwell upon a happy outcome, invest your faith there.

Takeaway: When conflict arises, your natural response will be to retreat or defend. Your quest will encounter obstacles that seem to be there to stop you. In reality, the opposite is true. Tension builds strength. Obstacles cultivate your desires. Your desires, broadcast into the universe, set in motion the forces that bring you what you need to fulfil your desires.

Position yourself as the hero in your own epic adventure, and live your greatest dream.

Code #16: Steer clear of self-righteousness and self-pity

Either self-govern or the world brings governing experiences upon you. We are not here to be humble. We are here to be humbled. Arrogance leads to monumental downfalls. You see it in sports, politics and business every day.

In pursuit of mastery and constructing destiny, avoid self-righteousness at all costs. Assuming a position of superiority stunts growth since falsely elevating creates no room to grow.

The invisible forces constantly at work in the universe that maintain equilibrium and balance will naturally seek you out, all but guaranteeing a fall. On the flip side, never wallow in self-pity. This will lead to desperation – a repelling force of nature that pushes people and opportunities away from you.

The story of Xerxes, King of Persia, demonstrates the value of this truth.

In 483 BC, Xerxes attempted to avenge his father Darius' failure and set out to conquer the Greek mainland. He intended to cross his army by building a bridge over a strait of water called the Hellespont. Before it could be completed, a massive storm destroyed the bridge.

Xerxes, overcome with anger and desperation over a situation he had no power to control, had every engineer beheaded. In an arrogant, pathetic display of self-pity, he then sent soldiers to the banks of the strait to whip the sea 300 times for failing to comply with his plans. Xerxes had no choice but to recognise a power greater than himself, but his desire to place blame led to these irrational acts, sowing the seeds for the defeat of his army and the downfall of his empire.

Our natural tendency is to look at events we can't control and blame them for our failures. This is nothing more than excuse-making and failing to take responsibility for our outcomes and responses.

If you were there with Xerxes, no doubt his behaviour would have struck you as wrong-headed and irrational. Here is something for you to consider: behaviour patterns in others that rub us the wrong way are often a mirror for these same behaviours we do not like in ourselves but do not consciously acknowledge.

For example, let us say you have an argumentative co-worker you cannot stand to be around. Ask yourself, "Have I ever displayed these characteristics?" Alternatively, if you feel the adverse effects of a jealous person, ask yourself, "Have I ever been jealous?" Acknowledging that you are as capable of fault as those around you will keep your perspective balanced, increase your capacity for compassion, and help you find a way to a solution.

Takeaway: It's wiser to have a substantial insurance policy over the future; the easiest way to achieve this is to remain humble always; if you look at companies, athletes and individuals who thrive, this one thing will always remain consistent.

Code #17: Recognise that the greatness you admire in others is already within you

By cultivating, awakening and bringing forth what is already in you, you validate your faith in yourself and develop greater confidence. All great accomplishments are achieved through the awareness that all you need is within you.

Psychologists have classified about 4000 traits of personality in common. Some are productive and constructive; others are destructive. Each one serves a purpose, or evolution would have selected against them.

There is no such thing as a one-sided being. We have a light side, and we have a dark side. We are all whole and worthy of love because we contain both darkness and light. We are flawed and needy – worthy of the help and compassion of others and capable of loving and helping them.

The best way to stop placing others on a pedestal is to see what traits we admire in that person – ones we think are missing in ourselves – and search for them within.

For example, take Coco Chanel. Here is a partial list of her personality traits:

- Original
- Authentic
- Driven
- Confident
- Consistent
- Creative

Once you have identified these traits, ask yourself when you, too, have displayed these qualities. By recognising these admired traits in yourself, you bring them to the surface and begin the journey toward a more powerful sense of self-worth; the moment you see something in another you admire, immediately own it; it is there, you will bring it to life.

Soon you will see the primary reason certain things had not worked out for you in the past was because of your lack of self-belief. You had convinced yourself that you didn't have what it takes, and used either made-up or past outdated ideas as a reference point. You sold yourself on this gripping yet false narrative and bought into an idea of limitation until, at last, the limitation was sustained in your behaviour.

It is now time to reclaim power, take charge of your inherent confidence and apply yourself fully, watch your achieve evolve into something far beyond what you or anyone else thought was possible.

Takeaway: If you desire to possess a quality and you decide to 'own' that quality, it will begin to appear more prominently in your life. If you believe it is missing in you or you don't have it, it will forever elude you.

Code #18: Silence is golden

Tell the world what you intend to do. But show it first.

As we discovered earlier in this chapter, there is tremendous power in the spoken word, but it is a double-edged sword.

You can speak things into existence, but it is best not to do that in the presence of others. When people know what you intend to do, your ego may be triggered. If you do not achieve your desired target in the timeframe broadcast, your dream could be contaminated with a focus and energies on meeting the expectations of others, as oppose to your authentic target. Your creative powers may diminish.

This is a danger zone! Your dream is now in jeopardy.

The only people who should know your intentions are those working on your immediate project, and even then they need only see the outline of your vision; there is no need for a detailed explanation of what is in your heart.

Another problem with talking too much is that it diffuses your authentic desire. Never let ambition diminish; communicate in a language that inspires others by artfully illustrating to them that your success in these endeavours is their success. Furthermore, talking about your intentions may incur jealousy. It's better to allow your desires, drive and commitment to your goals to express themselves in your actions and attitudes, not by sharing detailed plans.

As mentioned above preoccupation with proving yourself is a dangerous path to take as this opens the door for your ego to move to the forefront. The mission is to bring value to the world and leave it a better place. There is no need to prove your worth to others. Human nature at time can be malicious some may actively seek your destruction or try to steal your ideas and run with them. This is why committing to excellence and doing your very best is absolutely crucial. If you create a product and work diligently at maintaining the highest of standards, your product will be difficult, if not impossible, to replicate. On the other hand, if your creation is half-hearted, someone may take the concept to a level beyond yours, leaving you (deservedly) behind.

On a caveat in sports, music or entertainment some may be touting brilliance in a bombastic way as a necessary part of a marketing machine; this is easy to detect in the super-successful individual who at heart is more than likely to be humble and grateful, so never take appearances at face value.

Code #19: Accept that nothing is missing

Nothing is missing. It is just in a form that you may not recognise yet – take money, for example: if you presume a lack of cash, perhaps the wealth resides in the form of an idea or the contacts you have acquired or even in the form of the information residing in your skull. When you spend money, it's transformed into goods, services and even experiences it has never left you, simply its form has changed. If you warm a block of ice, it turns to water. Boil that water, and it will turn to steam. The water is still there in one of its other forms – it did not disappear, and it was not destroyed. In the same way, everything you want, need and desire is already present in one of its many forms.

Have you ever felt desperate for cash? Maybe your rent or mortgage is due, and you don't have the money. Doesn't it seem in those times that money eludes you?

Yet during periods of surplus, excess money seems to show up in your life effortlessly. Imagine how the energy you put out into the universe would change if you lived with the acceptance that everything you need is already present in one form or another. This recognition, expectation, gratitude and acknowledgement will work on your behalf to hasten its arrival in the form most useful to you.

Takeaway: We live in an expanding universe, and the idea of scarcity or limitation is both wrong and dangerous. Shortage of one resource represents an opportunity to refine its use or discover new alternatives: kerosene replaced whale oil, electric light replaced lanterns, telephones replaced the telegraph, and the list can go on.

Code #20: Recognise what you need to stop doing – and stop doing it

My father told me that my job is to observe and reflect. And anything that gets in the way of the telescope has to go, including the self. – Tom Hardy

Very often, we feel we need more of something – information, confidence or happiness – when we should recognise that what we presume we need is already residing within us. We only need to stop doing the things that inhibit its emergence. Let me explain with the following example:

Some years ago, I was visited by a presidential candidate, though the people of his country well knew that he would tacitly inherit the presidency. He sat in my office and observed my magnificent book collection. Being a bibliophile himself, we struck an immediate connection.

I had no idea why he had requested the meeting, so I asked, "What brings you here?" He said, "I have a fear of public speaking and cannot address millions of people. I need confidence, an expression of power, and the ability to ignite the desire and passions of my nation."

"You don't need the confidence to do that," I replied. He looked at me, puzzled. "That doesn't require confidence. Besides, you are super selfish. You may even be in the wrong profession."

He was startled by my reply, dumbfounded even. "Why do you say that?"

"Because you have been blessed with this position of authority, instead of showing concern for your people, you are focusing on yourself and afraid of how your body may react or how you may be perceived in the presence of others."

I continued, "A simple shift in your attention will neutralise your anxiety."

He protested, saying the finest training in public speaking in the world had yet to relive him of his fears.

To which I replied: "Public speaking doesn't require training. It's merely a matter of learning the etiquette and organising the information you are going to deliver."

"It's just not that simple!" he replied.

Then I shared a personal experience with him.

"Last night, I was heading to 5 Hertford Street in Mayfair to meet my significant other. I was super-excited and had so much to catch up on. On top of that, she loves to journal. To surprise her, I had picked up a personalised Aspinal Journal.

"She is involved in functional medicine and in the process of launching her first spa. I had new ideas to share, and I felt my suggestions would help. I didn't need to rehearse what to say. I was not self-conscious about how I would come across in conversation, and I didn't imagine all the worst scenarios. I couldn't wait to see her and share my ideas. All I could think about was what an incredible night lay in front of us.

"Two things were going on inside of me that were subconscious: I felt *optimistic and energetic*. I was so excited to see her and share the latest news. I felt *confident and secure*. I did not need to build myself up to a peak state to speak to her.

"I felt this way because my focus was not on how I was going to come across. My focus was on what I could bring to her. In the same way, your confidence and positivity will increase if you focus on how you are benefitting your audience, rather than focusing on yourself."

He grasped the point immediately.

Recognising his heritage and being fortunate enough to have read numerous books on etiquette and customs of various cultures, I was schooled to offer further examples. There is a particular etiquette about being a gentleman, of course, chivalry is timeless; when attending a banquet, your partner interlocks with your left arm on reaching the table; one always offers the best seat to their guest. And when walking on the pavement, a gentleman is to take the side closest to the vehicles. This demonstrates that you are putting your companion first.

But when you put yourself first, becoming self-centred and overly concerned with how you come across, you set yourself up for disaster. You must focus on your audience, on what you can give them, and then you will connect as easily as if you were having a heartfelt conversation with your closest friend. In much the same way, public speaking is just sharing what you feel. Focus on your audience and deliver your very best. This does not require confidence; it requires compassion and present moment awareness.

And don't forget your etiquette: put your audience first and remember, everyone is looking for a hero.

Let us look at this example. Frank has two PhDs and is an absolute expert on his topic. Before his presentations, Frank worries about forgetting his words, how he will be judged, obsesses that he may blush. In other words, he is fearful of being afraid. All these self-defeating thoughts create an influx of neuro-inhibitors which practically immobilise Frank. He looks more like a deer in the headlights than the next Einstein. His reaction is proof positive that the ability to perform is directly related to one's state of mind.

Now let us look at Sarah. Sarah dropped out of school at 15 and has no accreditation to her name. She is now 30 and is a self-made success. She understands the property market like the back of her hand. She stays abreast of the latest news and has mastered this topic, knowing how to buy, sell and flip properties. She has also trained countless others to do the same.

When she presents at a seminar, she recalls her turbulent beginnings and knows that, just as she broke free, others can too. She is ready to pour out her experience because she knows that with the right knowledge, commitment and perseverance she can help hundreds of people make something of themselves.

Sarah is genuine, authentic, has a sensitivity towards others and wants her audience to win. She cannot contain her excitement about sharing her blueprint for success, realising that by adding value to the lives of others, she will be handsomely repaid. Her focus is on what she is bringing to her audience, not on how they may perceive her.

Another way to view your present situation is to acknowledge that you don't need more. Instead, you need to remove what is stopping you from achieving your desires so it is no longer a dominant force. For instance, someone who is overweight does not have a diet pill deficiency. And a depressed person isn't depressed because they have an antidepressant deficiency. In most cases, an overweight person is taking in too much food. A depressed person (outside of a chemical imbalance) may be obsessively overanalysing and ruminating on negativity or in a life situation that they are afraid to address or change. Think about what would happen in either case if the person stopped the negative stimulus such as the reduction of refined sugars and emotional eating and the depressed made serious life changes refusing to dwell on the negative. The problems would take care of themselves, disappearing as quickly as they had come on.

A month later, after working with the soon-to-be-president, I received a personal call, and a heartfelt thank you for helping him negate a fear that could have cost him his position.

Takeaway: Allow what is lying dormant within you to come to life and rise to the occasion. Focus on what you can give to others and use your gifts to change your world.

Code #21: Free thinking

What you shout out, you pound in; don't put your brain in chains, you can only progress when you learn the method of learning. – Charlie Munger

According to the late theoretical physicist and cosmologist Stephen Hawking, if we can develop a way to expand a wormhole, we can travel back in time. Let us imagine that possibility and that you return to the dark ages to contradict people's beliefs about the earth being flat, or the planets revolving around the earth, or that women lack souls and have no rights. You would very quickly be burned at stake.

Throughout history, anyone introducing new ideas is condemned vehemently. As philosopher Arthur Schopenhauer put it: "All truths pass through three stages. First, it is ridiculed. Second, it is violently opposed. Third, it is accepted as being self-evident."

My question to you is this: do you have the flexibility of thought and the openness to accept a new idea?

For instance, imagine you were born and raised in a war-torn country, a communist state, or an excessively religious community held to a very particular set of beliefs. Even the media continually promoted appalling ideas that everyone around you adopted as normal. Would you have the flexibility to recognise the absurdity of your situation? Would you be able to discern right from wrong? Could you think for yourself and entertain new ideas in such a situation?

Don't be too sure; it's easy to accept new ideas in hindsight – after they are adopted as the new 'norm'.

But I'm challenging you here and now to be a visionary.

Here are some examples that demonstrate what I'm talking about:

When antiseptic was first discovered, it was condemned by the Church as evil.

Huge uproars and campaigns were organised to oppose the new idea of transportation by train.

Millions resisted seatbelts as destroying the enjoyment of travelling by car.

The list goes on.

Here is my point: any new idea that has the potential to change the world is always met with fierce opposition.

It is human nature to go with the masses. It takes incredible strength to recognise the truth. This is why it is essential to have a sincere connection with the forces of the universe and a genuine desire to do the right thing. These traits can turn you into a visionary.

You will always find that great thinkers, leaders and EndGamers looked in the direction of the masses and chose to turn the opposite way.

Suppose you adapt your mind to accept and internalise the universal laws that bring about the change you desire. In that case, you will naturally find yourself more open to new ideas, concepts and possibilities never before attempted or manifested in reality. This is the emerging EndGamer in you – a natural result of being authentic to your true self.

Takeaway: You must ask yourself two questions to keep in check at all times:

1. What is the number one piece of evidence that supports my claim?
2. What would it take for me to realise I am wrong?

These questions can be modified to ask and help others who are trapped in ideas.

Code #22: Ruthlessness

Though this term carries a negative connotation, it has an appropriate time and place.

For example, it is entirely appropriate to develop the skills necessary to ruthlessly ignore the ideas that hold you back, no longer attach any importance to the things you fear and fearlessly slay the demons of your self-doubt.

Accepting the lessons of this book, in theory, is easy enough while you are enjoying reading about them on the sofa. But what happens when you enter the arena of life?

Let's say you are driving down the road, and someone cuts you off, then swears at you.

Your automatic impulse will likely be retaliation. However, events like these are the real tests of whether you have the internal balance to remain serene. Now, that's real strength.

Code #23: Taking the initiative

The following story gives an incredible illustration of someone who was prepared to do whatever it took at any cost to contribute powerful change for his nation, and what transpired, as a result, is sure to leave you astonished.

The year was 1970. America was in the throes of turbulence. Communist influences, racism and illegal drugs were wreaking havoc on the country.

With the timeless words from John F Kennedy's 1961 inaugural address still ringing incessantly in his ears, *"Ask not what your country can do for you – ask what you can do for your country."*

The time came when something inside was nudging him to take charge. Unable to contain himself, he began to follow through and figure out steps he could take to make a change for the country that had given him so much. This man knew he had to do something, so travelling up from the mid-South, he booked a room at the Washington Hotel under the assumed name of Jon Burrows to keep his true identity private. Later, from his room, he wrote a letter to the president:

I have done an in-depth study of drug abuse and the communist influence brainwashing techniques, and I am right in the middle of the whole thing; I can help our country, I will be of any service that I can, I would love to meet you.

A meeting was arranged, and a convoy of limousines and armoured vehicles escorted Burrows to the White House. On meeting Nixon, Burrows gifted the president a Colt .45. He began explaining his mission to mediate the communist threat on America and undermine the destructive influences of racism and drugs. He was granted permission to become a federal agent, working under the code name Fountain Pen.

And who was this EndGamer?

The most recognisable face in the world. Jon Burrows was none other than Elvis Presley.

Elvis had taken the music industry by storm. He made an incredible contribution to people around the globe with his singing and acting. Now he was about to embark on a mission that he felt would help the country that had created him. For the next seven years, from many accounts, it is believed Elvis served his country as an undercover agent in whatever limited capacity he could, even while touring as the casinos were rife with Mafia activity.

On August 1977, Elvis and his father Vernon Presley were scheduled to appear in front of a federal grand jury to indict some of the most notorious crime personalities operating underground with the information he had uncovered. That morning tragically, Elvis was found dead on his bathroom floor. We probably will never know all the intricacies of what took place over those years.

No one can deny the fact that Elvis led the music industry by using his initiative to bring forth his own talent and originality, influencing millions of people globally and changing the industry as we know it. That same initiative was now being used on a very personal and private level throughout the remaining years of his life. Without the approval of anyone, Elvis was putting himself on the front line to give back to his country, leading by example in making the world a better, safer place.

Code #24: Activating the imagination

If you think of or dwell upon the form of something that already exists, you are focusing on a thing of limitation. This is why you have to think of the idea behind the thing and become one with the very essence of that which you have intended to emerge and bring forth. *This is also the mechanism needed to birth original ideas.*

The next phase, once an idea emerges, is to present the idea back to the subconscious with the intent of allowing a free flow of images to come to the surface. This is how the creation will evolve and be allowed to work through you.

It would be best if you adopted this as your self-concept. Seeing the product, service or desire already in existence will impress ideas on the subconscious and open a line of communication. Emotion is the only medium of transmission; hence by evoking the feeling, every fibre of your being gets to work.

So, as you think about the desire while *in a state of gratitude*, as that is what you would experience when the result is accomplished, the mind once again pre-supposes truth in the assumption and hastens its arrival. Once you have arrived at this moment, your mind will finally bring forth the feeling of it being part of your everyday life.

When we feel something is missing in the world, or an urge appears to create something new, that is the universe communicating with us, giving one the honour of being the custodian to bring that very thing to life. The instructions for achievement are always provided in the accompanying forms of both pleasure and pain. This roadmap may appear complex at first, yet the closer one gets to the destination, the clearer the path becomes. Any resistance that may appear along the way is used to strengthen and refine the will in preparation for the final hurdle. Though normally just prior to accomplishment, the universe appears to set one final and nearly insurmountable obstacle. This is perhaps to make victory sweeter so that you will feel that greater sense of gratitude in its accomplishment.

Soon, the obstacle fades into oblivion, and upon closer inspection, the roadblocks were nothing but a mirage.

Code #25 Decisivness

*The decisions you decide to do, **get done**, while the decisions you decide not to do, **do not get done**.*

People have problems because they make a poor decision and then re-decide to make the same decision. If you think of a person looking to quit smoking, it's a decision. Each step along the way is a new decision – a decision to buy the pack, to take a cigarette out of the packet, to light it, to inhale it. When people say they have no control, the reality is that they are deceiving themselves, and they always do. What we need is a mechanism to learn from a bad decision, and then forget to make the bad decision, and then learn to make a good decision and link it to the motivation to not only *not get started*, but the motivation also then links to follow-through and completion.

Conclusion

I hope you can see why at the outset I stated that this is one of the most significant chapters in the book.

Because it is so vital, I will repeat what I said at the beginning: Succeeding at the level of a EndGamer requires that you *become* the person who can achieve the results you desire at the magnitude that you wish.

You must take responsibility for becoming the person you want to be. You must dismantle the old self – override whatever is holding you back – and take yourself to your core strength. Then reconstruct your personality based on who you want your new self to be.

The first step is the necessary awareness – the conviction that you are now on your heroic mission and that there is no turning back.

Now, we turn to equip you with the tools that are indispensable on your journey.

CHAPTER SIX

Your Heroic Mission

Myth is much more important and true than history. History is just journalism, and you know how reliable that is. – Joseph Campbell

You are as individual as your fingerprints. As this unique creation, you have been given a set of gifts all your own and a unique calling that only you can fulfil. You are here for a purpose. You are engineered to succeed. You have an inbuilt blueprint – *a roadmap that is rigged in your favour.*

And you are rewarded every time you move in the direction of your dreams.

A similar principle is even demonstrated in other aspects of nature. Take monarch butterflies, for example. These butterflies have an inbuilt destiny that steers them instinctually and without choice. Monarch butterflies taken from their home and their offspring, having no awareness of where they came from, will by nature return to their original home.

In much the same way as this butterfly, your inbuilt mechanism is guiding you toward your true calling, even if you have no conscious awareness of what that is. As part of that mechanism, the universe also 'nudges' you with pain (physical and emotional dis-ease) if you get off track. These same forces often bring resistance into your life to help refine your character along the way as well.

There is at least one distinct difference between you and this insect, however:

You are gifted with the right to be an Architect of Destiny.

Privileged – and honoured yet full of complaints – as humans, we have a choice and the opportunity to be the grand architects of our own lives.

(Now, just because you have the ability to do so doesn't mean you *will* do it. In fact, the percentage of people who actually take charge of their own destiny is minuscule. Nonetheless, this ability is inherent in our genetic makeup.)

The heroic mission begins the moment you arrive on this planet. During the formative years, both triumph and tribulations can be utilised as the raw materials necessary to develop the tenacity required for success. Many misinterpreted tribulations continue to be the tormentors until observed how the resistance and breakdowns naturally led to the breakthroughs.

Guilt turn to gratitude once the required lessons have been taken and amendments made; then depression has the potential to turn into dynamic energy. Negative sensations arising in your body are nothing other than raw fuel and indicators of the things you have denied or lessons yet to be learned; they can be channelled, utilised along the way. Only through correct interpretation and redirection of the energy, only then can you get to choose what to do with it and how to use it. The stars become illuminated to your eyes only when darkness casts its shadow. It is the contrast of darkness that allows one to see the light.

Some may recognise their calling early in life and some much later.

Enzo Ferrari. Though Ferrari was most widely known for the elite brand of handmade Italian automobiles that bear his name, he was happiest when he was suited up behind the wheel of a race car. Young Ferrari was first inspired to become a racing driver at the age of ten after seeing Felice Nazzaro win the 1908 Circuit di Bologna. But it wasn't until some years later, when his family's carpentry business collapsed, that he began pursuing that dream.

Landing a job as a test-driver for a Milan-based car manufacturer, Ferrari was eventually given a chance at his first race. And, not surprisingly, he finished fourth in the three-litre category in his debut event – the 1919 Parma–Poggio di Berceto hillclimb.

His first win actually came in 1924, and he continued racing until 1932 when he founded his own racing team – Scuderia Ferrari.

You should not only note the duration of Ferrari's dream here but his unwavering commitment to excellence. *Close to two decades passed before Ferrari actually struck his vein of gold.* So, it seems quite fitting that after almost forty years of living his passion a top-of-the-line sports car would bear his name.

And it's also quite appropriate, once you know his story, to hear Enzo Ferrari say:

"Think as a winner and act as a winner. You'll be quite likely to achieve your goal."

When we are living out our true purpose, we bring value to the world, and we are rewarded in kind. Not only that, but the greater number of people we serve, the greater our reward. The symbol of Ferrari has been used in perfume, music, film, video games; the sheer volume of people benefiting from one man's dream and inspiring others, whether to own a car bearing his name or an item with its symbol would be impossible to calculate.

The mission is constructed twofold; firstly working on yourself by unlocking your latent potential; secondly, simultaneously and synchronistically bringing value to the world, by pursuing your raw unadulterated desire and being paid handsomely for it. The greater the value, the greater the reward. For example, some may argue that a basketball player gets paid too much for just 'playing a game'. But what they fail to realise is this simple truth: this athlete is actually bringing joy to millions, and sometimes even tens of millions, of people, the sponsorship and deals rendered keep industries alive from textiles to television. It is an exchange of value.

This principle of value exchange is also impartial.

Consider this. Even though arms and drug dealers appear on the surface to be evil and destructive, they still offer a service that supports millions of people, and they are paid for it accordingly. Of course, in time, they will also have a heavy price to pay for their desire for immediate gratification and ignorance of a better way to create personal significance, power and wealth. But the principle remains the same.

While doing some consulting work for a financial firm in Madrid, I asked the 26-year-old CEO entrepreneur how he had accumulated such a great fortune at an early age. Here's how he answered me. Growing up on a rough council estate in the North of England, he had two groups of friends. The first were involved in selling drugs, which for this group was exhilarating and a means of affording anything they wanted. There were another group of friends who decided to knuckle down and study finance as a better alternative for a way out of mediocracy. Both the drug dealers and the financiers were making substantial amounts of money. However, he wisely observed that he had never met a happily retired drug dealer, so he made the better choice and went into finance.

There is such a valuable lesson in this. We choose our destiny. But there are always two routes and choices.

Certain nations (and even some individuals) aggressively exploit the wealth of various countries. Or they use the masses to create an Us vs Them conflict – like men vs woman, white vs. black country vs country, religion vs religion the lists could go on ad infinitum, ad nauseam. Wealth can be acquired through conflict and conquest or via creation of outstanding products and services the world yearns for.

Be careful of falling into the pitfalls of immediate gratification and recognise you always have the 'choice' to develop other means of generating revenue and value. Make the better choice by creating products and services that help the world. Become part of the solution that saves the planet and conquers the stars. War has a time and place; wage it against your inhibitions, slay fearlessly self-limiting beliefs, aim to annihilate poverty and become an exemplary model for generations to follow.

The process of bringing the EndGamer in you to the surface began the moment the book was started, keep moving forward.

Remembering the Future and Predicting the Past

Remember with the same certainty you had about past events, the future you intend to create. Any psychologist or researcher will tell you that many of the past narratives you carry around may be either misinterpretations or entirely inaccurate accounts. I feel it's better to begin to predict the past and assume you were better than what you thought you were and then begin to remember the future as it begins to unfold.

In other words, become a *mind explorer*. Mind explorers are people so deep in thought that they lose track of reality, and explore the inner recesses of their mind and draw out ideas of things not yet created. In other words, the crystallisation of their heroic mission *in their own mind* is such that at times they cannot tell whether they are dreaming or they are awake. As a result, the mind explorer becomes so compelled to act on their dream to bring it to fruition that nothing else matters.

These are the people who leave a golden footprint on the planet – people like Newton, Princess Diana, Steve Jobs, Madame Curie and Mozart. They continue to live in our hearts and minds, and because of them, the world is a better place. And by living out your own true calling, you have the opportunity to not only follow a clearer path laid down but also leave your own footprints in time.

Your heroic quest is your entire life's work, not just a single snapshot of where you are currently. Developing a border vision is paramount. Many media outlets never report the twenty years of painstaking hours, heartaches and tears that are inevitable along the journey that leads to the pinnacle of success. They only report on the massive size of a celebrity's mansion, or the drama behind some scandalous affair.

Take Bill Gates, for instance. Between the ages of 20 and 30, he never took even one single day of work. The Beatles accumulated more rehearsal hours than any other pop group in history. But you only hear the glamorous side of the story. As a result, we are left with people who have the impression that success comes at the turn of a wheel, like winning the lottery, which is a complete misrepresentation of the hero's journey.

Here's another example of someone who realised the path to follow very early in life.

Lights, Camera, Action

It was the early 1980s. At the tender age of six, Ravi Chopra would help in his family's video store based in the UK's Midlands, serving customers with a healthy diet of Western movies with a trickle of Eastern matinée.

As children, when we watch the array of dazzling stars in a film, we become the character; we learn, mimic, imitate and evolve by what we see and the things that naturally draw us. The young Chopra was watching these movies from a slightly different perspective, from the angle of creation.

It's a common theme we hear all too often of children watching too much TV or playing too many video games, but this may not always be the case, as this was the spark that was required to light the fuse that would set Chopra in the direction of his destiny. The hours spent in front of the silver screen were never wasted. Each thought, expression and interaction was building the foundation for this child to one day grow up and create his own productions.

The rebellious phase teens go through played a slightly different theme for Chopra. The pursuit of films was the agenda, so making applications to his favourite TV show was the only logical way forward. Unable to handle rejection, Chopra's response was different to what we most regularly see in others who typically give up or run away and hide, feeling sorry for themselves. Young Chopra bombarded the production company with enquiries, offering free assistance as a runner and securing an interview with the Bafta-winning owner of a production company. He memorised answers for fifty questions he was likely to be asked, and after an hour-long interview he got the job as a 'production assistant' at the age of 17. He found out three years later that a question he asked the owner was what secured him the position: *Is this a company where I can get promoted and work my way up the ladder? I am very serious about this industry and if this is not possible, this is the wrong company for me.* Everything serves us when directed correctly, even rebellion.

College and university were not on Chopra's agenda; impatient and determined he could not comprehend spending thousands of hours studying something theoretically without a guarantee of true application. Chopra's premise was that your craft may be studied, but nothing is as powerful as immersion, so being on a production and being mentored would have no substitute. No matter how much we attempt to mimic the conditions and skills, the true environment and building the tangible expertise that is necessary can never be substituted. Chopra's endgame was cinema, so he set his sights on the BBC's Film Department and no other, irrespective of the time it would take. To qualify and be recognised by this juggernaut, Chopra began working with many TV and film companies, building the necessary foundation and exposure to qualify for a position with the very best. The BBC.

After eight long years of applying they finally accepted him. During the course of this time Chopra was establishing relationships with everyone he could in the industry, honouring everybody from the caretakers to the senior executives, every compliment and complaint genuine. With careful tact taken not to involve the ego, something taken from his cultural upbringing, it comes down to a pillar of truth. He shared with me a near magical story that took place at the *Empire* Film Awards where he attended as a guest. He was seated on a table next to rising film actor Jeremy Irvine, who had previously starred in *War Horse*, directed by Steven Spielberg. At the time Chopra had started scripting an idea for a sci-fi movie that would be both mesmerising and metaphorically serve to deliver a message of following one's dreams. Irvine would be perfect casting as the main star of his future film. He put it out in the universe that if it's meant to be it will be, and he forgot about it.

Now with a solid foundation in place with the BBC, it was time to build upon the dream. Chopra put a script together for one of the boldest short films to come out of the British film industry. It was going to require some serious investment. Chopra's wealth was already far greater than any bank account, no matter how sizeable. His wealth was in the form of a finely developed imagination with mastery of his craft to back it up. Then came the contacts and friends that had been established over the years through genuine agenda-free interactions. They were now being rallied together to be part of a dream that would not only serve Chopra but serve them immensely as well. Chopra began to organise some of the most credible names in the industry to be part of his film *Cognition* and, as a stroke of luck or destiny, Jeremy Irvine did indeed become the main star of the film, a flourishing seed that was planted years previously. Bafta winner Andrew Scott was also cast, the BBC Concert Orchestra performed the score, and he managed to secure use of the BBC's helicopter for the aerial shots. The production design team who had previously worked on *Star Wars* and *Guardians of the Galaxy* came on board, joining the quest, and finally the Emmy Award-winning sound editor from *Jurassic World* fine-tuned the acoustics for the film.

There comes a stage in one's life where you no longer chase the dream, the dream finds its way to you.

The movie to date has been released in more than ninety countries and has won over eighty international short film awards, picking up Best Sci-Fi Film at the British Short Film Awards and making it onto the long list at the Oscars for Best Live Action Short. The film is now making its way to the big screen as a full length feature film.

Live in the moment and treat everyone as the miracle that they are and observe how smoothly life will pan out as each individual is a reflection of you.

Chopra learned early on that persistence is the most powerful way to paralyse resistance and moving forward is the only way forward.

Building a Time Machine

The year was 1955, and he was a loving and proud citizen from the Bronx, both a model husband and devoted father working as a humble TV repairman to support his young family. At 33 years of age, he was entering the prime of his life. The value of an education and upright morals were the principles that he emphasised for his children, and in particular to his son, ten-year-old Ron. Being prompted toward engineering and science, Ron idolised his father and naturally found his dad's wisdom fascinating.

One night, Ron awoke to his mother's whimpering and the harrowing sounds of police sirens outside his house. Quickly running to his parents' room, he was horrified to find his father lying still and motionless. *His father had died of a heart attack.*

In the blink of an eye, Ron's world had been turned upside down.

Nearly a year after his father's passing, the depressed young man stumbled across a book that was about to change his life. It was as if an aura of light had appeared from the darkness of despair. The book was an illustrated version of the classic sci-fi novel *The Time Machine* by HG Wells. Though entirely fictional, to the unrestricted, uninhibited and flexible mind of a child *it was a story of possibility.*

Some men see things as they are and say why. I dream of things that never were and say why not. – Robert Kennedy

Influenced by the novel, Ron spent every evening in the basement of his home attempting to build a time machine, tinkering with bits and pieces of scrap metal, plastic and electronic parts. Ron began devouring books on both science and electronics.

As the years progressed, the dream didn't drift further away; it began to gravitate closer to Ron, yearning for discovery. With his wealth of knowledge and his learning through experimentation, now more practical answers were found. A glimmer of possibility came one evening when Ron was reading *The Universe and Dr Einstein*, a 1948 layman's explanation of Albert Einstein's relativity theory. This was the affirmation Ron was after. When the student is ready, the teacher appears. Perhaps this is an overused adage, but the truth cannot be denied.

In the book, Einstein indicated that space and time were part and parcel of the same thing: time being a fabric, theoretically there was nothing to restrict one from moving forward, or even backward, in time.

Einstein soon became Ron's second obsession. The raw pain of having lost his father so suddenly, coupled with the greatest desire to see his father once again, set a trajectory in Ron's life that still continues to this very day.

Ronald Mallett became the first-ever African-American professor in the University of Connecticut's physics department and a real astrophysicist with a doctorate from Penn State. There he stayed, quietly whittling away at the problem of time travel. For the bulk of his career, Ron concealed his true intentions in order to prevent ridicule from the scientific community. Ron used a cover story about researching how black holes affect time. "I knew that if I studied black holes, it was considered legitimate; as opposed to time travel," Ron would say later on when interviewed.

Who hasn't dreamt of turning back the hands of time? Or peering into the future? Einstein, Hawking and Nobel Prize winner Kip Thorne have all entertained the possibility of time travel. Although it may still be out of reach utilising our present technologies, let's remember that each step forward towards a noble cause creates a fringe benefit: further innovative technologies being discovered and manufactured.

It's about doing your best with what you have every day and falling in love with not only the Endgame but the process and the journey in the attempt to get there. Newton himself was highly criticised for the volume of work he performed using alchemy, and yet we cannot deny, for even one moment, that his efforts directly correlated with his discoveries in the field of optics.

Ron Mallet's personal breakthrough came around the turn of the century in the form of a simple and elegant formula he believes one day will allow one to travel back in time. According to Newtonian physics, only matter can create gravity, but Einstein disagreed: *light*, he said, *could also affect gravity*.

Mallett's ah-ha moment was when he put this missing piece of the puzzle together.

"According to Einstein, gravity affects time," he said. "If gravity can affect time, and light can create gravity, then light can affect time."

Mallett's formula calls for a device called *a ring laser*, which is exactly what it sounds like – a series of mirrors that force a tight beam of light into a continuous loop. Put enough energy into that laser and you may actually be able to warp space, creating what physicists call a closed-time-like curve or CTC. Though still to be proven, Mallet stands as one of today's pioneers in the theory of time travel.

Mallet's life serves as a beautiful example to us all: in pursuing a dream that may take lifetimes to fulfil, even though the result may not be visible at present, *learning to enjoy the path and journey as much as the destination is one of the keys to a truly adventurous life.*

Ferrari, Chopra, Mallett and many others recognised their dream early in life. Others discover their purpose later, sometimes much later.

We each find the path which works best for us. There is no right or wrong way.

However, living out your higher purpose does require a commitment to excellence and a consistent follow-through that never ends. You see, your life is a beautiful masterpiece. A blank canvas that is evolving, refining and improving with each stroke of the brush. We each have a unique life purpose, a purpose that is inherent inside of us and that arises out of what we value most.

And we are the most fulfilled when we are living in sync with our highest value and purpose. This is what gives our life meaning. We need no motivation to fulfil that purpose because it is a spontaneous living-out of who we are and what we are about.

There's a biological reason, as well, behind the fact that we function best when we are living out our unique purpose.

In Chapter Two we talked about the neuroplastic quality of the human brain and how neurons associate with one another along common neural pathways. Neurons are constantly at work perceiving and processing data. And thanks to your brain's reticular activating system function (also discussed in Chapter Two), your brain continually filters out information that is unimportant and irrelevant to your purpose and highlights those opportunities that help you fulfil your dream.

Whenever you encounter an opportunity that is congruent with your highest values and dreams, here's what happens biologically in your brain. The neurons 'myelinate' (nourish and facilitate) the coordinating nerves, causing your brain to neurogenically remodel itself. It is in this electrically charged 'thought state' that the most highly developed anterior part of the forebrain – the 'executive centre' – goes to work, strategically planning, awakening and inspiring vision.

And in the process, your brain releases certain 'highly addictive' chemicals. The more often these chemicals are released, the more your body craves them. So, even *biologically* as you succeed, you create a path that makes way for even greater growth. In other words, your brain actually 'rewards' you when you are progressing in the direction of your highest value, your purpose, and the fulfilment of who you are and what you can bring to your world.

You and I have already won the greatest lottery that there is going… the lottery of life. The question for you is this… What are you going to do with that winning ticket of yours – Simon Alexander Ong

In one of the most conclusive studies done on billionaires in the book *The Self-Made Billionaire Effect*, it was determined that mere 'habits of the mind' is the one factor common to self-made billionaires.

So, how do you develop these billionaire 'habits' of the mind?

By applying the principles and practices we've already discussed in earlier chapters to create thought patterns that lead to success.

According to one of the richest men in the world, Warren Buffett, "The more you learn, the more you earn."

Buffett also said: "We learn from mistakes, but they don't have to be ours."

This explains why people who succeed at an extraordinary level are part of a Mastermind group. It also explains why they are voracious readers – learning everything they can from others who have already succeeded. Why? Because they realise their brain is a simulation machine, allowing them to learn from others' successes as well as failures without having to make the same mistakes they did. Celebrated evolutionary biologist Richard Dawkins explains how it is not really the survival of the fittest; it is the species most adept at learning from the mistakes of others that thrives.

Bill Gates was once asked if he could possess any superhero quality, what would it be. His answer? *The ability to read fast!*

Having the opportunity to increase your earning capacity simply by learning and being able to simulate learning from others' mistakes without going through the same trial-and-error process puts you at a significant advantage.

But let me say again, you can't just 'learn'. You must also apply what you are learning as you go. This is the only way to legitimately advance yourself in the process en route to your desired life.

Inheritors of the World

The EndGamers have an image in their mind's eye of a better future. Every step forward begins to create greater clarity until it gets to the point where they live in the assumption that the dream is already complete. Knowing full well it may take many lifetimes, as legacy runs through their bloodlines, they know a part of them will continue forever.

In the current, divided world, no sooner do divisions disappear in one area, they continue to reappear in some new form as racial tensions reduce, political or religious frictions increase. Gorbachev of the Soviet Union in Oslo as the winner of the 1990 Nobel Peace Prize, surmised perfectly that peace cannot be achieved through unity in similarity but through unity in diversity – by learning to enjoy comparisons while respecting and honouring everyone, irrespective of colour or creed. It's the only way we will achieve balance. Diversity is the only thing we all have in common. For centuries, the attempt to communicate that idea, or have people adopt tolerance toward different cultures, appears to have moved the needle only slightly.

Could there be another way?

When meaningful relationships are formed with people and the planet, advancements in civilisation and greater peace become a by-product. View the earth and all inhabitants as both extensions and reflections of ourselves.

It is strange and marvellous how the world organises and orchestrates change and solutions in the most unpredictable ways. The intense heat and pressure deep in the earth's crust produce the diamond, and the butterfly, hidden and confined in the caterpillar, undergoes an internal transformation – an apparent struggle and darkness awaiting its metamorphosis before it has earned its right to soar into the light. You, the reader, are the inheritor of the earth, the very offspring of creation. You are one in a trillion – that means you bear the responsibility for the planet, the people, and all living beings.

Learning is by experience. In fact, many researchers agree that learning a language is not something one does academically to install information in the brain; instead, it is acquired. The introduction of language to toddlers does not begin with one's parents sitting them down and directing their eyes to a string of abstract letters – *it starts much sooner* – as early as several weeks after conception. The resonance of sound and emotions make its way into the body as the foetus develops. Immersion, absorption, experience and interaction have always been key to how we learn. Take a look at great composers, athletes or thinkers. They are undeniably amongst people thriving in their particular niche. True learning and transformation can only occur through osmosis. Therefore improving the planet and bringing one another together cannot be achieved with mere words; it can be through real and empathetic connections.

A key figure in a new movement designed to reverse the effects of climate change and improve global relationships with one another is Laurent de Brabandt, a young philanthropist and founder of the De Brabandt Foundation. De Brabandt is on an Endgame mission to lead generations to engage in philanthropy geared toward saving the planet and clearing archaic divisions between nations. Just shy of his 30th birthday, Laurent had already combined his love of travel into a stealthy grassroots movement to protect the planet, now established in 100 countries and growing. The vehicle is using sustainability in the tourism industry to turn the practice of responsibility toward the planet into the norm of modern-day society. In doing so it also serves to highlight the real link between tourists and the locals thus creating lasting and real connections between all the inhabitants of our world. With the correct approach, relationships can be formed, improvement of economies established, as well as both land and sea protected, saving the very planet. If, as a guest, you are welcomed and have a window to peer into other cultures, you will readily find barriers are brought down readily establishing the environment necessary for peace.

Wherever you are at any moment in time or point in space, that fleeting signature is yours and only yours. An imprint is established, both your mind and your location. Today, as travel to the most remote corners of the planet is easily accessible, it's time to connect everything to one another and to protect the world as we know it.

The Myth of the Shortcut

In an attempt to debunk the myth of the shortcut to success, you need to look no further than the field of sports. Even the most naturally gifted athlete, if they haven't properly prepared, will rapidly deteriorate into the worst player on the team.

There is no way around it. All great entrepreneurs put in the painstaking hours necessary for studying, learning and modelling others – while holding fast to their dream in every waking moment – until everything turns around.

How on earth did we come to believe in the magic potion or pill, or some other chance to 'get rich quick? Because we are bombarded daily from every angle with the promise of the miracle fix, humans are inherently lazy.

However, there is one true way to truncate the time necessary to reach your destination, and that is being blatantly honest with yourself and recognising you can never have enough time to learn everything and figure it all out on your own. The only actual 'shortcut' comes when you seek mentorship and *apply what you learn.*

The most significant factor in astronomical success is the ability not only to take feedback but be humble enough to apply it, even if you disagree.

The late founder of Walmart, Sam Walton was at one stage worth $20 million; he still hired experts for counsel and advice. He then took it a step further and travelled the country, visiting every competitor's department store to figure out how to streamline things even more efficiently. The results? When he died, he was worth over **$191 billion**.

Michael Jordan is believed to be the greatest basketball player in history. In biographical accounts of Jordan, every trainer he ever had mentions his outstanding ability to listen to advice and apply it, even when it was from players who were less successful. He was open to feedback.

You should take heart in this fact: none of the above examples is someone who claimed or believed they knew it all. Yet, no one would argue with any of them if they did. So be open to learning. Let the world be your teacher.

At the same time, you must also understand that the ability to learn from the mistakes of others is not to be confused with the myth of whimsical thinking – that is, hoping that by mere fate you may be able to achieve success without having to do the necessary groundwork. Forever looking for success at the turn of a wheel, without being willing to value the process and commit to it with your whole being, will only lead to disillusion and void.

Jim Rohn described it best when he said: "You can't pay someone to do your push-ups, and you can't fake strength."

Because while you can certainly learn from others' mistakes, as well as their achievements, there is a process you go through to prove your commitment and to earn the right to have reached your desired destination and claim the prize.

Thank God I didn't listen to people that said I should work eight hours! – Edison

Let me offer a word of caution. The many challenges and roadblocks that test your resilience and commitment to the process of becoming an EndGamer can also cause you to get off track and lose your way and even grow hard along the way.

You see, your brain is constantly at a crossroads. Here's what I mean by that.

Every day you wake up, you decide whether you'll have eggs, toast and juice or oatmeal for breakfast. Then you decide whether to wear the red shirt or the blue one. Whether to call your friend to schedule lunch or stay at the office and work through lunch. We are continually confronted with choices – yes or no, right or left, here or there. And each one of these decisions brings forward another decision. Therefore focusing on getting your best self to each moment and clarity in the direction helps create the resilience necessary to follow through; a great question to ask yourself throughout the day, in the words of Brian Tracy, "What's the best use of my time right now?"

This is why it's important to uncover your life purpose, living each day as if it were your best and your last. If you don't know what direction you're headed in, how do you know if anyone choice is the best choice or not?

American philosopher Will Durant summed it up this way: "We are what we repeatedly do. Excellence then is not an act but a habit."

(By the way, if you're having trouble determining your life purpose, I have some exercises toward the end of this chapter that will help clarify that for you.)

Never Begin What You Can't Finish

Most people work until they feel like stopping. Champions keep working until they are complete.

This is a profound truth, so please read this, re-read it… and most of all, **live by it**.

EndGamers do What is Necessary to Win, Despite How They Feel

Olympic swimmer Michael Phelps has won twice as many Olympic gold medals as anyone else in history. Twenty-three to be exact. Many of Michael's character qualities contributed to his phenomenal accomplishments, but I just want to mention two of them here:

He hates to lose. And hating to lose is a LOT stronger motivation than liking to win.

Another characteristic of Phelps is his resolve to perform no matter how he feels. Many swimmers don't swim well if they don't feel good. Not Phelps.

According to his swim coach, Bob Bowman, "Michael performs no matter how he's feeling. He knows exactly what he wants to get done, and he's able to compartmentalise what's important at any given moment."

Once you possess clarity of vision and the recognition that your actions are moving you toward your goal, and you have faith in the realisation that the universe is on your side, who is going to stop you from success?

The only person who can ever stand in your way is You! Get out of your own way and make something of yourself.

Modern psychology affirms that when we begin something that we end up not completing or make a promise that we do not keep, we are conditioning ourselves to fail by forming habit patterns of failure.

Here's how habit patterns work. Why do you default to choosing the same restaurant, the same grocer, the same hairdresser? It's because we are naturally drawn to the familiar. A routine behaviour done often enough becomes a habitual pattern that we do 'without thinking', that is, unconsciously. These are all benign examples. But the same principle holds true when it comes to forming both positive – and negative – behaviour patterns.

This means you are better off not starting a project at all than taking on a task you never intend to complete and conditioning yourself to fail. If you commit to doing something, then be sure and do it. Don't allow anyone or anything to stand in the way of your completing it. Sink your teeth into it. See it through. Never give up. Otherwise, you are breaking your word to yourself and sacrificing your integrity.

When a person finally breaks through and strikes their vein of gold, it's because they have persevered. They determined to see their idea through to completion. They kept their commitment to themselves and, as a result, developed habit patterns of follow-through and eventual success.

How else can someone go from what seems like a string of insurmountable challenges to a place where everything they touch turns to gold? I submit that it's because of the strong habit patterns of success they have developed in the neural pathways of their mind as a result of their persistence.

Remember, your very biology is engineered for success. Each time you move in the direction of your life purpose, your brain chemistry 'rewards' you. You grow, and expand, and develop habit patterns of success.

Once that is accomplished, winning becomes inevitable.

CEO of In Touch Networks, Matt Roberts, has been instrumental in building one of the fastest-growing tech companies in Europe. His philosophy sounds simple enough, yet under closer scrutiny, incredibly profound. Over lunch one afternoon, I asked Matt what he attributes his phenomenal growth. Matt replied, "Only two rules I live by and I instil in my staff: the first is never lie, the second is work hard."

Let's look at this closely. If you commit to a job and are upholding your own personal truth as well as your promise to your employee, or if you are self-employed your customer, then slack would not only be unlikely but contradictory to your self-concept. If you are working half-heartedly, you are not only lying to your company but breaking your own commitment to yourself. The second part is self-explanatory: if you do work hard, which essentially means being present in each moment and doing your job as effectively as possible, you will become irreplaceable, raising your ranks to the upper echelons of society and by setting a new benchmark, your voice, wealth and power will put you in a potion to shape the world.

Turning the Impossible to the Possible Left an MIT Professor as the Number One Enemy of the Mob

The owner of Sand's Casino was so powerful he once kicked out the legendary Frank Sinatra. Now, accompanied by two large security guards, he took a seat next to a quiet professor who was amidst his card game.

The owner briskly instructed the professor it was not only time to leave but that he was never to return.

"Why?" he asked.

The owner replied, "No reason. We just don't want you here."

The professor departed with his group of six colleagues. Hours later, speeding down mountainous Arizona terrain, the professor's accelerator pedal suddenly jammed. Swerving from side to side, the vehicle was moments from a horrendous crash before he was able to recover safely.

It was the third attempt on the life of the humble mathematician. The previous days had seen two attempts to poison him. What would prompt a number of the Mafia-run casinos of the 1960s to put out a death warrant on an obscure academic?

Our story begins at a Los Angles house party in 1956. Edward Thorp, a then-teacher of mathematics, was deep in conversation with Nobel Prize-winning physicist Richard Feynman. He had heard stories about Feynman calculating the odds of winning in casinos and asked the physicist if it was possible to beat any of the casino games.

"No," Feynman replied. It had been proven to his satisfaction that the games of chance in Vegas were precisely that. No amount of statistical analysis would lead to regularly beating the house. Rather than taking the legendary Feynman at his word, Thorp took his statement as a challenge, and it was, in fact, precisely the answer that he was looking for. Most, on the conclusion of an authority, stop. Thorp saw this as his opportunity to be the first to discover the way.

Thorp began looking for a solution to a conundrum, which he had been assured by a world-famous physicist was impossible to find. This is confidence of the highest degree. Thorp would have to think laterally to create a breakthrough in an area of probability that did not yet exist.

Yet Thorp *did* figure it out: a way to beat the casinos so thoroughly he could essentially print money – until he was unceremoniously disinvited from ever entering a Vegas casino again.

Thorpe had found the secret to predictable winning based on a precise formula. Could such a method help a player to win predictably in the game of life? His story inspired me to seek even greater control over my own destiny.

I learned that Thorp's success resided in his ability to formulate the right question and follow up with rigorous testing of hypotheses until he found an answer. He eventually proved that, no matter what was occurring on the table, if he followed his rules long enough, games of chance could be turned into a predictable science.

I launched a quest to test if Thorp's process was replicable. Numbers were never my strong point, but I knew I could overcome that weakness with enough practice.

I enrolled in online courses on mental arithmetic, statistics and the mathematics of games. Equipped with a mountain of jargon and equations that looked like something out of a sci-fi movie, I went to work on replicating the professor's findings in the casinos. I lost. Then I lost some more. Then I lost even more. Deep in the negative, I was afraid recovery was impossible.

The key to victory is not the will to win. Everyone wants to win. What makes a champion is the will to prepare to win. – Bob Knight

Talent is overrated, as every coach knows. It's no exaggeration to state that with enough determination and time, you can do practically anything. Professor Anders Ericsson has researched the secrets of exceptional performance for more than thirty years. This 'expert on experts' concludes the sole reason you are not a violin virtuoso is that you have not engaged in sufficient 'deliberate practice'.

There is too much emphasis on how we *compete* when we should be concentrating on how we *practise*. Olympic records are a culmination of a lifetime of *deliberate practice*. Breakthroughs do not come mid-game or during an exam, or when the entire world is watching. Breakthroughs happen in the laboratories, training rooms, practice studios and during lonely late-night hours of hard work, which no one ever sees. In this sense, we create our potential for success by working harder, starting earlier, and staying at it longer. It is the right kind of practice over time that leads to improvement.

Now I was undertaking to prove this to myself. I researched commentaries on Professor Thorp's work and any previous attempts at replication.

I came across an acclaimed writer who had a fantastic proposition. He claimed to have met with and had underground meetings with several MIT professors and tested over ten million perturbations of a particular card game. He claimed that he had invented a system with a 97% success rate. He offered to share his findings under the following conditions: anyone interested must meet him in Switzerland, pay $50,000, and agree to pay 10% of their winnings to him for one year.

As you can imagine, my scepticism was through the roof. Suffice it to say, my emotion won over my logic. My desire to learn was overwhelming.

Forty-eight hours after learning the seminar materials, I now had two theories for beating the casinos with the luxury of combining them in any number of ways. I decided to test the models, recover my losses and begin compounding my wealth.

I set a training schedule that included optimising my physical and mental performance and supplementation via blood testing, using a company called Bioniq (they would show me tangible data each month on what their supplements were doing to my body). Then came conditioning my emotions using meditation techniques to observe my thoughts and behaviours, learning to detach from moments of loss and learning to respond deliberately to events rather than react uncontrollably.

If you cannot control your emotions, you cannot control your money. –
Warren Buffet.

I borrowed a concept from engineering – the margin of safety theorem – so I would have a percentile yield so low it would be nearly impossible to fail. My conditioning included listening to affirmations whilst gamma frequencies were playing (allowing the information into the auditory part of the brain). To enhance and get the ideas into the visual cortex of my brain, targeted sessions were conducted in a Somadome (a futuristic meditation pod). This had the effect of bringing my visualisations to near life. Next, the physical act of writing with my left and right hand would be embedding the information into my kinaesthetic memory. I further utilised an advanced sequence of questions and answers called *"Yes of course I know I can do this because…"* This eliminates any iota of doubt in my potential to succeed.

After that, I would speed-read associated materials/formulas and books at rates so fast my conscious mind could not react – speeds of 25,000 to 60,000 words per minute, delivering information directly to the subconscious.

Daily I would have that part of my mind run scenarios of positive outcomes. I used speed modelling, a modified technique from neuro-linguistic programming (NLP), to enter a deep trance, instructing my mind to associate with all that I knew of the target persons, in my case Professor Thorp and other geniuses. The subconscious picks up this programming, making it an advantageous method to leverage the skills of others.

The actual training came with the practice on simulators, allowing me to mentally recognise stakes for each hand and various patterns; the amount I would bid would be calculated using what is known as the Kelly criterion.

Finally, imagined the outcomes I desired and their supported behaviours by instructing the higher dimensional part of myself (the subconscious) to provide me with the recognition of the feelings I would be experiencing once the tables were conquered and I saw my bank balance quintupled.

Thirteen months later, my girlfriend surprised me with a weekend away in Bristol. We had just finished supper and stepped out of the restaurant next door to a casino.

"Do you want to see something cool?" I said to her.

"What do you mean?" she asked.

With no notice given, hands held, fingers interlocked, I smoothly opened the casino door and whisked her in.

When we left, only about an hour later, she was dumbfounded.

"How did you do that? How was that even possible?" she asked.

"Beginner's luck," I replied with a wink.

Unstoppable

Live life as if everything was rigged in your favour. – Rumi

You only have a finite amount of time on this incredible planet; it's up to you to make the most of it. You should never allow your fears to stop you because your fears are nothing more than an illusion.

How do I know that? Because I know we can't trust our senses.

We are hurtling through space on a hard rock that is spinning at thousands of miles per hour. But our senses tell us the earth is still. Our planet is an orb. Yet our senses tell us the earth is flat. The fears you dwell upon are nothing more than future projections of things you do not want to experience; once again, your mind deceives you. Fear is a belief in something that isn't real; further arguing and defending a fear wastes not only time but also the finite number of thoughts one has per day.

We are not our thoughts. – Buddha

Just because a thought passes through our mind, causing us to feel a certain way or 'believe' a particular thing, does not make it true. (That's why in the previous chapter, I elaborated about never making assumptions, unless it is an assumption you wish to be true.)

Realise that random feelings of fear of the unknown and unfamiliar are normal. If you set a goal to do something you've never done before, you should expect to have some angst about stepping out of your comfort zone and into the direction of your goal. But you are a winner. You are on a mission. You are here to fulfil your purpose. It's time to lead the field.

And in the process, you can learn to enjoy the journey.

Reframe the challenges as steps that are bringing you closer to your destination. That way, you won't get emotionally caught up in inevitable difficulties, allowing you to more diligently decipher the correct steps to take. Let's say, for example, that you are not currently in a profession you like or want to be in. You can use it as an opportunity to discover how it helps you and what skills you are developing. Then when the time is right, take the leap to your chosen path. Remember, time is moving in one forward direction, and you are swapping your gift of life in exchange for what you are about to do. When you do what you love, and there is a purpose behind it, you expand and evolve, and life has greater meaning. And as you improve, the whole world improves.Never permit a dichotomy to rule your life, hating what you do to have pleasure doing what you like in your spare time.

Look for a situation where your work will give you as much happiness as your spare time. – Pablo Picasso

Before you can tap into the infinite reservoirs of the universe, first and foremost, discover that thing you enjoy. Then decide how you can not only get paid well for doing it but also how you can use it to serve the greatest number of people. In the words of one Las Vegas tycoon, "We are all morally and ethically obliged to serve as many people as well can in our lifetime." What a powerful philosophy to live by.

Begin by looking at those things you are naturally inclined toward. Things you would dream about as a child. There are clues buried in that; things that made us different or may have even attracted ridicule are at times the treasures we easily miss right beneath our feet. Schwarzenegger's bedroom wall covered with images of muscular men and gladiators, would have seemed strange to his school friends. Musk, talking about Martians and space rockets would have appeared sheer fantasy, even weird and Coco's obsession with images of royalty would have appeared delusional.

The kinds of things that you and I do, even now, that take no effort whatsoever. We could even describe these behaviours as automatic and impulsive. I will also reiterate why the draw toward Hollywood icons, business EndGamers and great leaders is so strong. This is because they are following their own original path, consistent with their dream, without emulating another's. In doing so, they harness great power, and we are subconsciously influenced as observing them triggers our dominant archetype embedded in the untapped recesses of our minds. We see our own reflection mirrored back at us and identify with them. They are plugging into archetypal energies, and the hero begins to play through them. We will be looking at this in greater depth in later chapters as it will be instrumental in creating things that are original and brand new.

Awakening the Traits of Greatness

You can begin your journey by first recognising that the character traits that are being displayed by your heroes are already residing in you and have expressed themselves throughout your life. Though it may not be to the magnitude of the hero you admire, however, they have been displayed in you nonetheless. Next emulation is to do with recognising the essence of the archetype being expressed through them, ensuring originality. Much like acquiring a foreign language, you repeat the word enough after hearing it from another until it can roll off your tongue with no effort. But this is only the starting point. From there, you must branch off into individuality and your expressions.

The interim phase requires that you take off the stabilisers and begin riding on two wheels. A point where you stop emulating and start creating. Then once gaining some level of mastery, you can turn your idols into your rivals.

Success is a Team Sport

The young Scotsman Andrew Carnegie came to America with nothing… and retired the richest man in the world at that time.

But he didn't do it alone.

In his pursuit, he met an inventor named Elmer R Gates, who was famous for sitting for hours in a soundproof room with nothing other than a pencil and paper and his mind, waiting to receive the information he needed to create his inventions – much like Tesla and Edison, two other great inventors who also had specific methods for tapping into the realms of the subconscious.

So Gates, the inventor, first gave Carnegie a framework of taking the intangible impulses of thought and bringing them to life – this is the alchemy of really transmuting nothing other than thought into pure tangible gold.

Carnegie as we mentioned earlier on in the book sold his company for an astronomical sum, then went on to spend the remainder of his life as a philanthropist, looking for the most effective ways to distribute his wealth even building libraries around the world, the value of education he believed, was the way forward for the world and a personal void he was looking to fulfil having never completed school. Yet one thing in particular Carnegie felt above all else was missing in education a practical framework and formula for creating success. He believed the development of such a philosophy would hasten our evolution and significantly improve the world as we know it.

So as destiny would have it when Napoleon Hill interviewed Carnegie, the meeting sparked the creation of 'The Science of Personal Achievement' and the work that Hill is so famous for *Think and Grow Rich*. And though Hill is rightly credited with this work, the idea actually began in the mind of Carnegie years earlier and grew out of his association with Gates and others in his own personal Mastermind. You see, Carnegie created the real framework for his wealth via his Mastermind.

It takes a team of 24 Formula One pit technicians to support one racing car driver to the winning line. He cannot win alone.

Bill Gates owes most of his success to his ability to surround himself with the best minds. He couldn't have built Microsoft without them.

And you are no exception. You must surround yourself with winners if you want to win.

In the following chapter, we will cover how to develop a magnetic personality and naturally attract people to rally behind your ideas. But to do that, you must first recognise that just as these people need someone to follow, you as the leader must become the one worthy of pursuit.

The Path of Discovery

How can I do what I love and get paid handsomely for it? – Dr John Demartini

The first clue on your path to discovering your heroic mission is to realise that your purpose is deeply rooted in your inclinations. Think of it this way. When you go to a restaurant, you don't choose what you don't like. You go for what you are inclined towards. The people you like, the activities you enjoy, all come as a natural part of you, steering you in the correct direction if you consent to it.

And though you can indeed find people with whom you have things in common, you will never find someone with the same values. Our hierarchy of values (what's most important to us in life) is as unique to us as our DNA.

To further uncover your inclinations to your higher purpose, ask yourself these questions:

- How do I spend my free time?
- What energises me?
- What do I talk about more than anything else?
- What do I think about most often?
- What do I spend my money on?
- What inspires me?

These and other inclinations are embedded within the fibre of your being, emerging and attempting to put you on the correct path to unravelling destiny. Your ability to decipher what this is will require you to become aware of, and follow, these signs, and if ignored will only be to your own detriment. And the reality is that when you are doing what you naturally love, you are operating out of your forebrain's 'executive centre'. This allows you to follow your own inherent success blueprint that activates your inborn genius.

Persistence is Key

As this process unfolds, however, it is important to remember that creating anything outside of the ordinary takes persistence. It won't require a lot of additional effort, as this is something you are naturally drawn towards and inclined to do. But it will require *consistency*.

Look at the common thread among all the true masters of their craft – Michael Jordan, Mozart, Tiger Woods, Margot Fonteyn, the Beatles. They rose to the top because they accumulated more hours of practice than anyone else in their professions.

I was an overnight success… after ten years! – Madonna

As Madonna's quote so beautifully illustrates, you see the principle of duration once again. Most people quit after a couple of attempts. But the ones who break through never entertain the terms *quit* or *fail*.

You may observe others that seem to work as hard, and yet they don't achieve this level of mastery. Here's the truth: either they don't expend enough effort, or the quality of their thoughts is contaminated with the only two things that halt progress: anxiety and fear. Their dream is not on the same level as the winner. The dynamic power of the universe responds when you have faith and go the extra mile. Moving toward your ideal without requiring a guarantee of success activates an unstoppable force.

Don't Ask Permission – Just Do It

Who hasn't had the urge to drop everything and go in pursuit of their dream? – Paulo Coelho

In contrast to the examples given earlier of Enzo Ferrari, Chopra and Mallet, there is another camp of people who discover their calling later on in life, as if by chance.

But when the idea seizes them, a power takes over and they find themselves swept up in an epic adventure. This is the point at which their lives truly begin.

The question is: *Do you have what it takes to drop everything if need be and pursue your true quest?*

A disturbing fact is that people rarely ever realise that they are capable of doing what they dream of at any time in their life. Just because you hold a certain image of yourself in your mind doesn't make it true. In fact, the *real* truth is that it could just as likely be completely false. Now to be sure, you will think, feel and behave consistently with whatever you choose to believe about yourself, and in so doing, that becomes your reality. But you can just as easily *choose to change* your image and what you believe about yourself and *create a new truth* in your life. Remember when you were at school? You naturally enjoyed – and excelled in – some subjects more than you did others. This is another clue about your natural, inherent blueprint.

I want you to stop right now and consider your natural inclination. What you *could* do and who you *could* be if you determined to rise to the top 5% in your field. Sure, you may be a diamond in the rough right now. *But with some focused effort and unyielding determination, you could create a world-class version of yourself.*

Remember the earlier point about your mind is always resting at a crossroads?

Now think of that, and you can see how these steps would allow you to drastically reduce the time it takes you to reach your desired destiny:

1. Gain clarity on what you want.
2. Set that image and intention solidly in your mind.
3. Then at every apparent obstacle, ask yourself: *"How would the person I want be do what I am about to do?"* Then proceed accordingly.

Bruce Lee declared: "I'm probably the best fighter in the world!" That was his heroic mission. And he lived it. He accepted every challenge that came his way, and even though his life on earth was cut short, he will live in the hearts and minds of martial artists forever; in doing so became immortalised. The primary point of this chapter – and particularly this section – is that you have the right to live out your heroic mission without having to ask permission from anyone.

I'll go one step further. Outside of medicine and law, you probably won't even need a certificate, permission or some qualifying degree to do what you know you want to do.

Here's a perfect example.

Though his rugged good looks, beard and biker jacket may make you think otherwise, Marc Jacques Burton is London's new breed of the serial entrepreneur.

Burton established a philosophy early in life that he would do what he wanted, when he wanted, without restrictions, permissions or rules. So he creates his own rules and as a result, lives his dream. Burton is the new breed of entrepreneur – the kind who proves one can live their dream *and* leave their permanent footprint on this planet.

Burton has an unquenchable thirst for knowledge – learning from books, mentors and life. By reading the biographies of the likes of Conrad Hilton and John Paul Getty, he plants in his mind the belief that *"I, too, can create great results."* And by recognising he too had similar qualities of success that are displayed in his own life, he was able to bring them to the surface and began living by them.

Burton was one of the original founders of Tonteria, the internationally acclaimed Mexican-themed bar/nightclub that is packed every evening and had even been graced by Prince William and Prince Harry. As word spread, Leonardo DiCaprio chose the venue for his after-party preceding the premiere of *The Wolf of Wall Street* at the Chelsea nightclub. Marc helped build this club with nothing other than an idea and a powerful way of conveying the concept.

In his words, *"I fell into nightlife by chance."* While studying at Bath University, he frequented nightclubs and was fascinated with the way social barriers dropped and very different worlds merged into one on the dance floor and around the bar. He marvelled at the way locals, celebrities, business tycoons, models and royalty all intermingled without regard to who they were; everyone wants good times, irrespective of title, wealth or degree. And this was the spark that ignited his desire to create such a dreamland community of his own. While at Bath, Burton learned the model of creating 'success' without financial investment through inspiring shared success with others. In the process of moving in the direction of his desired goal, he took good notes of what other clubs were doing right as well as wrong. As a result, he had gone on to create a world-famous club designed around his own unique preferences.

But Burton's pursuits didn't stop there.

A significant part of being among some of the most successful people in the world is developing your own statement about who *you* are. And clothes, more than anything else, give us an immediate impression of a person. When put together well, clothes can look like a work of art.

Burton had always been interested in fashion. Going back to his French roots, on a visit to Paris he saw a pair of slippers that caught his attention. The idea sprung to mind of how fashionable those would be with a suit if put together correctly. Again, with no concern for obtaining 'permission', he went to work in the laboratory of his mind. When his ideas took shape, he poured them forth onto paper. And with the assistance of a fashion designer had his first unique pair of slippers created. Wearing them in the club one evening, Burton was approached by one of the most famous rappers in the world who wanted a pair.

Before long, he started taking orders and began selling the slippers from the back of his car. At the same time, the slippers were taking off; an idea to design a leather jacket came to mind. No jacket of its kind could be found anywhere in the world: the finest leather bearing a unique 'power quote' inside, as well as a concealed pocket for a Kindle, iPad or notebook (carried by every successful person, of course). So, Burton went on a mission. Tracking down one of the finest coat makers, a man who had sewn jackets for some of the biggest names in the fashion world. With no permission and no special invitation, armed only with his dream, Burton found himself knocking on the door of the coat maker's home in Florence. Now it took convincing, but after some time, the designer agreed. So, they set to work and within 18 hours had created a game-changing piece of fashion.

The MJB brand was born, quickly gaining momentum and popularity around the world. With strictly limited runs, MJB is becoming one of the most sought-after clothing lines for the entertainment industry not only attracting collaborations with DC comics and video game brand Mortal Kombat, also gaining custom from icons such as Mick Jagger, Gigi Hadid and Tom Hardy all proudly wearing these statement garments.

The MJB creations positioned at a premium may not be accessible to all but carrying desirability speaks volumes; much like a supercar or an expensive timepiece, its very presence and craftsmanship earns respect.

His heroic mission should solidify in your mind that it is not necessary to gain permission or certification to pave your own path. Had Burton attended fashion school, it is highly unlikely a traditional route would have led his brand to be world-famous since the sheer competition and traditional routes would have set too many barriers in the way. Burton took a smart cut to the top.

MJB now stands as a British brand. Born in London. Bred in Italy. Rocked by artists it stands in a league of its own.

If you want to do it, then do it. That is quite enough.

Every day you are writing a chapter of your own story – the hero's journey. You have a mission. And you have everything inherent inside of you to complete that mission – your highest purpose – so don't wait a moment longer and turn the page.

CHAPTER SEVEN

Personal Magnetism: The Key to Attracting All the Support You Will Ever Need for Your Mission

Become the person you would notice in a room." – Warren Buffett

Imagine having a direct channel into another person's mind. Some researchers say the first three seconds create an impression. I think they are too generous; perhaps there is no time-lapse.

You'll be discovering a way to draw attraction, intrigue and respect by your very presence; this is how you get noticed.

If you have a specific person or target in mind with who you want to create a connection, in this chapter I will be providing you with methods to produce a relationship and response even before any word has been spoken.

Nothing about Ben Feldman would lead you to believe he had any chance of being successful: a high school dropout and one who never ventured for work past his home town, Ohio's 60-mile radius. He looked more like a gnome than a salesman – short, stooped, overweight and balding. He didn't sound like a salesman either. He was shy and spoke with a lisp.

But at his peak in the 1970s and 1980s, he sold more life insurance by himself than 1500 of the 1800 insurance agencies in the entire United States. When Ben Feldman died at age 81, he was without question the world's greatest salesman, making it into the *Guinness Book of World Records* – selling more life insurance in one day than most agents sell in a year.

We'll be looking at the hidden secrets behind Ben's unmatched success. It had everything to do with his intention. His intention was genuine. From the depths of his heart, he believed he was saving individuals, families and businesses from financial disaster. And he drew courage from this worthy

cause. His passion for his mission was the energy that fuelled his ability to persuade. According to chroniclers of his success, Ben was a master of metaphors, using language effectively to have the prospect understand the importance of the product to purchase. There was no pressure on the sale. Ben would say, "When you walk out of life, your insurance money walks in."

At the same time that Feldman's business began to gain momentum, the New York Life Insurance Company limited a single life insurance policy to $500,000 worth of coverage. Thanks to Feldman's influence, that limit was pushed to $20 million.

Speaking at his funeral, the chairman of New York Life, Harry Hohn, said of him: "Ben felt everyone in the world was underinsured." As a result, he made it his mission to do whatever it took to insure them.

If we look at Arizona State's Professor Robert Cialdini, he states that one of the most potent ways to influence someone is to have them recognise you genuinely care. This is powerful because the person then feels you have their best interest at hand, so what you say works.

Sincerity and persistence are key; after trying for weeks to access a prominent Youngstown real estate developer, Ben came up with a plan. He gave the developer's secretary five $100 bills to take to her boss – in exchange for five minutes of his time. "If I don't have a good idea for him, he can keep the money."

It worked. Ben sold him a $14 million policy that day.

This worked for several reasons, primarily certainty; Feldman dared to reach out in an unconventional manner capturing his prospects attention with a potentially substantial loss, which demonstrated that he was so sure of his inevitable outcome that he could not be ignored. This spoke volumes to his prospect before they had even met, the novelty creating a cognitive spike highlighting the significance of the proposal; further reciprocity was at play: the developer had already been given $500, so an unspoken commitment was reflected back.

A few years later, Ben decided this same developer needed to up his coverage another $20 million. But once again, the busy tycoon refused to set aside time for the required physical exam.

So Ben hired a doctor with a fully-equipped medical van to go to his office and wait for him. That worked, of course, and when Ben was finished with him, the man's life was insured for $52 million.

This is an excellent example of a genuine commitment to already existent clients. Feldman felt a responsibility to go back for repeat business and was morally obliged to ensure that cover was sufficient providing peace of mind for his clients.

It's time for you to step aside for a moment and look at innovative ways to get the result; you owe it to your customers. Feldman, furthermore, was an avid reader dedicating so much of his life to studying the influential art of communication. His field became the arena for providing services for the greater good; leaders are always readers may be an overused adage, but it can't be reinforced enough, much like regular exercise improves performance. What we are dealing with here is far more critical than only the physical aspect; we are dealing with the power of the mind.

Once again, we can note that success is no accident and, in fact, no gift.

A Genuine Intention and the Power to Influence

The intention is everything; please – reread that and remember intention is easily set by having an outcome. Any interaction or whatever you do must have a purpose. I cannot reiterate this enough. Or what happens is a wavering of communication and ultimately nothing.

When accompanied by a genuine intention, the ability to influence is one of the most essential skills in the world; this is because any significant target in life can only be achieved by rallying the right people behind your cause.

And the more robust your conviction, the easier it is to persuade people to adopt your vision. This is why a politician or a preacher who is also a strong orator can move an entire audience to line up behind a cause.

Research now uncovers how powerful oration causes the volume on the logical part (frontal lobe) of the brain to quieten, which explains the phenomenon of crowds getting caught in the current of the speech.

It is attributed to Gandhi that he once said, "Persuasion is an act of violence." Hence, ideally, you want people to find out the truth and lead to their own conclusions.

Selling is essentially the transfer of feelings. – Zig Ziglar

No matter what your level of intelligence is, one person can't know everything. Much of the wisdom, experience and connections you need to succeed must come from other people. In fact, as a species, we cannot multitask without massive compromise to mental ability. An entrepreneur or a major tycoon may appear to be running multiple businesses, though this is not the case. Cognitive resources are directed to delegation; the focus on the vision is the one thing being delivered to each person of contact. Entrepreneurs are entirely present with each task.

For that reason, your success ultimately resides in your ability to attract people to you. Your capacity to inspire them to act out the part they will play in your overall plan, a clear demonstration of how them delivering the best they have will directly impact what they too wish to achieve in life: *the why is always more important than the how.*

Andrew Carnegie, whose life we've discussed in great detail, understood this concept perfectly. He credits all of his riches to this one principle – what he refers to as the 'Mastermind Principle' – the ability to surround oneself with talented people who share your vision, adopt your mission and work together toward a common goal.

By developing within yourself the techniques of unspoken persuasion and traits of personal magnetism you will learn here, you can improve your relationships, create powerful bonds that draw others to you and at times, even without a word spoken, convince them to do their very best.

The Magic Behind Attraction

How is this type of attraction created? Is it based on one's looks? Body language? The words you use? The quality of your ideas? Your bank balance?

The answer may startle you. Because, though each of these components contributes to how people respond to us and a magnetic personality, there is a significant aspect of attraction that is not discussed in any other self-growth or success literature I am aware of, though it is documented in some of the scientific journals.

One of the most significant factors contributing to human attraction is the scent!

In essence, we are attracted to another person not only by sight but by scent.

Now, it's not what you can smell consciously or a scent that you are even aware of. *It's the scent your body naturally emits based on what you think and how you feel.*

In other words, your thoughts determine your body chemistry, which in turn determines how people respond to you.

And once you understand this mind-boggling phenomenon, by simply changing your perception of yourself, others will automatically begin to respond to you in new and novel ways.

Here's how it works.

Underneath the armpits, we have a gland called the apocrine gland that secretes a chemical substance known as a pheromone. Human pheromones are believed to influence the behaviour and physiology of the opposite sex, such as triggering sexual interest and arousing excitement.

But studies also indicate that the secretion of pheromones is activated by certain psychological factors as well.

For example, if you feel stressed or are overly self-conscious, your body releases cortisol or adrenaline – a stress-induced hormone. This 'scent' is picked up unconsciously by others around you, their brain interprets the meaning of the scent, and it may even repel.

So even if no words are exchanged, people pick up on it and somehow know that something isn't quite right, that something is making them feel uncomfortable.

Have you ever been in a room where you sensed the tension was so thick you could cut it with a knife? Your instinctive reaction to this was not just based on what we might call 'negative energy'. Rather, your brain was interpreting the dominating scent, much like how a dog smells fear. It's the same principle, and add to that the body language cues the interpretation is clear for anyone observing.

Now consider what happens physiologically when you feel calm inside – when you are comfortable with who you are, independent of the good or bad opinions of others – and when you respect and value other people.

In this emotional state, your body automatically secretes oxytocin – a bonding chemical. This is the same chemical a mother's body releases in response to her newborn baby that creates an incredibly powerful bond between them.

Think about it. You have probably experienced meeting someone that you seem to immediately and automatically connect with. You can't put your finger on it, but there's just something about that person that draws you to them.

May I suggest that though there are certainly other factors to it, a dominant one will be scent.

And you can experience the same magnetism… the same drawing power… *by learning to change your thoughts.*

This is a fascinating truth. Irrespective of who you are as a person, what credentials you may have, or how you look, you determine how people respond to you on a chemical level by how you feel about yourself and others.

If you're in a situation where you are stressing out, worried about what people will think about you, afraid you will say the 'wrong thing', then your body emits a scent that may repel those around you.

On the other hand, if you choose the attitude of, *Hey, let's go have some fun and see how many people I can meet, learn about and connect with,* without any preconceived ideas or underlying agenda, others will naturally be attracted to you. You will experience a very positive, favourable and almost predictable outcome – *and you will make some incredible connections in the meantime.*

Relationships are a true superpower – Dan Fleyshman

Another powerful mantra to keep in mind is: *I am going to make that person so happy they met me.* This will ensure you conduct yourself at your very best while ensuring you are cognisant of another's needs and wants. The person, more times than not, will mirror this right back to you. Everyone wins.

By simply changing how you view yourself, becoming more comfortable with who you are, you automatically become more attractive.

Dr Richard Bandler, the co-founder of NLP, suggests that you can't lead someone into an emotional or physiological state unless you are first in that state yourself. This is a very profound observation.

For example, I can't expect you to relax if I am tense. And I can't expect you to be comfortable with me unless I am first comfortable and at ease with myself... and with you.

This is a powerful and dynamic truth and one that allows you to take charge in developing the type of magnetic personality that attracts others to you, people who will rally behind your cause and facilitate you achieving your goals.

There are too many labels and categories when it comes to defining personality; ongoing discussions about preferentially being introverted or extroverted. In fact, neither is impactful without a solid internal environment. A powerful self-concept evokes the correct behaviours to be displayed in the appropriate moment. One such example is the founder of MNKY HSE, Mayfair; it is the creation of serial entrepreneur Boris Kofman. Kofman's results speak volumes, not his words. At first glance, he appears introverted though the external influence he projects attracts more people and opportunities than he has time for. Know your worth, and the world will reflect it directly back at you.

Display True Class in Every Interaction

Many people are struggling to find meaningful ways to live. As a result, they welcome the opportunity to join forces with someone who can attribute purpose and meaning to a common cause.

So the mission you undertake must be authentic with who you are. It must be genuine. You can't fake it.

Just like Ben Feldman, your intention is to come from deep within you. You must believe in your cause. Commit to developing a strong sense of self and identity where you recognise your inherent ability and genius without the need for external validation. Without this, you won't be able to stand by your cause when you meet with inevitable opposition.

And as a person of influence, remember first to serve. First, give. Do so because it is the right order. But also, you'll find that when you give first, the receiver is much more likely to reciprocate in kind by wanting to help you. Another principle for you to follow when attempting to persuade others is to ensure this is a cause they will equally benefit from. Make it a win–win.

And finally, determine that you will go beyond the golden rule: treat others not only the way they want to be treated but how they specifically *like* to be treated; make them feel like the most important person in the world because at that moment they are. In other words, treat a king like a king and a queen like a queen. In doing so, you are not minimising yourself. You are displaying social etiquette, as well as sensory acuity and class.

In particular, when engaged in conversation, don't rush to spurt out an answer or go rambling when someone asks you a question. Take time to process what they've asked you and answer in such a way as to honour their question with a well-thought-through answer.

Present moment awareness equates to a presence, a powerful one at that.

And never steal a person's thunder. If they are sharing a personal struggle or a tough time with you, don't immediately rush to talk about a tough time you also had. Put that person first. Honour them, and it will always be reflected back at you.

The same holds true when you receive a compliment. Don't rush in with an immediate knee-jerk reaction to reciprocate. That only serves to weaken the value of their compliment to you. Learn to receive compliments gracefully. If you look at great actors like Angelina Jolie, when given a compliment, she receives it humbly and graciously because she is aware of and comfortable with her own value and worthiness.

By showing genuine respect and deliberately treating others the way they like to be treated, recognising and matching their behaviour and sensory preferences, you allow for connections on a far deeper level. This is only possible when you take the time to listen, observe and communicate in a way that serves others.

There are Moments in Life that Change the Entire Course of our Destiny.

We are each of us angels with only one wing, and we can only fly by embracing one another – Luciano De Crescenzo

It was a storm in the middle of summer. I gazed outside my bedroom window. Dark clouds looked threatening, preparing for battle against the determination of a blazing sun. The lightning, though distant, pitched its roar until the resonance of thunder could be felt shuddering and sweeping through to the bone – the battle raging between the two mighty forces, both giving their best in this fight. For millennia, this grudge had existed between them. Could the clash be depicting a battle between two opposing forces, or was it simply natures symbol of making love? A sign to us all that no matter how ferocious the storm may appear in the moment, it can only ever be settled by allowing each force to play out its part and be what it is. Somehow, by patiently riding it through, the uncertainty and chaos ultimately subside, and pure tranquillity emerges.

Do you recall my chance meeting in the Langham with the girl with the inquisitive brown eyes?

We only live once, and whatever one chooses to do, *either give it all you have got or don't do it at all*. In life, I believe prevention is better than cure; equip yourself with the very best tools and whatever you undertake, do your very best. Happiness is so deeply rooted in thriving relationships; as much as we are told "learn to feel good within" there can be no denying a wonderful relationship serves to magnify happiness and propel couples to even greater heights. Inevitable moments of conflict arise. I called one of my dearest friends, a thought leader in the field of psychology, Dr Massimo Stocchi. *Could there be a way to manage the storms more effectively and build between two people a true eternity of happiness?*

"What do I do to really make this work?" I asked the good doctor and my friend. "I'm planning to propose to her and now viewing diamonds."

He replied, "Who did she fall in love with? If you ever stop being that person, allowing emotion to go unchecked and override your intellect, you may introduce a form of toxic weakness. That form of attachment, neediness and vulnerability *destroys*. Weakness is fatal."

"With her, learn to love both sides?"

"Yes, there are no one-sided human beings. Nature is chaotic. Embrace both sides. Be the vessel to contain the chaos while honouring and respecting all that she is."

There was silence as I thought about my wise friend's words.

He broke the silence with a simple question. "What was it about her that made you realise that she was the one?"

This answer came easily for me. "It was her essence, the way in which she carries herself. No garment, clothing or makeup could ever conceal that. When I first truly fell in love with her, it was at the Palace Kempinski in Istanbul. She had invited me to attend her friend's wedding."

In his silence, I knew he expected me to continue, and so I did not disappoint him. "An unexpected and unplanned moment – I had flown in a day previously to deal with some work before the event. As I made my way to our room, she was already standing in the corridor outside our suite to surprise me. Our eyes met. She was in her yoga pants and tank top, no makeup – and hair tied back. She was the most beautiful girl I had ever laid my eyes on."

Once again, his reply was astonishingly simple. "Be the one who opens the door for her future."

When we said goodbye, I thought I knew what he was implying.

It was now early December, and she was on a trip to New York with her sister, both for personal health reasons and for research in technologies for her soon-to-open health retreat. Our schedules were busier than ever with both of us at separate corners of the planet. Though I was abroad on a contract until the beginning of January, I decided long before to cut it short and surprise her on New Year's Eve. *How I relished the prospect of sharing the moment with her and her mother Nina when the clock struck twelve.*

There is just something about a high quality of love that invokes within us a desire to be even more... *a reason.* When we were to reunite finally, I wanted to be the best that I could be in every way. I had been following a consistent training regimen and was in excellent shape. This always gave me a great boost of confidence. Lazo Freeman, a multiple Natural Bodybuilding Champion and now Yogistic sage, was my fitness trainer. Though what he charged could be considered a small fortune, I viewed it as an investment, for I was cutting out potentially years of trial and error en route to developing an aesthetically flawless physique.

My nutrition plan was designed by celebrity nutritionist Rehan Jalali. A true, modern-day Michelangelo, Rehan chiselled the body into a work of art – although this time, the sculpting would be from the inside out. Rehan's approach consisted of analysing everything from blood markers, age, height and even looking at genetic signatures, and with a good supply of Vitabiotics supplements all my nutritional needs were met.

Nothing was left to chance, as world-class results can never be stumbled upon. Rather, they are the product of painstaking research and unparalleled work ethic.

I had also taken some cooking lessons with my friend and HelloFresh founder Patrick Drake. Whenever we went on dates, I watched the dishes she ordered and observed her tastes for certain things, especially desserts such as Gozinaki, a famous Georgian dessert. I had practised in advance preparing dishes, including a Chilean sea bass and a risotto which had me tossing a pan for close to 45 minutes. But I didn't stop there since attention to detail is everything. I built an entirely new wardrobe and began to restructure my business to ensure financial stability for our future. *She had never expected anything from me, and in some way, that had made me want to give her everything.*

Reflecting back now, those workouts, learning to cook, building my business... none of these were a struggle because they were all meaningful in pursuit of someone who had so profoundly affected my thoughts and my feelings. I was preparing to build my life with her, and just having had the privilege of experiencing that state of mind alone was something to be grateful for. It had become for me the fuel necessary to make more tremendous strides than ever before.

If we followed our dreams with the level of intensity that is coupled with love, I honestly believe our goals would appear in our lives much faster and in more predictable ways.

December 31st – my flights had been so severely delayed that on landing, I would have but a few minutes to race to Pall Mall Barbers for my haircut, shower, throw on my tux and head to the event in Holborn for the New Year. In my haste, I had left my mobile phone on the aeroplane and with no time to retrieve it. My heart raced as there was so much to consider. Gifts had been previously ordered to be delivered at the table for my girlfriend and her mother as a surprise. I finally arrived just a little after 11 p.m. at the event in Holborn. I knew I looked my very best. *I can't wait to see her and for her to see me.*

The systems are down, and the staff cannot locate my girlfriend's table or even find her name on the written guest list. I walk into the large ballroom, scanning the entire area. It is near impossible to walk through the hundreds of people who had come to the venue. *Where is she?* I race back to the front desk to call her number, only to be directed to her voicemail. She would not recognise the number, so why would she answer the call on such an eventful night?

The evening progresses, and it is nearly midnight. *There is still no sign of her.*

Sorrows are our best educator. A man can see further through a tear than a telescope. – Bruce Lee

Completely deflated, I determined to actively engage myself in inner reflection but was too tense to do so. I head outside to compose myself and catch some fresh air, closing my eyes. I reposition my thoughts, stabilise my emotions, and imagine her in my arms. For but a second, the sounds and chaos disappear.

Inside of me, I feel an inner nudge. *She has got to be here.* I head back to the main party.

I see the musicians are now on the live stage. My heart breaks as they announce… *the countdown before midnight.*

'One Kiss' by Dua Lipa plays. It was the same song playing in the background the first time we had met. *She is here; I know it.*

Though there are moments in life we just cannot explain, the chance of that song playing right now was highly improbable.

The thought flashes through my racked mind that nothing is missing in the universe. *It just exists in a different form.* People are a combination of qualities:

what they represent and what we experience from them. They never disappear; they just reappear in new forms. To get the form you want, you must engage in psychological alchemy. You do this by first recognising that nothing is missing. Then observe and declare the form it is currently in. Finally, shift your focus and emotionalised intent to the form you want, and you will create the catalyst for the universe to reorganise itself and give you what you want.

So, I acknowledge that thought for a moment and reflect on how she is in my heart. I close my eyes and tangibly zone out, thinking of her... if it's supposed to be, it will always find a way. I suddenly feel a tap on my shoulder. As I turn to see who was responsible for the tap on my shoulder, she looks at me, tears running down her face. She says, simply enough, "You came back for me! *Did you tell them to play that song?*"

How do you Express Love?

In his popular book *The Five Love Languages: How to Express Heartfelt Commitment to Your Mate*, relationship expert Gary Chapman outlines five ways that we express and experience love:

- By giving gifts
- By sharing quality time
- By words of affirmation
- By acts of service
- By physical touch

One's 'love language' is defined as their primary mode of *experiencing* love. Chapman suggests that to discover one's love language, you must observe how this person expresses love to others (because people naturally tend to express love the way they prefer to receive love), and what they request from their significant other most often.

In reality, we need to experience all of them. But as you decipher your own partner's primary love language, and you begin to fulfil that, you'll find you can connect and meet their needs at a far deeper level than ever before.

This principle extends well beyond our significant other, however, and has many lessons to teach us about personal magnetism and how to connect and influence others as well.

As we are morally and ethically obliged to serve as many people as we can in our lifetime, the ability to communicate love on a deeper level – beyond mere words – becomes a vehicle for us to influence the greatest number of people.

So, with that in mind, let's explore some additional personality traits and behavioural techniques that allow one to create rapport with others, facilitating your ability to persuade and influence others to support you as you move forward in pursuit of your dreams.

Flexibility

I'm not entitled to have an opinion unless I can state the arguments against my position better than the people who are in opposition. I think I am qualified to speak only when I've reached that state. – Charlie Munger

To be a person of influence – able to inspire and motivate others – you must be flexible in your thinking and communication. Flexibility opens the door for you to liaise with anyone and everyone, and this means being nonjudgmental. People are operating out of a worldview that they believe to be correct based on their environment and personal experiences; any attempts to change this, the greater you preach or force persuasion, the more resistance you will predictably encounter.

Why is this important?

Well, consider this. If you are only comfortable forming associations with others who are most like you – who have pretty much the same perspectives, social reach and talents as you – then your Mastermind group will be out of balance.

To fill those gaps you have in yourself, you need to reach out and connect with others who are *different* from you – people who bring a very different perspective and a more diverse social network than you currently have. And before you can ever persuade them to rally behind your cause, you must first exhibit flexibility in your thinking and suspend any judgments or foregone conclusions about them or their worldview.

You have to be seen as a friend, and not an enemy, if you want to successfully gain the support from others you need along the way. Any inflexibility or rigidity in thinking can very quickly put you in a place of opposition.

Besides, arguing your position, coming to conclusions and making judgments, and then assuming you are correct puts you in a position of risk

– for when you elevate yourself over another, you create both a psychological and energetic imbalance.

And what if it turns out that you were wrong? Do you have the flexibility to change?

Charisma

Charisma is defined as a *compelling attractiveness or charm that can inspire devotion in others.*

Think of someone you know who is charismatic, someone whose personality is simply 'magnetic'. What is it about them that makes them so? Though someone with charisma is certainly self-confident and feels comfortable in their own skin, it may surprise you to know that charisma has much more to do with *how they make you feel* than it does with how they feel about themselves.

It is the ability to connect and to communicate what you have and what you want, *regarding what others want and what is valuable to them, in a way that helps them get what they want.* That is the magic of charisma.

Charisma is a potent tool of influence; we cannot help but loop back to doing the greater good for all.

The Unconscious Hello – Establishing a Deep Bond Before a Word has Been Spoken.

This is a tool that will help create trust and instant likability to whomever you cross eyes with, even at first sight. It is a guarded secret in the communities of skilful persuaders and even operatives in the secret services and intelligence agencies; you will find very little literature on this; it's called 'the Unconscious Hello'.

When you first notice another person, be it face to face or across a crowded room, they will automatically communicate an acknowledgement towards you without realising it. The first communication will be nonverbal. It may be a smile, a movement of the eyebrow referred to as the 'eyebrow flash', a tilt of the head or a nod. Your unconscious picks up every nuance, every iota of the meaning of which your conscious mind may be utterly unaware

178

of – building on the premise that we like people that are like ourselves. If you deliberately mirror back the first signal received from another, you create recognition of trust and understanding, without a single word being spoken, as you have just matched their immediate unconscious signal. Now it will be near enough impossible for them to recognise what has just transpired because by the very nature of the unconscious, it is something outside of one's conscious awareness.

There is a second method, and this is for you to initiate influence by priming your person of interest and initiating that first signal which will be either be an eyebrow flash, a head tilt or a smile; these work as universally they are all expressions we do towards people we like and trust.

An Eyebrow Flash

This is a quick up and down movement of the eyebrows that friends use when they recognise one another, be it at a distance or in a crowd. As people approach a person they know, more times than not, the instinctive eyebrow flash sends a message of recognition.

Tilting the Head

The head tilt is a slight tilt of the head toward the left or right side. This signals that the person recognised is not a threat because by exposing your carotid artery, you communicate trust. The carotid artery is the primary source for blood to reach the brain; thus, exposing the artery sends a signal that the person exposing their carotid artery does not pose a threat, and the other trusts the person in view.

The Smile

A smile sends the message, "I like you." When you smile at someone, they instinctively feel compelled to reciprocate. The triggering of endorphin release in the brain from the smile promotes a feeling of wellbeing, as the muscles on the side of the mouth instruct the brain to promote the release. In other words, if you have the person smile back at you, you have just planted a good feeling about you through their own eyes.

Matching and Mirroring

In language, to express a feeling, you have to convey a thought. First, it is good to experience the emotional feeling inside your body and then communicate it. People often use ready-made templates that are just responses; this is not intentional. We are pretty much programable machines that spurt out what we have been told or heard, rather than actively taking a moment to process, understand and respond effectively. By learning to actively listen bring as much presence as you can, and give a moment for your feeling to transmit to the person you are communicating with, ensuring as well that you listen and pause processing what is being said and understanding the individual, you will not only impact them in way that they have never felt before, you'll be impacting yourself.

Leading is only by example, never by enforcement of ideas; the more an idea is enforced, the more you will find a person resists. Never in all of human history have ideas been able to be enforced on civilians even the most extreme cases of dropping bombs or annihilating groups of people have not caused them to change their views. An unfortunate truth that has plagued civilisation since the dawn of time. You must first capture the thought and feeling you wish to convey. Once you are in that state, speak from the heart; the emotion becomes contagious, and you will lead from there.

To create a sense of rapport and ease with others, you must remember that *people like people who are like themselves or who they would like to be akin to*. That is the premise behind this following technique of matching and mirroring, which is possible on many levels. So let's start by reflecting back to them the words they use.

Sensory

Mirroring requires a keen sense of awareness and a genuine intention to create a trusted connection and bond with another person. This will take some practice, but the more you practise, the more it becomes part of your natural behaviour and who you are.

Here's an example of a conversational exchange that demonstrates sensory mirroring. See if you can distinguish how this plays out.

Person One: *My wife and I are looking for a new home.*

Person Two: *What specifically are you in the market for?*

Person One: *We want something that **looks immaculate**, something that takes your breath the first time you see it.*

Person Two: *So, you're after something that **looks immaculate,** and that presents so beautifully people stop and take notice of it.*

Person Two did an excellent job of mirroring the dominant sensory experience of Person One – which was visual; some people are more auditory based and some kinaesthetic. Of course, we are a little bit of all; however, with careful observation, you will notice we all have a dominant preference for how we organise and interpret information. On a caveat, do not relay back in parrot fashion as this may appear condescending instead, make an emphasis on the type of words used.

The words used in the example above were primarily visual:

Looking, immaculate and *see.*

This can even be taken one step further if you take a moment to keep track of the words being said and even the subconscious hand movements, and you mirror it back subtly; you create even more of a connection. When the person used the word 'immaculate', that neurone had just triggered in their brain; if you use the same word, you will never be going down a dark alley.

Here's another example:

Person One: *My wife and I are in the market for a new home.*

Person Two: *What are you after?*

Person One: *We want something that **feels** warm and inviting… from when you first step foot on the grounds to the moment you walk through the door.*

Person Two: *In other words, you want a place that immediately already **feels** like home.*

Once again, Person Two hit a home run by matching and mirroring Person One's primary mode of sensory experience in this conversational exchange – kinaesthetic *feeling.*

We experience our world through our five senses:

- Visual – seeing
- Auditory – hearing
- Kinaesthetic – feeling
- Olfactory – smelling
- Gustatory – tasting

But we each have a dominant sense through which those experiences are relayed to us. Now, most people are not aware of what that is, but a keen observer, someone interested in creating rapport and establishing a bond with another person, can quickly determine what that dominant sense is and match and mirror it back to them. This is a very subtle – but very powerful – connector, causing the person you are communicating with to suddenly feel understood, accepted and at ease.

A study was conducted on shoppers in New York City who visited individual stores interacted with the staff but left the store without buying to further illustrate this point. On questioning why they didn't make a purchase, the overwhelming response was, *"The store clerk didn't understand what I was after."* In other words, the store clerk didn't mirror the shopper's dominant sensory mode so they could connect with the buyer in a way that made them feel heard and understood.

Speech

Matching the other person's rate, tone and volume of speech is another way to use mirroring and matching to connect with someone. If they speak slowly and softly, and you speak quickly and loudly, you will not connect. Because we speak at the same rate we process information, if you speak too quickly, you will lose them, and if you talk too slowly, you will bore them.

Breathing

A very subtle but potent and fascinating mirroring technique is to match the other person's breathing rate – breathe in sync with them.

Physiology

Of course, there's a lot of literature that speaks to mirroring the body language of another person to establish rapport and put them at ease. This is probably the most obvious and most straightforward to accomplish. However, you want to be sure and do this so as not to appear conspicuous, as that would, for sure, backfire. If someone is tapping their foot, you could tap your finger at the same rate at the same rhythm; this stealth influence allows one to fly under the radar. As the subconscious picks up millions of bits of data every moment, it also picks up on this outside of sensory awareness.

Anchoring

Each moment we are alive, we experience that passing of time in some emotional state. We are either happy, sad, curious, balanced, bored, excited, peaceful or any number of other emotional states.

We can be occupying one emotional state, and then something changes in our environment that triggers another emotional state.

For instance, you may be out walking at the park and see some children playing a game of tag. That triggers a memory from your own childhood, a very happy memory. All of a sudden, you feel that same happiness all over again as if you were back in that same space and time. That memory is an anchor of joy for you – a reference point that has the potential to trigger a powerful emotional and behavioural response.

As an influencer who seeks to persuade, you can deliberately establish anchors and tie them to an emotion someone is feeling at that time or emotion you have elicited. Then you can use that anchor to gradually return them to that same emotional state at a later point in time. One standard anchor is the use of touch. If you are in conversation with someone and you wish to show your care and concern for a problem they are sharing with you, a commonly accepted behaviour is to reach out and touch their hand or their arm.

Now consider you are sharing an idea or a concept with that same person at a later time – something you need their input on and would love to have their support for – and when you ask for their response, you reach out and touch them in the same manner. You will likely elicit the same concern and care from them that you demonstrated for them at that earlier time.

Another example can be something as simple as when an orator removes his glasses every time he intends to connect with his audience and make a major point. The audience becomes conditioned to that anchor and has a cognitive bias to that behaviour. So, each time he removes his glasses, they pay extra attention to what he is about to say. Or a comedian who takes a second to pause, then gets a quirky smile on his face, right before sharing the punch line. The audience is already conditioned to laugh before anything has even been said.

Most people believe the best way to convince someone of something is to pile on the information. Give them enough reasons, and you will be able to persuade them in a particular direction. But even if you win them over initially, that approach often falls apart once they forget all the reasons they bought into to begin with. A much more effective and lasting approach is to lead them toward a certain position by connecting with them on a deeper, emotional level using the technique of anchoring. It is an entirely covert way of moving someone in the direction you want them to go without trying to convince them with data.

I'm sure you've had this experience before. You enter a crowded room, *and no one notices.* Everyone there is already engaged in conversation with someone else, and you can't seem to get anyone's attention. You may as well be invisible.

The next time that happens, here are some subtle anchoring techniques that you can use to get attention anytime you want.

Approach a group already engaged in conversation, observe the person who seems to be leading the conversation. The one who has everyone engaged. Notice their tone, their volume level, the keywords, phrases and the gestures they are using. When you find an opportune time, interject your comments using the same volume level, tone of voice, words and gestures. Attention will then be transferred to you as you will be using the same anchors as the lead contributor had just established.

Another technique is to make sure you say hello to everyone individually when you first arrive. Then as they respond with a 'hello' back to you and acknowledge your presence, reach out and touch the underside of their elbow lightly with your hand (or some similar repeatable gesture that you're comfortable with) or you may even set a visual anchor by simply tilting your head to the left or right. Do this every time, to everyone. Then whenever you want to speak, all you have to do is repeat the same gesture you used as an 'anchor' of initial acknowledgement, and you will once again be given the opportunity to take the floor.

Anchoring can also be defined as a form of *cognitive bias used as a reference point for evaluating and making decisions.* It is an intriguing persuasion technique and if you wish to enhance the effects even more, ensure you infuse the anchor with the emotional response you wish to elicit with the person you are interacting with. Earlier on I touched upon the idea of transferring feelings; this becomes a perfect platform to not only establish good feeling but also have a method to trigger those feelings on command.

Conclusion

As long as what you want to accomplish in life is meaningful and beneficial to society, then believe in your mission and back that belief with a genuine, authentic intention.Next, develop a magnetic personality that attracts others to you and your cause using these powerful – yet subtle – techniques. In so doing, you will become a person of influence with an uncanny ability to persuade.

I will reiterate that the ability to influence others and persuade them to align with a common cause is one of the most indispensable skills in the world!

This skill is now yours for the taking; utilise the skill for the greater good.

Go... *Influence yourself first and foremost, and then influence the world!*

CHAPTER EIGHT

Your Invincible Power

There are powers inside of you which, if you could discover and use, would make of you everything you ever dreamed or imagined you could become. – Orison Swett Marden

Shivering in a dark motel room, I pour three large bags of ice cubes into the half-filled bathtub, then plunge my fractured hand into the freezing water, gritting my teeth and praying for the numbness to set in. Where and how I had injured my hand, I did not know. Tears of pain fill my eyes, and the swelling only seems to get worse. I barely recognise my pain-racked face in the mirror at the foot of the tub. Fatigue begins to settle in, taking a suffocating and dark hold over my body, and much like the sensation of a general anaesthetic, that moment finally comes where my eyelids become so heavy that they close all by themselves. My mind drifts back to earlier that evening as my subconscious attempts to process it all.

The bout had me pitted up against a division one wrestler. Although I had been trained in Greco-Roman techniques, I was in no way qualified to take on this seasoned pro, who had the bearing and the marks of one who had survived brutal battles. As soon as I put eyes on him, one of his prominent facial features caught my eye: *cauliflower ears*, the permanent and painful deformation of the ear resulting from repeated friction. For me, the sight meant only one thing: *trouble*.

It would be impossible to defend against athletes of this calibre without specific training in takedown defence. With my inadequate background, entering the fray against such an opponent and attempting to outwrestle him was like going up against Arthur Ashe or Emma Raducanu after taking just a couple of months of tennis lessons.

I knew my only chance would be to keep the fight off the ground, resist his takedown attempts, and force him into a standing altercation. In that setting,

I could utilise *holding and hitting inside elbows* and other techniques known as *dirty boxing*. Balance and control would become vital. If we went to the ground on his terms, I would be on the defence with an excellent chance of losing the match.

Armed with this insight and knowledge, I had prepared a game plan. *"Warfare is deception,"* I reminded myself.

There we were in our corners. I looked at him, and he did not flinch. No sooner did the opening bell ring than I am slammed on my back like a sack of flour. The top of my opponent's head drives into my mouth, splitting my bottom lip. I attempt to use his momentum to reverse his position, so I scoot my hips to one side whilst interlocking my feet on the inside of his knees. He posts to control my movement and rains down blow after blow. I attempt to shift my weight to create space but instead take several more shots to the side of my head; I fight through the pain and disorientation with sheer grit and intent to get out.

I sit up and immediately hook my arm around his head while tying up his left arm to stop further strikes. I clench down tightly to deny him the space he needs to continue his strikes. Now, with his left arm immobilised, I begin posting my knees into his hip. This creates enough distance to allow me to kick off and burst back up to my feet. I know the game well and using my footwork, I begin to create awkward angles. I then prepare to sprawl to smother his attempts to bring me back down onto the canvas. I know I must attack, or I will lose. Time is up: *it's now do or die!*

He lunges directly at me with the speed of an arrow, and suddenly we are both off our feet. As I am going to the ground, I hook my arm around his neck in the deadly choke named 'The Guillotine'. He did not see that coming, and my grip is so tight that he will pass out if he does not tap. *He struggles to free himself, refusing to tap.* We struggle for what seems an eternity, and the excruciating pain of lactic acid build-up, coupled with the flow of crimson fluid from my head, weakens my grip. He manoeuvres his head to the side and escapes. *We scramble back up to our feet.*

Time to change strategy.

My opponent gives me a scrutinising look, seeking to use his wrestling advantage to take me down once again. As we circle, he decides to strike with me instead and go blow to blow, undoubtedly demonstrating to the judges he can do it all.

It is a fatal mistake.

An exchange ensues, and we are soon in *the clinch*. I had excelled in the clinch during my Greco-Roman training, and as we struggle, I clasp one hand behind his neck, and the other begins to control his triceps. I pull his tricep to create the space necessary to launch a knee directly into his exposed ribcage; I feel the sensation of my knee caving into his bone. I keep the momentum going, and he is beginning to deflate like a punctured tire. *Dirty boxing ensues.* I grip the back of his neck tightly and pull him in for another strike to maximise impact, catching him with a clean uppercut. His head recoils back and to the side, allowing me the split second I need for a takedown of my own. And yet, my attempt is thwarted. His instincts kick in, and his form is too strong.

We continue to exchange strikes; his eyes display a determination to prove himself in this range. I strike with a solid right hand without retreating it back, providing me with the hand positioning to clinch again. He circles his head to undo my clasp and pulls back aggressively. I see the desperation in his eyes as he attempts to return to his basics. He shoots in for another takedown, but this time I defend well, sprawling in flight and launching my hips and legs as far away from him as possible. He is exhausted. I sense that I can stop him, and I need to go for the kill.

Fatigue makes cowards of us all." – Vince Lombardi

I feel alive for the first time in the fight. I finally believe that I might be able *to pull off a victory!* I shoot for a single-leg takedown, knowing he will defend, and so I end up positioned for another clinch; he now has no choice but to fight on my terms.

The tables have turned. I am now the hunter stalking my prey, progressing forward, and probing my target with decoy jabs to set up the correct distancing to land finishing blows. I begin utilising footwork known as the 'Jack Dempsey Drop Step', enabling me to transfer my entire body weight into my punches. The distance between us bridges as my opponent attempts to clumsily weave to evade my strikes.

He moves forward now in desperation, and I am ready to intercept. We are now head-to-head at the same distance between two people in a phone box. My body squares in an instant, and using the *floating punch*, my hand moves vertically toward his solar plexus. No sooner does my top knuckle touch the centre of his chest than my lower knuckle just as quickly replaces the point of contact. I drive the shot into him like a silver bullet and then recoil my fist back even faster than it had launched, creating a concussion effect that momentarily collapses his lungs.

My opponent buckles backwards, now stunned and unsettled, gasping for air, and finally crashes violently onto the canvas.

The bell rings. The match is over. The referee brings us to the centre of the mat.

"I've done it," I say to myself with an enormous sigh of relief.

But it is my opponent's arm that is raised.

It was like a physical punch in the gut, bringing me from the heights of triumph to the lowest low.

Still, even at this lowest point, I am able to remind myself: *one can be destroyed in a single battle but not defeated – there is always the recognition of self-worth and the extraction of experiential learnings.*

A loud knock startles me, wrenching me out of my deep slumber, and immediately I can hear an overstuffed letter edging itself beneath the door. My mind is hazy, and my eyelids feel too heavy to open just yet. The brilliance of the morning sun beaming throughout the room from the large and uncovered window acts as nature's alarm clock, forcing me to wince my eyes open.

I had passed out. In a feeble attempt to reorient myself, I head over to the bathroom and place my head under the open tap, running a cold stream of water through my hair. I then stagger slowly over towards the door and curiously pick up the envelope. I notice that it's stamped Pride FC, and there is a short pause wherein I feel reluctance brewing inside. I am too familiar with the frustration of opening a *'well done for participating'* message followed by the customary *'but you are not good enough,'* I realise that I cannot bear to open it.

Not wanting to deal with another blow of rejection, I crumple the envelope and throw it angrily into the bin.

I begin packing my suitcases, preparing for the long journey home, but this time it is a welcome farewell. I wedge one of the suitcases to keep the door open as I begin steering the remainder of my luggage out of the room. In my haste, the final suitcase catches the wastepaper basket, tipping it over, and the crumpled letter tumbles out. *What the hell?* I grab the letter within my clenched fingers as the thought flashes; *I guess in some way we are all addicted to pain.* I thrust the letter into my rucksack.

… On the aeroplane, as I prepare for take-off, I follow my all too familiar routine of reading away the journey. I place a copy of Daniel Priestly's bestseller

Key Person of Influence into the pocket in front of my seat. I then take the letter out of the crumpled envelope, open it, and cynically begin to read.

Pride FC would like to inform you that our judges feel the martial arts skills displayed, coupled with relentless tenacity and your camera presence, is a combination that will work well for our organisation. We would like you to consider fighting for Pride FC.

The beast had been slain! I had tapped into my invincible power and hadn't even realised the result had been achieved before I had even considered it could be. *I now knew I was worthy of the world's stage.* Was I to continue this adventure or revisit that chapter at a later date?

I've always said I don't fight because I hate what's in front of me. I fight because I love what's behind me and what's around me. – Brad Picket

Many have always stated the 'Why' is more important than the 'How'. If we peer a little deeper, we find that to achieve the result, the truest and shortest path will be the route of what we love. Done in this manner, finding our source improves our craft. *Our power resides in our desires.*

The Unicorn Man

Rising tides raise all ships; look at the direction the current is moving towards and launch into it, leveraging off of nature's momentum.

Contrary to what many so-called experts assert, knowing your true calling has never ensured success. Neither has passion, location, capital, purpose or marketing. Combine them all, and you will find more failures than successes.

There are two qualities, the elusive obvious yet so often overlooked, that separate the EndGamer from the other 99% of the planet. It made Ali an all-time great, Isaac Newton the mind who ushered in the scientific revolution, and Stephen Hawking a man who brought to humanity an unprecedented understanding of black holes.

Almost everyone overlooks these qualities because of a flaw in our consciousness that pulls us away from acknowledging or working with them.

Before I get into both these qualities in detail, I want you to consider the following:

Despite the ever-shifting complexities of class, race, gender, education, wealth and lineage, society's hierarchy has stayed the same throughout the millennia – there has always been a controlling elite, a '1%'. And history shows, over and over again, that one does not necessarily need to be born into this elite group to gain access.

All of us share the feeling of desire; it ignites a flame and gets us started toward our dreams. Consistency leads to excellence, and excellence leads to success and, ultimately, happiness. "Following your passion" is not the common element of the successful 1%. Blindly following your passion may lead you right over a cliff. Passion must be accompanied by an authentic desire, consistency, determination, perseverance and an emotional detachment to the processes used to guide you there.

It was August 2010; I was invited to Stockholm to speak to a small group of young entrepreneurs on the power of mindset. There I met Andrew Masanto, a former lawyer and aspiring tech entrepreneur. I was captivated by his talk on building a successful social circle en route to business success. Andrew emphasised that like friendships, business is built on trust – your reputation is everything. By creating value in all that you do, you will attract opportunity. By delivering what you say consistently, people naturally come back for more. Andrew made a strong emphasis on one deciding what they want. He said to me, "A turning point in my life tilted me toward a decision to supersize my income. I realised the worst exchange one could ever make is time for money." In my view, this was a subconscious driver as he was now only on the lookout for streams of income that could come independently of time exerted and a method of allowing money to continually compound itself.

Take, for example; you have £10,000 to invest; if you can increase that amount by only 1.58% daily within twelve months, that amount will compound so much that you would breeze past a cool million.

In your relationships, he emphasised strength and authenticity in both male and female interactions. If you come across as needy or unprepared to contribute, you repel others with good biological reason. In primitive times, getting what you needed was a matter of life and death, so approaching a tribe to obtain something carried a strong undercurrent of violence and bloodshed. A part of our brain still sees business and even social interactions from that ancient perspective. If someone whose reputation you do not know and with whom you have not established trust comes to you in an overly needy or desperate fashion, the brain may even evaluate this as a threat.

Remember, position yourself from a place of strength no matter what you are asking for; the attracting power resides in you and evokes coming from a place of abundance.

What struck me about this erudite was his iron-clad integrity, rare enough in most people but especially among trained lawyers, who often take up cases in which they are not adding value and have little or no trust in the person or case they are representing.[1] Andrew's legal training had honed his attention to detail and instinct for grasping the essential facts of a situation, which prepared him well for his journey ahead.

Andrew was soon my friend and mentor. I was fascinated by how smoothly and successfully he would build a company and exit, build another company and exit, always assuring everyone involved came out a winner. Here was a person who was a success at anything he attempted. He reminded me of the story of King Midas, which like many ancient stories, contains eternal truths embedded in metaphor. Andrew's success relied upon truths as old as humankind – from his grasp of statistical analysis first introduced by Pythagoras in Ancient Greece to his understanding of human behaviours, which one can study in the works of Cicero, Buddha and Shakespeare.

If you look at the people in your circle and don't get inspired, then you don't have a circle; you have a cage. – Nipsey Hussle

Though enviably situated in a bachelor pad in Soho, Masanto's late nights were consumed with his business projects, not the London nightlife. His aim was always 'passive income', an automated flow of cash. He shared a small office in nearby Berkley Square, surrounded by the affluence of Mayfair in London's West End, began to imbue his very consciousness. If a drop of water finds itself upon a block of ice, it becomes ice; should the same droplet find itself in the ocean, it becomes the ocean. The environment becomes your norm and your expectation; in this case, a 'wealth consciousnesses' was forming.

The initial illusions of opportunity very quickly subsided, and the stark realities emerged; the local communities had established themselves in a stringent framework for centuries; old money and connections were both

---

1   The exceptions stand out, such as attorney Gerry Spence, who has never lost a case in his career. His integrity manifests as a commitment to truth and honest dealing with all. He did not pursue a 'win' for its own sake but was a seeker for the truth of any given situation. Also worthy of mention Amal Clooney and Kimberley Motley both exemplary human beings.

tightly guarded and impenetrable. Masanto felt frustration and quickly leveraged himself beyond that. There is a particular trait in every one of us, though frowned upon by conventional wisdom, it serves a purpose and is triggered to the forefront when one can find no other way. Though buried under years of conformity the renegade within emerged. It was time for revolution, rebellion and innovation. Masanto constructed his platform and sources of new money exceeding anything that could have even been possible in that same environment. From London then to New York, proving that lifestyle is a choice – and the option is always before you. Now residing in New York as an angel investor and entrepreneur with an incredible portfolio and the freedom to pursue whatever he wants with almost no financial strain, Masanto's life illustrates that often-unrecognised quality that sets the 1% apart and allows them to go from success to success. At first glance, it's easy to conclude education, luck, perseverance, talent or any number of qualities or combination of qualities helped him succeed, and of course, they all play a role. But under the surface, there is a more profound force at work, elusive to even the well-trained eye. In fact, after many conversations with Masanto, I concluded that even he was not aware of the essential drivers contributing to his success.

The propelling qualities behind Masanto's rise are namely his *setpoints and application of First-Principle Thinking (questioning every assumption you think you know, then stripping them away and creating new knowledge from scratch).* His setpoints had naturally risen and expanded to a point where the mediocre disappeared into dust. As Masanto rode the arrow of time, continuous improvement became automatic.

Masanto had an *uncapped* setpoint and an undefined as well as unrestricted earning and creative potential, as in the numbers became so vast that his perception was no longer about money rather finance. When numbers hit the ten-plus digits, wealth continues to compound exponentially to a point where there is more coming in than one could ever possibly spend in a lifetime.

Hence why when you notice the philanthropy of the super-wealthy, it becomes a strategic endeavour to ensure the monies proliferate for the greatest good and find ways of compounding.

Setpoints are the aspect of our reality at work consistently and automatically.

The amount of money we make and the influence we express is an example of a setpoint. Of course, income fluctuates but usually in relatively minor margins around a consistent average; one is not rich one week then on welfare the next. Our happiness is reasonably consistent, too. One is not sporadically bouncing from depression to joy. Physical condition is another example. People are not muscular and fit one month, obese the next, then underweight after that. They are almost always the same.

When the world changes, such as in the upheaval of a financial crisis or a global pandemic this consistency remains and is much easier to observe. The very well off may deviate downward, but it is only a deviation from their normal average or setpoint. Economic downturns are often an opportunity for savvy investors, and in the end, they may have deviated from their normal average in a positive direction.

The fact is this opportunity is not for the select elite, but everyone. Whether you have the mindset to take advantage and become like the 1% is a matter of your setpoints and training in first-principle thinking.

Our setpoints bring about only what we already know; we automatically integrate the past into the present because the past is our standard reference; this is also the pitfall for the most prevalent type of thinking, which is thinking by analogy (meaning you only follow current paradigms and ways of doing things, because it has always been that way). The brain and body are rigged – programmed – to accept this, which is why our attempts to build the future often create little or no change. We may learn lessons from the past, but we also incorporate the patterns of the past so deeply they program our future, too.

When I asked Masanto about thinking by analogy, this was his response to me. *Default thinking goes somewhere specific and is predictable. I prefer adventure. A first-principle thinker can think against the norm and into the counterintuitive.*

Changing your future means deconstructing your setpoints, removing whatever imaginary cap you or anyone else had imposed upon you, then redesigning the setpoint to program a 'new normal' tuned to what you want, consistent with your internal values and no longer inhibited by false perceptions. Next, it's learning to think from 'First Principles'.

Masanto puts it this way: *There are many layers to what you see, and that's where looking at things in greater depth is of paramount importance; I analyse a system or an industry and look at the operations, then look at what would be necessary for disruption to occur, and shake an industry into its next phase of growth.* This is an excellent example of thinking which is not based on analogy or the existing way of doing things; it's the embodiment of improvement.

Masanto has no concept of a cap or limit on income, so it continues to grow and compound exponentially.

Throughout the book, the many ways I have offered you to improve character, set goals and build aspirations are all designed to naturally raise your setpoints. The keys to improvement and change that not only last but flourish over time require conditioning: training your reactions and responses so they communicate with the autonomic nervous system in a way that improvement becomes just as automatic as breathing.

Let's flip the paradigm right now. It's time to design the future the way you want it, project yourself to that time and see it evolving exponentially, then come back to the present with a clear goal in mind. This will help reprogram your expectations and adjust or even remove unnecessary setpoints. Remember, the future presupposes that the setpoints have been changed. This is what Stephen Covey meant when he placed *Start with the End in Mind* as the first habit of *The 7 Habits of Highly Effective People*.

Please reread the last paragraph. I want to strongly impress upon you the need to make every effort to think first of the end, improve it, and reverse-engineer to the present. This is the essence of a master strategist, an EndGamer.

Once success is achieved in one area, opportunities tend to arrive exponentially. Ignoring this is a fundamental flaw in many socialist doctrines, which suppress individual opportunity and enterprise as greedy and unfair. The point is, irrespective of gender, colour, religion or race when you become excellent at what you do, you win the respect of the entire world – and new opportunities abound. The natural world, even the universe itself, does not practise equality but rather the success of self-actualisation. City-states emerge almost out of nowhere. Some thrive, and some do not; the height of trees in the forests is not equal; certain stars in the galaxies attract more universal resources than others and emit more tremendous energy. Even mammalian primates have their hierarchies, though the leaders shoulder the responsibility of assuring all are cared for. There is a lesson in all of that.

Everybody has the *opportunity* to thrive, excel and become a leader within their world in their way. Nature teaches that lesson, too. All trees, whether straight and healthy or not, originate from identical seeds.

Tom Hardy no longer has to hope he can find a good agent or a worthy movie role. Angelina Jolie doesn't have to fill out job applications and try to convince casting agents of her skills as an actor, and certainly, Peter Jones doesn't have to advertise his business acumen. Once the paradigm shifts, everything is attracted in relation to the nature of the paradigm (Peter Jones doesn't get a lot of acting offers, for example). One who has reached the upper echelons of achievement becomes an attracting force. An individual whose excellence cannot be denied draws the world's spotlight – where gender, race, religion, background and social status suddenly play no part.

I will again remind you negative forces we battle on the road to achievement are often the resistance required to build the strength of character needed to succeed and prepare to lay down the path necessary for legacy. Madame Curie, Diana Princess of Wales and today's Arianna Huffington were not persons who allowed their power to be manipulated, controlled or defeated.

Why? Empowerment brings the strength to dare, to challenge, to persist and to create success on one's terms. The power of tyrants or jealous competitors rarely bring down an empowered person; an empowered person can never be overpowered. I do not know of any successful victims; the best thing to do when one is suffering is firstly hear them out, in doing so they feel understood Ensure though your emotions remain both firm and strong and gradually help build them up.

The one who is disempowered is easily overpowered. Many people who rise to the top of their respective fields, be they social change or professional enterprise like Malala Yousafzai or Coco Chanel, could have very easily decided to succumb to grim beginnings, past experiences and traumas or taken refuge in labels of victimhood to defeat themselves before they even started. Instead, they chose to take responsibility and rise above all odds.

Activating Genius

There is a part of every one of us that is alive, a livingness that flows through every atom of our being; in Ayurvedic philosophies, they describe it as the part that water cannot wet, fire cannot burn, and even a tornado cannot breakdown.

Our disconnect from the living energy that flows through existence is by either our own ignorance or death. In the earlier examples, I touched upon an idea that when water evaporates or a composite of rock is broken down, there is an essence of that thing that still exists. That is the part I coin as your invincible power; it's indestructible and came into form the void. By becoming aware of that essence, our own inherent genius is triggered. It can be likened to turning the key to the ignition or switching on the power to a computer suddenly, the potential for its usage is activated. However, the realisation of its pure potential has no restriction on what can be created and has no constraints of time.

Many remember the formative years and gauge their potential on either their performance during school or their future advancements in comparison to their peers. There is a fundamental flaw with this, as, by comparison, you automatically cap your future potential, or by presuming your true potential can be gauged by past reference points, stagnation becomes the only predictable outcome, and you are then locked into 'thought by analogy'. Let's look at an example below of one such pioneer with no early visible signs of genius and in my opinion, a pioneer in first-principle thinking.

You'd never think that a man whose name is synonymous with genius would show such little promise in his early years. But that was the case with Einstein. Born in 1879 to a middle-class Jewish family living in Ulm, Germany, Einstein's early development was nothing to write home about. For example, his speech was so delayed that his parents finally consulted a doctor. Later on, his rebellious nature and lacklustre performance at school led one headmaster to expel him and another to declare he would never amount to much.

And that prediction was accurate for some while.

After graduating from the Swiss Federal Institute of Technology, Einstein couldn't get a job no matter how hard he tried. He became so depressed over his lack of success that he wrote a letter to his family saying he wished he had never been born. *(Imagine what the world would have missed had there been no Einstein.)*

Finally, after many long months, he was hired at the Swiss Patent Office in Bern with the help of a friend, where he eked out a meagre living for his young family working six days a week as a lowly patent clerk. This third-floor office job, however, provided the perfect environment for Einstein to think. Working long hours alone in the patent lab, without any pressure and no one to compare himself to, he began to regain the use of his greatest asset – his imagination.

In early 1905, while still a patent clerk, Einstein wrote and published four scientific papers, which were destined to not only change the course of history but catapult the planet into the information age. Einstein good scientific training though not at the level that would have predicted a breakthrough of this magnitude. Einstein's keen interest in physics, mathematics and philosophy served as a stable foundation and combination for training his thought process. So how does an unknown patent clerk possibly challenge some of the greatest scientific minds in history, including his own idol, Sir Isaac Newton?

Here's how.

The secret to Einstein's discoveries was not hidden in schools of knowledge. The secret to this power was already in Einstein himself. It was in his mind. *In his imagination.*

Einstein's ability to question without restriction or an imposed framework of thinking allowed his imagination free rein. As a result, his scientific papers, particularly his theory of relativity, proved to be genius propositions that rocked the world of physics. But Einstein's real genius came from his keen ability to use his mind to see pictures, play out scenarios and 'what ifs…' These 'thought experiments' set his mental processes in motion, leading to some magnificent discoveries.

You – and virtually every human being with a capacity to think clearly – can perform these same kinds of thought experiments and create your version of genius using the wonders of your imagination. Thousands of hours' research and a spirit of curiosity laid the foundation. By no means are discoveries and genius ever random. However, it can always be traced back to countless hours of attempting to unravel an unknown puzzle, essentially playing that game of life at its highest level. The world stands in awe of Einstein's discoveries – and rightly so – but during the early stages of his discoveries, the majority were resistant to his ideas and the new ways of thinking that were primarily responsible for his breakthroughs. As powerful as Einstein's discoveries were, it was his ability to think and even challenge the ideas of his own idols that allowed him to make these discoveries – by imagination and thought alone.

If you are talking to an audience, ideally you should not try to persuade them to accept your position, there is no point in persuading a student that you are right. You want to encourage them to find out what the truth is, which is that you are probably wrong. – Noam Chomsky

This is how virtually all of our planet's advances and discoveries are made, by the way. There will always be a cognitive bias to what society indoctrinates us with: 'The scripture says this…' or 'My doctor says that…' One can collect and study exhaustive amounts of research, which is excellent. But what's more important than learning is a quiet time to think and extrapolate the knowledge you have just digested and the ability to bring it to life as opposed to leaving it in the realm of abstract philosophy.

It all comes back to authenticity and absolute truth, one that resonates with us and is not the conclusion of someone else. Being open to new learning without rigidity is what produces independence.

There is a concept so powerful in the world of nature that supports this truth. Nothing in nature is identical, *nothing!* Even the smallest units of light shine forth with different parameters and activities. The goal is to become self-reliant, where you bring *your originality* and embrace *your uniqueness*. Just as we explored in the earlier chapters about becoming your best self, *your authentic self is what releases the latent powers of your mind.*

Let's consider another example of the mind as the workshop of the imagination and another one who tapped into the reservoirs of his invincible power.

During World War II, Ferruccio Lamborghini served with the Air Force mechanics corps and became a wizard at engine conversions and repair. So, after the war, Ferruccio set up a small car repair shop in northern Italy.

He got the idea to buy surplus military machines that he could convert into tractors, as tractors were in high demand in the agricultural region of Italy where he lived. So, he founded a tractor factory, and backed by energy and determination, the strong-willed Ferruccio was soon building an average of one tractor a month. After a while, his business became so successful that he expanded his product line to include air conditioning units and oil-burning heaters. It is essential to note that his natural zeal, energy and inclination towards growth and expansion was constructing a foundation for his future.

Not surprising, Ferruccio had a love of cars, especially luxury sports cars. And once he became a wealthy entrepreneur who could afford what he wanted, he owned a small fleet of them. One such prize was his Ferrari 250 GT, which unfortunately had an ongoing problem with the clutch. To get to the bottom of it, Ferruccio paid a personal visit to Enzo Ferrari himself to complain. But instead of offering to help with the problem, Enzo put him off, stating, "The problem is not with the car but with the driver!"

This was not what Ferruccio expected to hear, and it was quite an insulting response for a mechanical genius and successful entrepreneur. So Ferruccio took it as a challenge and decided to build his own sports car, and whether the insult was true or not, Lamborghini utilised and leveraged off this incident to success; the success would not only be for him but the entire luxury car industry. As one individual strives and improves, everyone improves. Although

Ferruccio had already made a name for himself in the tractor industry as a powerful, well-respected businessman, when he announced that he would now proceed to build the best sports car ever, a lot of his friends thought he had gone mad. And many voiced their opinion. They believed this would be a "hazardous leap in the dark" for Ferruccio's company, an extravagance that would cause him to lose his entire fortune without ever turning a profit.

Of course, he proved his naysayers wrong. In less than a year, he had purchased land and built a large, ultramodern factory unrivalled in its field. After hiring three of Ferrari's ex-employees, Ferruccio set out to create a luxurious and powerful GT of his own – one that would reach 150 mph on the famous Italian motorway connecting Naples and Milan. Thus, the Lamborghini 350 GT was born. More importantly, the name 'Lamborghini' soon became a respected legend in the world of luxury sports cars.

Though there is a lot of conflict and disparity about how competitive we should be, competition has its advantages. For example, a racehorse will always run faster when competing against another horse. Without a competitive market environment, we fail to evolve and develop to our potential, as the competition itself keeps us on our toes. Just remember, it's not about mimicking or copying the work of a competitor; it's all about taking a competitor's idea and improving on it.

Planting the Seed of a Dream

Embedded in these three examples are clues to the secret to accessing the residing power: immersion in the world of the things you love – the very same power you have at your disposal to realise your own goals.

Let's consider these clues:

At the early age of five, Einstein's father gave him a compass. This simple gift fuelled Einstein's passion and an insatiable curiosity to understand the laws of physics, eventually directing him down an unlikely path to fulfilling his dream of becoming a physicist.

Young Lamborghini's mechanical knack for small engine repair became evident while serving his country during wartime. That skill, sparked by a brilliant idea to build much-needed tractors out of surplus army vehicles, gave Ferruccio just the opportunity he needed to create a lifetime of success for himself and his companies.

The two examples illustrate:

1. Einstein had a passion for how the universe worked.
2. Lamborghini had a passion for motors, engines and cars.

These examples provide a good illustration of how natural inclinations lead to inspired and creative thoughts, which dictate ones behaviour whilst simultaneously moving one toward their life purpose.

That's the correct order. You start with your heart.

Physically speaking, your heart is the most selfish organ in your body. It takes the *finest blood first* for itself, and then distributes the remainder to the rest of your body. But this is the correct order. This is the only way it can work if you are to live and be healthy. Now, maybe you don't yet know what all your passions are or where your natural inclinations reside. But if you've worked through the previous chapters, you probably are a lot clearer than you have ever been before. If not, it's time to listen to your heart, as that's the only way to live *spiritually* healthy and happy, fulfilling your purpose and loving what you do.

Here's a mental exercise that will help you identify your calling.

Let's imagine for a moment that you have just won an all-expense-paid year-long vacation to one of the finest resorts in the world; you also are given Satoshi Nakamoto's Bitcoin wallet. Everything you are responsible for is fully taken care of – bills, family, work – so that you can *truly* go away for a whole year with no care in the world. And you get to choose what you want to spend your time doing. Maybe it's reading; maybe it's some recreational activity; maybe it's devoting your time to creating a project you've had on the back burner for years.

Whatever it is, it has to be exactly what YOU want.

Now, pause for a minute and think about this. What would you choose to read? What would you love to study? What would you enjoy spending your time doing? Take the time to listen to your heart, and you will discover your natural inclination; it is easy when you look at where your mind naturally wanders. Go further back to the unrealised dreams of a child.

You have had life experiences that offer clues to your natural inclinations; it's now time to start putting the pieces of the puzzle together. If we are attuned we can recognise that there is indeed mercy in the universe and compassion in the way it communicates with us. What natural inklings have come your way, what life experiences have you had – possibly even painful experiences – that may be nudging you in the direction of your natural inclinations and onward towards success? It is our perceived voids that we most actively attempt to fill. Those are the signals one must listen to, as they are the keys to deciphering the language of the universe.

Steve Jobs appreciation and practice of calligraphy, his engagement in yoga and regular meditation, coupled with his ingenuity in computer science, may have been the foundational ingredients necessary to build his creations. By keen observation of Apple products, one may conclude his training in 'thinking less' as in clearing the mind during meditation also contributed to the creation of sophisticated products that are simple to use artfully concealing their power and aesthetically pleasing.

Never permit yourself to entertain negative messages from others – and even often from yourself – that try to convince you that you can't do something just because you haven't been trained or don't have experience. Remember Einstein? He was a nobody in the world of physics. He had had no extraordinary scientific training. But instead of waiting for permission to pursue his interest in unravelling the mysteries of the universe, he decided to listen to that silent voice within and took the initiative himself. Not only did it work, but his very name is synonymous with scientific genius. People are always subordinating to authority; though I believe there is a time for authority to be understood, respected and honoured, there is a massive difference between respect and subordination.

To punish me for my contempt for authority, fate made me an authority myself.
– Einstein

You, the EndGamer are now learning to drop any and all mediocre standards as well as let the illusionary boundaries and inhibitions melt away. At the outset, there will be many times that you may not *feel* like the successful person you want to be. Doubt is on standby looking to trip you over at any instance. It is no wonder; we are all naturally plagued with self-limiting beliefs and fear as a result of past experiences. So, when it feels like you're swimming against the current it's time for you to start backing yourself up and believing in the one reflecting back in the mirror. The insidious adversary of self doubt only has power if you consent to it; dwelling on it is the only source of its fuel. The enemy has the ability to go unnoticed flying under the radar and even conceals its very presence in front of others. The courage to break free of these negative influences is embedded in our very own DNA. Conquering this foe is your only true route to salvation. The enemy is not external to you and cannot be overthrown with brute force or hate.

And God said "Love Your Enemy", and I obeyed Him and loved myself. –
Kahlil Gibran

When stars collide – and, as a result, collapse – in the universe, the intermingling of elements create other elements such as gold. Unlike carbon or iron, gold cannot be created within a star or a planet on its own. It must be born in a more cataclysmic event. There are certain moments in life that can be likened to a collision of stars. Rare treasures emerge from these experiences that you can take and make something great out of. Your ability to extract what's necessary depends on how you respond to these moments and what meaning you give them. Our alchemy (discussed in Chapter Three) is all about converting some of life's cataclysmic events into gold.

So, just because your gifts have lain dormant inside you for years – decades even – it doesn't mean they don't exist. I'm here to tell you it's your time. It's time you believe in yourself as I believe in you and discover the gold mine of potential that resides within. This is why authenticity is so critical. No one can walk your path; no one can achieve what you can achieve. That opportunity is yours alone – as long as you follow your heart.

Explorations of the Mind

Once you explore your heart and determine the natural inclinations, it's time to employ the use of your greatest asset: your mind to direct and coordinate those actions.

Let me establish something of importance from the outset:

Whether you know it or not, whether you feel like it or not, you have a degree of control over your mind; focus is everything. To crystallise your focus, learning to bring your energies to one thing is more important. Remember, we only have a finite amount of attention and deliberate thoughts we think about per day, so use it wisely. The mind is that one thing in life that we have been assigned greater control over than perhaps anything else.

For instance, you can't control other people. You can't control events in history. You can't even control what you might encounter if you get in your car and drive.

But one can have control over thoughts dwelled upon, and one can learn to keep them sustained in the right direction. Which, by universal benevolent design, is the only thing one *needs* to control. Doing this well enough gives everything else the room to take care of itself in time.

The next point I want to make is that you (and me, and everyone else on the planet) are of *two* minds, something we explored earlier on in the book. I felt it necessary to add this point again as the review will help elucidate how it works. The 'objective' mind that you can directly control, and the 'subjective' mind that responds to orders and impulses from its objective counterpart. In other words, you can only control your subjective mind *indirectly* through your conscious, objective processes.

The objective and subjective minds are two separate *functions* of your mind. But because they each perform a specifically unique function relative to what you are thinking, feeling and behaving, it's much easier to distinguish them as a separate 'mind.'

At the most basic level, here's how the objective and subjective minds work.

Data from the outside world is relayed to your objective mind through the window of the senses. Your objective mind analyses and interprets the data and then sends signals, impulses, 'meanings' and then orders to your subjective mind relative to how it has analysed the data. Whatever you believe about everything in your life – yourself, others, and even life itself – you believe because of experiences you have had and the meanings you have assigned to those experiences. So, when a new thought enters your conscious or objective mind, it is immediately analysed based on whatever you believe about that subject via past references. Then it signals the subjective mind to respond accordingly.

Let's consider a basic example to show how this plays out.

An aspiring actor is en route to an audition and is pressed for time – the cars are slow-moving during a rainy morning in London traffic.

As her objective mind realises she may end up late, her heart palpitates faster. The objective mind within jumps to worst-case scenarios, bad first impressions, messing up the audition. She begins to worry the other talent may have the advantage, thinking that they might be more experienced, favourable, attractive, and the list she rattles off in her mind goes on and on!

The objective mind now takes these two pieces of data and starts analysing them: assigning meaning to this predicament – if one is late, naturally, this has a negative connotation attached to it as there can be no excuse for lateness. The subjective mind recognises the signal that trouble is brewing: the potential late arrival – now the mind is looking for reasons to justify the anxiety and seeing a late arrival as a threat, fight or flight triggers.

The subjective mind doesn't evaluate, analyse or question anything; the objective mind passes it over. The function of the subjective mind is not only to control the billions of natural processes automatically going throughout the human body and its surroundings but also to respond accordingly to deliberate messages, impulses and orders passed on to it from the conscious or objective mind. So now the subjective mind goes to work.

Naturally, if one is in trouble, it tells the body to respond with a sense of fear and dread. So the stomach knots up, and blood pressure rises. In the case of our actor, she is now preoccupied with what to say in defence of the delay while ruminating over thoughts of blundering the audition. As our actor attempts to distract herself, she scrolls on her phone and begins rereading her emails, where she then notices that she has misread the appointment time. It is, in fact, one hour later.

Instantly, she feels relieved, and her entire physiology changes. Suddenly there is a smile on her face, her appetite returns, and she recognises with additional time for practice, her punctuality may even deliver a more favourable impression.

Here is a solid example of control over your mind.

Now let us rewind to the moment of distress for our actor. Let us say that instead of the internal turmoil, she reframes the situation in a different way. The initial interpretation of lack of time may even provide less time to think, and her best performances have been delivered in moments where there was no overthinking. The pressure of the traffic could be seen as surrendering to the present moment without judgment. Regardless of the outcome, good or bad, the audition adds to her equity of experience. Even by the law of averages, she is now a step closer.

She now relinquishes the idea of comparing herself to others, recognising beauty can be capped and is limited while attraction is unlimited. Projection of her best qualities will result in both beauty and brilliance of performance.

First of all, the truth is our actor has no idea of the outcome of the audition if her performance would be up to scratch, or another actor would be selected for the part. Immediate feedback will be given on the areas to work on in order to improve next time. Next, by automatically asking the question "How can this serve me?" or "How can I profit from the result of this?" the mind will have no choice but to search for better outcomes and improvements.

Further, she has positioned her dreams in the present tense and believes in the assumption that she is already the person she is destined to be, so regardless of the outcome today, she has no need to worry. She only needs to have patience within for the inevitable result.

Second, the truth is, the feeling of comparison was not warranted. Authenticity attracts a greater audience, and feedback is at times of greater value. It provides the areas necessary to improve and refine. Performance is a moment in time and not a reflection of one's true worth.

Third, the truth is she was en route to the audition, and the error was in her future projections. So, the focus would have naturally been better thinking of how she would like it to evolve. If her imagination was on leaving the judges spellbound and swept away by her very performance, there would be a greater probability of the body delivering that. This is so because, for that image to be actual, the mind presupposes that the performance went smoothly, unlocking the body's potential to deliver at its best when it matters most.

When one sends the message they desire, reframed to the subjective mind, it recognises the reinterpretation. Then, naturally, the worry begins to dissolve.

Our actor just controlled her thoughts, feelings, and even circumstances by acknowledging the truth. One has the potential to direct and take charge of the objective mind along with the conscious thoughts which result. Doing so indirectly instructs the subjective mind, as well as the physical symptoms. Worry is simply a focus of attention on what one doesn't want to occur, and so it's time for you to train yourself in those very moments to pivot to the outcome you want.

Further, I would like you to consider the following: if you fear, you are not thinking; you are remembering an experience and then predicting a future outcome with the same feeling emerging in the future.

It's time to learn to be in the present moment and learn to think in the direction you wish to go.

For centuries, the clergy of all religious denominations, the philosophers and the scientists, have all thought about, debated, researched and experimented in great detail the functions of the subjective mind. The predominant positions held are about its impersonal nature (in other words, it acts without question according to the impulses received from the objective mind). However, it is also the part of you that engineers and builds your body – the actual temple you reside in.

Think of how you started as one cell, the beating of the heart, etc. There is an intelligence directing that and, as such, houses the creative power of the individual. Just like in the example above, the subjective mind took whatever thought meanings were transferred to it from the objective mind, and the subjective mind communicated to the body to respond accordingly.

In the initial case of our actor, the individual was worried, nervous, fearful, unable to concentrate, and developed physical symptoms, all because the subjective mind acts without question based on whatever the objective mind pictures and dwells upon.

In the second scenario, the subjective mind acted on the message from the objective mind that everything was fine with a correct reframe, suggesting that there was no reason to be worried. Our feelings and behaviours are the physical, bodily reactions to the subjective mind carrying out orders from the objective mind.

In essence, the body is under no influence from the outside stimulus. How one interprets an event or message will always affect how one feels. The images in the mind and the internal conversation create the output and stimulus in the body. We will be looking at a model below of how the same inner intelligence once evoked through inner conversations and images not only affects how one feels internally but is also part of what influences and constructs the entire outside world.

So, in order for one to have more control over emotions and have a base level of good feelings most of the time, thoughts need to be present, accurate, equilibrated, and there needs to be a hiatus before reacting to a situation, and then the interpretation will be guided to the outcome one is looking for.

If you think about the explanation and example we've just discussed, you can readily see how the subjective mind is intensively sensitive to suggestion. All our actor did in the example above was think trouble. Immediately, the subjective mind went to work to respond according to that suggestion, creating feelings, behaviours and situations relative to that thought or belief.

It works the other way too, not only in the negative – whether you feed your subjective mind good thoughts or bad thoughts. Your subjective mind doesn't evaluate the difference. It merely works responding and creating feelings, behaviours and eventually circumstances to substantiate the initial belief.

So, since you can decide what thoughts you hand over to your subjective mind to act upon, you can begin right now to move in the direction of your dreams, merely by determining what thoughts and 'thought experiments' would move you toward your desired goal… which brings us right back to listening to your heart.

First-Principle Thinking and Beyond

It is commonly thought that nothing moves faster than the speed of light. There is something however that moves at a velocity far greater and that is Space, in order for the universe to continue to expand and light to journey into an ever expanding nothingness. That something, scientists today postulate is outside of the very fabric of the universe and even time itself. This maybe what dark matter is the discovery could be on the horizon or this revelation may take eons of time to reveal itself. Yet what we find is that every new idea, creation or invention is birthed out of a nothingness; perhaps it's in this nothingness where the potential of everything that exists or will ever exist resides. The more frequently we enter this silence and peek into this realm, the more the mind has a tendency to find its own unique way of drawing out the answers we are looking for.

I was first introduced to the power of first-principle thinking, unknowingly, whilst I was at a roundtable discussion where a property start-up team were pitching an idea to tech entrepreneur Vasily Koledov and other Russian investors. Koledov only in his mid-twenties at the time, began picking apart the idea and exposing its fundamental flaws, much to the dismay of the team. To them, it appeared their plans were being dismantled and destroyed. But eventually they saw that Koledov was performing a creative service; crumbling the framework into a nothingness needed to create the space necessary to rebuild it into something that would actually work.

Koledov using his training in first principle thinking via his company Geo-Alpha, is now one of the few stealth pioneers delivering key information to the United Nations in helping reach their sustainability goals by using natural systems to provide the resources for societies and the economies around the world.

First-principle thinking is key, as the masses are bound by thinking from analogy and more times than not, restrict themselves until it becomes the default. This is the realm of seeing things as they are and presuming this is the only way things can be.

For example, there was a point when cars only ran on petrol, so thinking by analogy would have the individual go out in search of oil as oil is the only fuel that can run a motor. Nations control and direct the fuel line; hence, the thinker by analogy can only operate from this framework. Let me gather the people and equipment necessary, dig for oil, help run economies, and make a handsome fortune.

The first-principles thinker would ask: would it be possible to construct an engine that would run on another fuel type instead of oil? Perhaps a source of energy and not a limited or controlled resource. What would it take to create a form of transport that uses renewable energy? Could solar be used, electric, or even a yet undiscovered resource?

Why have we not returned to the moon?

If we think by analogy, the answer is simple: it is too expensive to fly a rocket to the moon, and the monies to be allocated could never be justified by heads of state, and only a government can authorise space travel, after all; and furthermore, rockets can only be used once, and it's always been that way.

Elon Musk posed the question from a first-principle perspective, asking why rockets only be used once? That's as absurd as making an aeroplane that was only good for one flight. The cost of travel would be unjustifiable and out of reach for everyone. By designing a reusable rocket, you have dropped the costs drastically and created a potential for frequent flights. Now let's break it down further. The components to build a rocket are so expensive that only governments could allocate taxpayer funds to finance such a venture. The first-principled thinker, Elon Musk, posed the question: what would happen if one were to build the manufacturing unit, then directly sourced the components necessary to construct a rocket in house? This birthed the company SpaceX.

First-principle thinking is a methodology of thinking most common amongst physicists. It's breaking a problem down to its constituent parts and rebuilding it from there. Original thinkers and visionaries tilt more towards first-principled thinking than anyone else.

With the current explosion of cryptocurrencies, the world has been forced to re-evaluate currencies of exchange and begin to conform to change accordingly. The ingenious creation of the mysterious and unknown Satoshi Nakamoto, cryptocurrency, built a method of decentralising currency into a means that can operate without banks, governments or regulatory bodies.

It includes a seal-tight way to protect the asset more securely than the World Bank and Federal Reserve, further a currency which by its very nature would be impossible to go to war over. This is another example of a first-principled thinker: why should currencies be regulated? The only viable answer would have been: it's always been that way.

We are about to go a layer deeper. Bear with me and take time to digest these ideas, they will be invaluable and help develop the original thinker in you.

Idea Prototypes

For example, playing a game with pebbles is no different than playing a virtual reality video game. The essence remains the same: they are both games that have rules, entertain their participants and observers, and they both have a conclusion. One is, of course, incredibly more sophisticated than the other, yet the fundamentals are the same.

To better understand this concept, take a minute to look around you. First of all, you are likely sitting on a chair or a couch while reading this book or perhaps listening to an audio version and maybe driving or walking with headphones on. If you think about a chair, it is a material, physical object existing in time and space. But there was a point in time and space where that chair did NOT yet exist. The first creator of a chair was compelled to build it for the reason of 'comfort'. Not until the creator of that object first 'saw' the prototype of that object in the realm of imagination could they even begin to consider creating or building it.

In essence, everything that exists in the physical realm had first to be conceived as a 'thought image' in the non-physical realm before it could ever be created. That is natural law and is why the imaginative powers of the mind are such a necessary tool in creating one's own reality. Our ability to imagine or 'see' anything at all with our mind's 'eye' allows us the opportunity to create anything at all we want to make. That thought image, or idea prototype, precedes its physical representation. The creation of the physical expression is a process implemented by the subjective mind, per orders from the objective mind.

Everything came into existence in this same way. First comes the impulse of desire; when one consents to it (meaning believes it is possible) the mental picture appears, the subconscious goes on to transmit the request feeling of ownership then the prototype of the thing though nascent in nature finds its own way to emerge. And once that mental picture is put in place, nothing can prevent it from becoming a concrete reality except the same power which gave it birth – YOU.

If you think of the idea prototype as the essence of a thing, and the material, physical form of the prototype as its outward expression, you can quickly see how the first step to creating any external reality is the creation of its idea prototype. Being quantum in nature, this prototype can only be formed by the operation of thought. And to have substance and staying power long enough to create its physical equivalent, this prototype must be thought of as actually existing in the quantum realm already.

As children, both Jeff Bezos and Musk were avid fans of the popular sci-fi show *Star Trek*. It is no coincidence that the playful imagination of a child will set into motion the very mechanisms that will take our species into new frontiers of deep space. The technologies are being birthed out of pure desire. Progression may be near impossible on many levels if the past is used as a reference point. If you keep looking at the past, you end up creating more future scenarios of what transpired. If you project a thought into the future, it will keep pushing that thing you desire into the future like a carrot on the stick in front of a donkey.

If you build the image in the present tense without a future projection and carry an expectation that it has already occurred, your mind no longer differentiates between what's real and imagined. Remember, the subconscious mind is like a computer and impartial to what you program it with. Further, by presupposing it is real in the present tense, the mind has no choice but to build a justification for that premise, as we surmised earlier on in the book.

Our very belief about a thing unlocks our potential to achieve it. Believing it can't be done is the quickest way to shut down the mental and physical processes necessary for achievement. Now let's turn back to the topic of idea prototypes. To better understand this concept, consider that the distinctive characteristic of the quantum realm is 'thought', and the unique characteristic of the physical realm, the world of matter, is 'form'. Also, a significant aspect of physical matter is that it occupies space and therefore has certain boundaries or limitations. Thought is immaterial in nature, however, and is therefore not limited by boundaries of space or even time itself. Now let's consider the degree to which something is 'living' in relation to thought and form… and the fact that the amount of space a form occupies has no relationship to the degree that form is 'living'.

For example, you may watch a bee in pursuit of nectar from a flower. The bee occupies very little space. Nevertheless, it is as 'alive' as is the cat who paws it away if it comes too close. Or the elephant, who may not even be aware of their existence. In other words, thoughts are just as 'alive' as any living form in the physical world of matter.

Let's take this one step further.

According to Einstein, the core idea is that space and time, which seem like different things, are interwoven. Space has its three dimensions: length, breadth and height. Then there is a fourth dimension, which we call time. All four are linked in a kind of giant cosmic sheet.

The scientific definition of time is that period occupied by a 'form' while passing from one point in space to another.

By that very definition, then, where there is no space, there can be no time. So, if 'thought' is not confined to the limitations of space, neither is it bound by the limitations of time. Putting all these concepts together, we can see that thoughts are living things that are entirely independent of time and space. So, anything you can think of, any idea or thought you could imagine represents the immaterial idea prototype of its material counterpart and is present in the here and now.

Further, any idea, goal or dream you can conceive of in your mind has the potential to come to life in the physical present (space and time) by exercising the sheer power of thought, then moving into physical action.

You may accurately consider your thoughts in this way: thought is the necessary component of the first cause. You, the originator of that thought, receive an impulse of desire, and by consenting to the desire, you become an active participant in the entire creative process. Thus, the idea prototype is triggered from there, and if the belief accompanied by desire is stabilised, you can then know it will happen. From there, the Universal Intelligence takes over your thought 'seed' and goes to work to organise the necessary additional components that will turn that thought from immaterial into material form. This will happen right in front of your eyes.

Remember the example above of *Star Trek*. It cannot be viewed as a coincidence that today's current science and technological conditions have evolved to a level where those early dreams of space travel and landing humans on Mars are coming true.

St Augustine asked where time came from. He said it came out of the future which didn't exist yet, into the present that had no duration, and went into the past which had ceased to exist. – Graham Greene

In an attempt to make this clearer, let's return to the example earlier on with our actor.

She had a 'thought' (idea prototype) that she would arrive late to her audition. It was confirmed in her mind, as real as if she would have been rejected at that very moment. So, the reality of that thought already existed in her mind – in the present tense. That is why her physical reaction was so immediate and debilitating. She saw it playing out in her mind as reality. She believed it was real. And her belief presented itself in the physical realm (her physical body) in the form of anxiety.

Remember, the idea prototype is the essence of the reality – it is precisely what that reality represents. It is not the reality itself. So, in this case, the idea prototype was the 'thought image' that she was in trouble with, and it was not the audition itself.

Now consider what dream you want to pursue.

Maybe you want to live in a stunning apartment in the heart of the city. That's the physical reality of the thing itself.

But what's the prototype of this dream? What is the purpose of its existence? What do you want to experience from the reality of this dream? Serenity, prestige, contentment a comfortable abode or the joy that comes from experiencing a home that gives access to the immediate exhilaration of a big city?

Using the concept of the idea prototype, you can plant the seed of contentment, prestige, serenity and beauty in your subjective mind using the powers of your objective mind. Then using your powers of imagination, surround that prototype with the specifics – the image of the home, the skyline you are viewing, the way rooms are oriented and furnishings are positioned, paintings on the wall, the standalone brass bathtub, on and on. Paint an accurate, vivid picture in your mind and hold it there. Next ask yourself whilst in a relaxed state, the way you would fantasise as a child, what would feel like to have ownership and the happiness on a day-to-day basis. Take a moment to give your body the opportunity to recognise that feeling; next you fall asleep in the assumption. You continue this practice to the point where it feels natural and normal for you; you are no longer in a state of wanting it because you already have it.

And then tend to it properly, just like you would a seed you plant in fertile soil. As long as you tend to it correctly, the kernel will naturally germinate and grow into a plant. The idea prototype or 'seed' you plant in your 'fertile mind' will, when tended to properly, germinate into your external reality as well. Of course at this stage strategies, ideas and work conditions will begin to appear; work with all your heart and the results will begin to appear.

To find the idea prototype for anything you desire, it is only necessary to determine in your mind the *purpose* of the thing you wish. For example, suppose you want a new car. Determine the reasons for its existence, which would be the ability to reach one's destination swiftly and safely and what that kind of car (make, model, colour, style, etc.) will do for you. What does it mean to you? What does that car do for your lifestyle? Your image? Whatever purpose that car serves for you would be its idea prototype.

By continually bringing your attention to the reason for its existence, it will also train you into being an original thinker and a skilled innovator because you will not be bound to only the form that currently exists.

In actual practice, you must first form the ideal concept of your desired object in your mind, fleshing it out as much as possible using your gift of imagination. Draw the picture of your desired goal in full colour, with everything just as you want it to be, and establish this full-colour picture as a reality in the here and now. Closing your eyes and using the powers of your imagination, you can 'feel' it, 'smell' it, 'hear' it, looking through your own eyes... just as if you were sitting right square in the middle of it. In other words, lose yourself in the image, bathed with its prototype. Now feel the gratitude of having this in your life and edge a little further into the future to place just past the realisation of your dream; this will hack your mind by creating a presupposition as if it's already happened. Your mind will need justification for this premise therefore it will actively seek a tangible expression.

There is a form of originating energy within you that is activated by the directed mind and the 'will' (discussed a bit later in this chapter). When self-directed, you can plant seeds of your desired reality through your objective thoughts, which then relay themselves to your subjective mind – the creator of your reality. And if the requisite feelings are appropriately sustained the mindset for accomplishments will be underway, the planted seeds will eventually attract to themselves all the conditions necessary for manifestation in outward visible form.

So, to summarise this understanding, your thought of anything forms its corresponding idea prototype, which in the model I am presenting to you creates a nucleus or centre of attraction for all conditions necessary for its eventual externalisation in the physical world, directly related to the nature inherent in the idea prototype itself. In other words, if you plant a tomato seed, you won't grow a cucumber. A tomato seed, by natural law, can only result in more of its kind – tomatoes. That's why the nature of the idea prototype is entirely significant here. The quality and characteristics of your thoughts – the seeds you plant in your subjective mind – will be what determines your eventual reality. It's not fate; it's not purely circumstantial. It's natural law.

This can be viewed as both comforting and reassuring, however. Once you plant the seed – the idea prototype of your desired reality – in the ground of your subjective mind, and you nurture it properly, then the responsibility of the outcome is your actions in its direction. You can go about your daily affairs with certainty, knowing that with the idea prototype in place, natural law has taken over, and in time, the reality of your desire will begin to show itself.

It may be a very small circumstance at first. Like a seedling, when it first begins to break through the ground and show itself, it is very small, fragile, and seemingly insignificant. But it is the direction of the thing, and not the magnitude of it, which is to be considered. In turn, this slight circumstance will lead to further signs illustrating the direction until you find yourself pulled into the flow of the fulfilment of your desired goal. This is when your pursuit, persistence and going the extra mile will ensure your actions are consistent enough to produce the physical effect of the thing desired.

This is the way life is to be lived, the way dreams are to be realised. Complying with the natural laws of universal principles and a perpetual source of health and happiness in abundant supply will be yours to seize.

Magnetic Expectations

Positive thoughts accompanied by feelings attract corresponding circumstances. Negative thoughts if accompanied by feelings will do the same. This is natural law. The only difference is in the nature of what is attracted. It works the same either way. This is great news, and considering the premise that you have control over the nature of your thoughts and thought impulses, you will be choosing the nature (positive or negative) of the circumstances you attract into your life as well.

Now, let's take this premise and apply it to the process of creating our dream reality.

The power and strength of your thought images are enhanced by the 'energy' you assign to them. So, if you allow your mental image to serve as a vehicle to provide you with the specific feeling of attainment accompanied with gratitude, the sooner it will attract the necessary corresponding circumstances and the sooner the object of your desire will present itself in visible form. Once again, it is not about forcing a contrived feeling or pushing for an outcome, it is receiving a transmission for the mind of the feeling of attainment. If what you are aiming for is not delivered on schedule its also having the recognition that, firstly you had not sustained the requisite feeling and secondly, having the faith that it is already there enjoying the journey will always hasten its arrival.

Initially, your thought power, or attracting magnetism, won't be that strong and consequently can only reach so far. But the more perfectly you guard your desire as a secret within your own mind, the more life you give it, and the stronger your ability to broadcast your intention, which in turn becomes a power of attraction. It is best to keep the desire concealed as mentioned previously draws greater energy to it. Think of it this way if you're dealing with a problem by bringing it out in the open, most of the time it causes the problem to weaken. Hence you do not want the target desire to weaken, so guard it.

The only time this isn't the case is when you're working with a team or Mastermind group toward a common, collective goal. In this situation, you amplify the attracting force and power by discussing it. However, it is still not advisable to discuss what you are doing *outside* of your team; have your team collectively visualise, with expectancy always the best.

And it certainly is not necessary to share your desire with anyone in order for it to be realised. The reason is that your thoughts themselves house all the positive energy required for attracting what you have planted in your subjective mind. This energy is the attracting force that is released through the vibration of thought impulses into the universe. The universe then takes that energy and goes to work to put in order the conditions necessary for realising your dream.

Once your desire has been firmly established, it is the assumption that the desire is already complete that ensures your goal or dream is not uprooted or replaced by an opposing idea. The positive 'expectations' that you have set up in your mind are the triggering mechanisms for attracting every good thing you desire into your life. However, negative sensations and feelings will as rapidly destroy your dream. Successful entrepreneurs or anyone in the realm of pushing industries forward are not naive to think they won't find obstacles in their way. They do, of course! The difference is they develop contingency plans to manoeuvre around the temporary failures on the route to success.

The nature of your expectations, or the quality of your mindset, will be the determining factor that either realises or destroys your dream. This is an invisible but powerful force and truth of nature. As we have already explored in earlier chapters, if you dwell on your past reference points, you create the same rhetorical cycles. To break these cycles requires a shift in not only your perceptions but a massive turnaround in identity. Develop the self-concept to change to that of a winner.

But the good news is that it works just as well with positive expectations because it is a natural law. These are gifts we have been given by the universe to direct and create the life we want to live, as long as we obey the universal principles that are in place. If we understand how they work, and we are willing to put forth the effort necessary to self-determine our own reality, then life will bless us with an abundance of good things – *as long as we keep expecting it!*

The mind will then put the things we want as focal, and the opportunities that appeared hidden become apparent.

Just remember, your desire cannot be realised without the proper, supporting expectations – the nurturing necessary to see your idea prototype manifest itself in your physical world. But once you reach the state of mind where you don't just believe or hope your idea will manifest in physical form – *you know it will* – then this is the point where you truly begin to receive the physical expression of your desired reality. The only thing necessary is that you see it in your mind, and you believe it in your heart. *Expect it… feel it… attract it… and you will take the required steps and ultimately receive it.*

Projecting a Powerful Will

Years before anyone would accept the idea of a man travelling to the moon and back, Dr Wernher von Braun, renowned aerospace engineer, was asked, "What would it take to make a rocket to reach the moon?" His response was quite simple. "The will to do it."

Once you become clear about what your desired result looks like, the next step is to *declare that it will be so.*

This is important, so let me repeat it. If you want to achieve a goal you have set, the next step is to *decide to manifest it.*

Don't waste your time sitting around wondering *how* you're going to make it happen. Don't wonder whether or not you *can* make it happen. It doesn't matter if you can't see how. It doesn't matter if you feel this goal is outside of your control. It doesn't matter if you don't know the necessary steps to get from where you are right now to where you want to be. Because you know what? No one who's ever achieved does. Steve Jobs, Bill Gates and Richard Branson never followed a well-defined plan. They had zero guarantee of success when they started out. That's the way it works. Many people think they must have a clearly defined blueprint before they start, or they get stuck figuring out the process and forget the objective.

But the only thing necessary in the beginning is the ability to see the end result. Much like an architect designing a home: the completed image is in the mind before any foundation is laid. You don't need to know the names of each bricklayer and how each piece of equipment is procured. You just need to have the end in mind. Then as things begin to evolve, plans start to develop.

As long as you are distinctly clear about what you want, then all you need do is decide to make it so. Like Dr von Braun and the rocket – have the will to "make it so"

The moment you begin to doubt whether or not this will be possible is the moment you begin to lose ground. It is the universal principle at work. You will get the results you intend. That is, if you declare your intention to be so, then it will be so. If you believe in yourself, then you will get it done. If you believe it may not work, then you will get what you ask for. It may not work.

Because when doubts occupy your thoughts, what you're doing is creating images of what you don't want. Remember, your subjective mind doesn't analyse your thoughts; it only implements them. Furthermore, doubts start shutting off parts of the brain that are so important in actualising ones potential.

To the subjective mind, every image with feeling IS. Negative, anxious and doubtful feelings contaminate; if you catch yourself in that moment, begin to revise the image into the reality of prosperity and success. *It all depends on what thought pictures combined with feeling that you are passing over to your subjective mind to implement.*

We can quickly sabotage our goal if we don't fully understand this truth. You must see that EVERY thought is an intention, whether you realise it or not – *every thought.* So, if you're wavering back and forth between… *this will work, this won't work, I don't know if this will work…* you are sabotaging the outcome. There's no way it will work.

To make it so, you must remove words like 'maybe', 'hopefully' and 'can't' from your vocabulary. You must not allow yourself to think *negatively,* as a negative thought is nothing more than an intent to manifest what you *don't* want. You will simply be manifesting conflicts and obstacles. Whatever is inside you will eventually be manifest on the outside, in your world. This takes some practice, of course, because we all succumb to doubting ourselves from time to time. But keep in mind, when this happens, you are using *your power against yourself.* If you think you are weak and powerless, you are 'intending' weakness and powerlessness. And that will be your state.

And never forget… *you are already in the process of life, co-creating the reality you awaken to each morning.* You are simply manifesting whatever your thought images and thinking processes have been telling your subjective mind to manifest. If it isn't what you want, then you know what you have to do is replace those undesirable thought images with pictures and feelings – the idea prototype – of what you DO want, and your subjective mind will do what it does naturally and produce the desirable outcome instead.

The instant you become aware of thoughts that create doubt, stop wherever you are and internally take charge, by affirming (loudly in the mind) STOP! It also helps to engage in some thought-taxing puzzle like those you would find in Mensa or some form of mental arithmetic; this forces the brain into logic and out of anxiety, allowing the mind room to settle. Once in control relax and imagine yourself sitting squarely in the middle of the life you desire, being and doing exactly what you want to do with joy, grace and ease. This will adjust your thought images back to where they must be to continue moving you toward your desired result.

This is the power you have inside of you – the key to living your desired purpose.

The ideal state is when *who you are* is congruent with *what you want*, and all your thought images and intentions are consistent with your desired goal. You don't need anyone's permission to do this. It is a natural human ability. Trust it. Just remember, it will take practice to hone your objective mind to the point where *you take control* of the natural process and design it to produce the outcome you want.

One more thing here…

Don't ask the universe for what you want in a submissive manner; take charge, have certainty. Declare it through your actions and your inner words. Then embody the attributes of one who can easily attain what you are after and immediately begin acting upon whatever comes up. And finally, see that your goal is for the greatest good of all – not selfish or out of a personal need. As architect of destiny, you will readily see that more value you bring the rewards will always be exponential. Intentions made both for your good *as well as* the greatest good of all will tend to build both abundantly and run through generations to come.

The desire has been given to you to fuel your mission on earth. It is your responsibility once that fire is lit, however, to fan it and provide it with greater oxygen, so it turns into a roaring furnace spreading like wildfire. When you think about well-established brands and commodities you will find it extremely difficult to pinpoint an advertisement that converted you. More times than not it was via word of mouth, loyal followers, who proudly propagate their use.

Remember, you are the one in charge of it. Let your target embody you, and always ensure utilisation of your secret weapon – the invincible power of your mind. Ensure the heat of your desire never diminishes; as the intensity increases, you will not be left with ashes... *but gold!... Now it's time to turn the page and learn to lead not only yourself, but the masses and generations to come.*

CHAPTER NINE

The Leader in You

Always lead, never follow, strike for perfection in everything you do. –
Henry Royce

The men were a quarter of a million miles away from home, the furthest distance
any human beings had ever voyaged. They were on an awe-inspiring yet perilous
journey. If victorious, they would be humanity's first step toward colonising the
stars. As the men gazed at the Earth, it appeared to have a life of its own. It was not
barren, in contrast to the other visible planets in the solar system. The Earth had
a refined quality as if it was communicating to the men and boasting its majestic
appearance as the prize of the galaxy, teeming with life. The blue and white swirls
resembled a marble that had come to life and one which had an appearance of
being so close within reach, yet simultaneously as distant as eternity.

Commander Neil Armstrong's voice crackled over the radio transmission
to Mission Control, and the signal began to rapidly fade; all communication
with Earth had been lost as if disappearing into the abyss, his heart palpitations
sped up. Beads of sweat relentlessly broke through his pores. With just minutes
to land, a deafening silence came over the craft, and this was immediately
followed by the jolting shock of screeching alarms that had been triggered by
the onboard landing computer. It was indicating dire warning of an overload.

Armstrong and Buzz Aldrin were on the craft, which had just entered lunar
orbit. The two men were beginning their descent towards the untouched
silver orb. They had no idea that their moon landing plans had already
been modified due to a miscalculation that had led to an overlooked effect
of Newtonian physics. Minutes before touchdown, their focus went to high
alert. Armstrong realised they were about to overshoot their landing site and
miss by as much as three miles.

If this happened, the result would be fatal, as the surface of the moon is
layered with countless boulders and craters. Even a slight degree from the

landing spot and the craft would either be hurled into space with no return possible, or they would crash. If they survived the crash, they would become stranded prisoners on the desolate and unforgiving moon until they painfully suffocated as the oxygen in the tanks in their suits became depleted.

The planned landing site had been precisely calculated, as it was comparatively smooth. With the modified flight plan, the astronauts urgently had to find another suitable place to land. Avoiding the multitude of large boulders and deep craters was essential, so Armstrong took the craft off autopilot and manually controlled its descent. Minutes flashed by at supersonic speeds, and with only 30 seconds of fuel left in the tank *it was now or never.*

The world held its collective breath in horror as the thread of communication evaporated, and the craft disappeared. *Suddenly there was no contact at all.*

Almost all of our thoughts are on autopilot. Even before you decide what to do, your brain has already chosen the response outside the limits of your conscious awareness. Tension and pressure draw out who you really are. Years of preparation for our space travellers had etched responses in their reactions and may have even reconfigured their genetic code. Millions of different variables synchronised and were calculated with no lapse of time or moment to consider beforehand. *Fight or flight* kicked in, triggering access to the entire brain and every cell within their bodies. The subconscious took charge, throwing the conscious mind into the back seat and buckling it down, then taking command over all other faculties. It was now in control of the dashboard.

Armstrong guided the *Eagle* softly down onto an undesignated landing site – *within moments, the signal of transmission reconnected and reached Earth in perhaps the most significant achievement in all of human history.*

Leadership on every level is exemplified in its truest form when preparation is so thorough that in moments when there is no time to think, instinct kicks in, *accessing the hidden knowledge, experience and information stored in every fibre of the body.* It is at this moment when visions of outcomes become so clear; the mind renders images so distinct that the universe has no choice but to construct the intangible image into reality: *its physical formation comes to fruition.*

Leadership on every level exemplified in its truest form when preparation is so thorough that in moments where there is no time to think, instinct kicks in accessing hidden knowledge and information stored in every fibre of the body and visions of outcomes become so clear that the mind renders images so distinct that the universe has no choice but to construct the intangible image into its physical formation.

In this chapter, we will be learning to lead, and leadership by essence, is the ability to thrive in uncertainty. If there is less certainty it means there are fewer boundaries, and if there are fewer boundaries, it naturally follows that there are fewer limits and what you are left with is more possibilities. You have to have faith that if you step off the map, you will not fall off of the edge of the world. When Columbus was told he would sail off the edge of the world, the reality was that he sailed off the edge of their map.

As a leader, your goal is to enable each individual to do their very best work. Empower them, become the example in a way that they too recognise the traits you possess reside in every one of them; as these rise to the surface, not only elevate them but transform your own growth to the next level.

Success breeds success.

Inside every EndGamer is a great leader waiting to emerge. But well before you can effectively lead others, you first learn to lead yourself.

And how do you do that?

By taking those authentic qualities you already have dwelling inside you, mixing them with the opportunities right in front of you, *and transforming your own life*.

Transformation has magnetism. It is an attracting force. Once transformed, you become an influencer, leading and inspiring others to do the same. That's how great leaders are made.

Leadership comes in many forms, and in its truest form is a selfless act and a result of taking charge and moving forward with genuine intention. A leader may not always be vocal. It is never the long-winded monologues but short, pithy speeches and potent words that strike chords with the heart and inspire generations. However, the most powerful way to move people is through your example and your actions; they always speak infinitely louder than words.

Whenever you notice something isn't right with yourself, your family, the nation or even the world – no matter who you are or what is going on – it's your responsibility to take the initiative, take immediate charge. You have been gifted with this life and the power that resides within you. It is there for a reason and is to be utilised in the very best way.

In a divided world, no sooner do divisions disappear in one area, they continue to reappear in some new form as racial tensions reduce, political or religious frictions increase. Peace cannot be achieved through unity in similarity, but through unity in diversity – by learning to enjoy comparisons while respecting and honouring everyone, irrespective of colour or creed. It's the only way we will achieve balance. Diversity is the only thing we all have in common. For centuries, the attempt to communicate that idea, or have people adopt tolerance of everyone, appears to have moved the needle only slightly. Everyone has a mandate in life, and everyone is playing their own role.

When addressing the students at Oxford University, Mark Cuban was asked what would be the very first thing he would do if he were to be voted president of the United States. His answer was pure brilliance. "I would first gather the people who didn't vote and understand why and look for some form of common ground and win them over." A nation is as strong as its shared vision. If we look at the term 'divide and conquer' it says it all. The quickest and most effective way to fragment countries, nations and citizens, even down to families and the world itself, is to divide them when they are quarrelling. When they are distracted, you can easily control them and then take over.

Stop for a moment and think of how ridiculous racism is: *one person is offended by the pigmentation of the skin of another human being.* Even so with religion, people have divided over ancient scripts thousands of years ago that would be impossible to validate, and all are open to interpretation from so many angles. The idea of a proof being in the realm of miracles can never be replicated, as each scripture claims its miracles; *hence, you are left with faith, feeling and emotions, which are purely subjective.* Furthermore, many parables are beautiful and artistically convey life lessons, and the human brain is designed to be stimulated and enriched by stories and not logic. Logic requires mental training of the highest calibre, whereas stories do not require such mental clarity. If you can convey your message in a picture, you can build upon understanding for anyone.

The ability to unite and move the masses in the direction of good is the cornerstone for any great leader; as the consumer of this book the level of understanding you have brings to you the responsibility to be a thought leader and one who leads generations to come.

Deciphering the qualities of a great leader is never a simple task, as there are countless variables. However, integrity and following one's own truth with the flexibility to change will always triumph over everything else.

What follows are seven traits of great leaders. Look at where in your life you have displayed these traits, then take ownership and recognition that these traits already reside within you; by recognition you evoke the state, bringing it to the surface for your own personal use.

- Leaders lead and never follow, they need no roadmap as they are the roadmap.
- Leaders calculate the odds and put contingency plans in place so when things appear to not go their way they have the ability to navigate around potential disasters.
- Leaders never settle for second best and carry an unspoken recognition that they stand in a league of their own.
- Leaders take ownership of life and full responsibility giving them creative control as an architect of destiny.
- Leaders are passionate about their mission taking the initiative always; by doing so the presence and energy brought to life creates a cascade of effects that reflects that energy right back to them, the fuel needed to continue.
- Leaders have the confidence to be original without concern for what others think, and they are wise enough to recognise that both support and challenge lead to growth.
- Leaders treat themselves and others with respect, giving of themselves without expecting anything in return; though the moments of being stern, harsh or even outbursts of anger may appear to the uninitiated as ego-driven, rather the master can recognise that it is an act of love to get the body of work delivered to the highest standard.

The leaders whose stories are relayed in the journals of time come from all walks of life. With so many industries emerging and information being discovered at truly astronomical rates, never have we needed more leaders to help direct the masses. Art, music, technology, healthcare and fashion are evolving faster than ever. When you follow your authentic path and are sincere about what you do, others naturally follow. That is the point where you capture momentum and take the lead.

One such example is David Gandy, the world's only international male supermodel. You might think that to achieve such a status, Gandy himself would have aspired to model from an early age or that he at least had some inclination to pursue a career in fashion as he grew older.

But Gandy's beginnings resembled nothing of the sort.

Born in Essex, England, to working-class parents who ran a property and freight company, Gandy aspired to become a veterinary surgeon. But his grades weren't good enough. So, with no real plan in mind, he enrolled in university – the 'cookie cutter' thing to do – and was a mediocre student at best.

Then quite serendipitously, the opportunity that set him on the path to his illustrious career showed up. While working part-time and attending the University of Gloucestershire, Gandy's flatmate entered him into a model-search competition on a British daytime television program without telling him.

On June 2001, 21-year-old Gandy won the competition, which included a modelling contract with an agency in London. That was enough. That was all Gandy needed to take charge of his life and begin making things happen.

In his own authentic style, Gandy brought masculinity to male fashion. He noticed a fundamental flaw in the male modelling industry: a world dominated by slender men could never create any real momentum, and men themselves never aspire to be thin. Men generally neglected fashion as a subsequent by-product of this approach. Gandy chose to ignore the rules and came forward with a solid muscular frame, naturally attracting attention and evolving into the much-needed role model, bringing back the consummate English gentleman to once again take pride in how he dressed.

As you can see, Gandy didn't set out to be a leader. He simply took what life offered him, infused it with his own unique set of gifts and abilities, poured his heart into it, and transformed himself into a person of influence and renown. And he did it by the most powerful means possible – embodiment and example.

In other words, he led himself first.

The significance of this truth cannot be overstated because leading, or influencing, by example is not just one quality of a leader... *it is THE ultimate requirement!*

Gandy's fine physique and stunning good looks may have kicked off his modelling career, but it's who Gandy is *inside* that made him into the influencer he is today.

"What I have learned is that being a gentleman isn't about what you do, or what you wear, it's about how you behave and who you are." – David Gandy

Not only that, he is the perfect example of a leader going from strength to strength, as Gandy capitalised on his earliest opportunity and subsequent success to explore many other ventures as well, from launching his own fashion line to various charitable works. People may argue that he was born with good looks, but realise this: so were thousands of other male models. It is not what you are born with; it is what you do with what you are born with. The world rewards us for our original efforts and fearless pursuits.

If there is anything we can learn from Gandy's example, it is the importance of making the most of every opportunity… to take what we've been given and with it build a legacy.

What lies behind us and what lies before us are tiny matters compared to what lies within us. – Ralph Waldo Emerson

We will now continue our exploration of further qualities that make up the consummate leader. Take a moment and pause after each one as you reflect on it with understanding:

- Leaders inspire others to excellence by making the very best of who they are and what they have. Think about doing whatever you do at a world-class level. Most people settle for mediocre. Differentiate yourself by aiming for the best.
- Leaders are self-reliant. They are humble enough to accept direction and ideas from others, but what differentiates them is that they trust their intellect and reasoning abilities, they think for themselves, and they make decisions based on facts without bias or emotional attachment.
- Leaders continually strive to improve. 'Failure' is not in their vocabulary. They may suffer temporary defeat or run into obstacles along the way to victory, but they are never down for the count.
- Leaders do not set themselves above others. They are aware of their own attributes *and* shortcomings. In an interview at MIT when Charlie Munger was asked what made him and Warren Buffett so competent, his answer was profound *"It is not a competency if you do not know the edge of it. We do not go beyond that; we know our competency better than other people do."*

At first glance, that comment may appear as if he is capping his potential. It is, in fact, quite the opposite. Recognising your strengths unlocks your potential, so you use your mind to leverage off the strengths of others or other forces. Look at it this way: if you want to fly to Mars, you cannot rely on your strength to leap. You can, however, rely on rocket fuel or the development of anti-matter devices utilising the minds of scientists to figure out formulas and create the materials to make that a reality.

- Leaders do not seek to please others. They aren't afraid to speak the truth, and they aren't afraid to say no. This quality provides the distance you need to gain clarity on your task and focus on its creation.

Steve Jobs illustrated this beautifully in the following quote:

People think focus means saying yes to the thing you've got to focus on. But that's not what it means at all. It means saying no to the hundred other good ideas that there are. You have to pick carefully. I'm as proud of the things we haven't done as the things I have done. Innovation is saying no to 1000 things.

Discovering the Leader in You

How do you discover this higher version of yourself… this leader waiting to emerge?

Over a decade, I have worked privately one-on-one with individuals across the entire spectrum of culture and class, using different techniques without conforming to a traditional framework. What I found was that I never did anything for anyone other than help them see truths about themselves that they had been denying. The brutal honesty about their potential to change was enough to get people on track and surprise themselves. This is one of the secrets I use to create champions. It's the same for a person breaking a sales record or an athlete winning gold. It's about breaking an imaginary plateau in the mind of the person and getting them to see a result before it ever materialises and then bridging the gap to reality.

Self-Discovery is Everything

As much as books, lectures and seminars help, our own experience teaches volumes if we listen. That's why dogma is so dangerous. Dogmatic individuals will always claim as fact what they've been taught by others whom they've allowed to do their thinking for them. Without the flexibility to question, they wreak havoc. There are good people in all races, religions, creeds and colours, and true Endgamers are never dogmatic. Remember to keep company with those that ask questions and steer clear of those who claim to know all the answers.

Discovering the leader in you is about having a vision. It's 'legacy thinking', which means investing in yourself while simultaneously seeing the potential in others and investing in them.

Become what you aspire to be. Scooter Braun saw the potential in a 12-year-old Justin Bieber. Cus D'Amato saw the potential in a street boy named Tyson. Gates saw the potential in home computers becoming a global industry. Jobs saw the future in creating something that was aesthetically pleasing and practical in every sense. Musk went toe-to-toe with multiple industries, including oil which, for centuries, has refuted any and all ideas toward alternate energy sources.

In each case, you'll find that the road is difficult. Establishing a foundation for a new idea has never been glamorous. But fortune favours the strong. Survival of the fittest provides a playground that is fair. The opportunity to become a leader in your chosen path no longer requires physical prowess, culture or social class.

The prerequisite is something we all equally share. In much the same way as we share time and the air we breathe, we share the ability to imagine! Anyone can cultivate an idea in the fertile ground of their imagination, using the strength of the mind. We are all given equal potential; it's just a matter of using what you've been given and never giving up until your mind images become your reality.

Right now, you stand on the precipice of launching into a whole new world. By focusing on continuous improvement at every level, inspiring and developing anyone in eyesight or earshot of you, the leader in you is crafted relative to what you see those around you need.

It may be through challenging or supporting them (which is where emotional intelligence comes in), being acutely aware of what is needed at the moment and delivering it with finesse. Throughout this book, I have deliberately encouraged the refining of your character because it is your personality that puts you in a position of sustained organic growth. You are the only one who can lead you to where you want to be; no one else can or will.

The unique leader you are evolving into creates opportunities that other leaders can't. This is how you create a legacy and how, in turn, people naturally follow you without question. We unconsciously gravitate to those leaders who truly add value to the world. Their leadership earns a 'standalone' reputation, which transcends their own industry. They become iconic – ironically by teaching people to initiate themselves and become leaders in their own right. In turn, you become the ultimate leader.

Set yourself in the direction of leadership as you easily absorb and apply what you are reading in this chapter. Become a symbol of possibility to others. Look at the history of the greats who, irrespective of what era in history they lived, their examples remain timeless. Like the explorers and adventures of old, let your virtues, your life works and your creations continue to live in the minds and hearts of generations to come.

The effective leader's map of prosperity is impenetrable, irrespective of what conditions to the senses. With an etched bias in their DNA toward truth and not ego, the leader is able to provide the flexibility necessary for progress. Biography, or even history, are artful descriptions, though never a prerequisite – the effective leader writes his own history.

Take, for example, Mustafa Kemal Atatürk, widely regarded as one of the greatest leaders of the 20th century – a centennial for him was declared by the United Nations and UNESCO, still remaining as the only person to receive such recognition. In 1916, during the First World War, after centuries of global rule, the Ottoman Empire was on its last legs. This Major Commander was the underdog, and yet he was able to stage a battle of such magnitude, resulting in the victorious expulsion of the sheer might of all the combined colonialist powers of Britain, France and Russia. The victory was so ingenious and well-calculated, and to this very day still earns respect and even celebration by those nations who attempted to conquer his land. The aftermath of the battle had Atatürk dismantle a fallen empire and resurrect an entire nation. In doing so, he established the sovereign state of Turkey. Atatürk had no model to go by, no fable to follow or roadmap from history. He wrote his own chapter for his nation. A national hero and a great symbol of possibility was born.

You, the mothers who sent their sons from faraway countries, wipe away your tears; your sons are now lying in our bosom and are in peace. After having lost their lives on this land, they have become our sons as well – Mustafa Kemal Atatürk

The Language of Your Body

It is accurate to say that every part of you is whispering your truth if you just listen. Your body is a total feedback mechanism. From physical illness to psychological pain, your body and mind continually nudge you towards growing and improving as long as you are willing to correct whatever is going on as you discover it. Observe the events of your life because paying attention to your body through present moment awareness – both physically and emotionally – is of paramount importance.

When I first discovered this reality, it was a moment of 'satori' or 'sudden enlightenment'. As you recall from my earlier story, at one point in my life I suffered from excruciating, debilitating back pain. A specialist ran scans that indicated collapsing discs. My logical conclusion was to either fix it or build enough muscular development in the lumbar area to support and compensate for the damage.

That's when I started searching and discovering my own truth. As bizarre as it seems, my back pain was not the result of any physical abnormality or injury. Rather, it was a cry for help; it was my body begging me to take ownership and charge of my life by confronting my inner demons and making changes. In other words, the physical pain was phantom.

The body learns through association. So if you are in pain and someone tells you your pain is due to poor posture or over-training and you allow that idea to take root, then your body starts behaving as if it is real. This is why obliterating ideas that don't serve you is one of the only ways to move ahead. You must learn to condition both mind and body to respond optimally in the direction of your goals and desires.

The organs weep the tears the eyes refuse to shed. – Sir William Osler, 18th-century physician

The late Dr John Sarno, orthopaedic surgeon and acclaimed expert on the subject of the mind–body connection, came to the conclusion that millions of back pain sufferers are experiencing signals from the brain resulting in painful spasms. Also, these assumptions have been clinically documented. In an overwhelming majority of cases, all that is necessary for the pain to stop is a change of signals. The pain itself, in fact, is harmless and not indicative of any physical abnormality. So even though the scans show misalignments in columns and abrasion in the spinal discs, according to Dr Sarno, it is almost always harmless. A cross-section of people scanned showed that most people have similar wear and tear in the spine and never experience any pain whatsoever.

So, had I believed the scan and acted on the doctor's premise that I needed spinal fusion, strengthening, etc., to correct my back pain, I would have gotten nowhere.

Not only that, but what the doctors failed to tell me was that the spine starts to deteriorate in all of us around the age of 20. It is therefore normal and to be expected, just like when someone's hair turns grey. It's certainly not a sign that something is wrong. Had I not discovered the truth, I would've been spinning my wheels forever.

This all makes sense when you understand that the subconscious mind is the builder of the body, the intelligence instructing us to develop according to design; think about it: you started off as one cell there was an intelligence causing you to develop, take shape and form. It is now time to use both your intellect and intuition by expanding your awareness to what is really going on, and you do this by recognising the feedback from both.

Nature demonstrates this universal truth in a myriad of ways. For instance, leave breadcrumbs on the cabinet long enough and you will soon have a trail of ants making good on your oversight. There is universal intelligence in the behaviour of ants, knowledge transmitted in an unseen field that allows them to innately sense (via pheromonal scent) when food is nearby. What do you suppose is orchestrating that?

In the same way, goats can detect signs in the mountains that they follow to more nourishing pastures in order to satisfy and sustain their needs.

Is it not logical then that this same intelligence – the initial First Cause that directed the creation of the universe – would put signs in front of you and me?

Indeed, if this intelligence can govern ants and goats… and your own growth and development from a single cell into a living, breathing, viable human being… this same intelligence can communicate to and through your body using language that your mind and spirit understand.

We presume shooting stars are a rarity. However, they frequently occur in the night sky, if only you could see them. In the same way, signs that direct you to your destination and the next logical step in your journey are right before you every day. You just have to expand your awareness and wake up to what's going on in your life to see them. This is why bringing your awareness and directing your mind with clarity to what you desire is so important; this helps filter out the continual bombardment of unrelated information.

Besides, life is more fun when you become like Sherlock Holmes, observant and aware of the mysteries unravelling right before your very eyes that will lead you to your own pot of gold – *your destiny*.

Many such clues are delivered to you through your emotions. Every emotion is a message, a lesson, a signal for you to pay attention to. By learning to listen, you can understand the message your emotions are communicating to you.

Are your emotional charges telling you to take ownership of a disowned part of yourself? Is the charge reminding you to change your interpretation of a redundant signal so you can upgrade how you think? Are your emotions pulling you to acknowledge the truth about yourself with balance so you maintain an emotional equilibrium? Pay attention to your emotions and the messages your body is trying to deliver through physical pain and dis-ease.

Work diligently on understanding the following examples so you can use your emotions more effectively instead of allowing them to control you. In essence, learn to control how you feel, and you will develop greater power in all that you do. Getting caught up in emotions, particularly negative ones, for hours and sometimes days wastes valuable energy and time. You are reading this because you are en route to doing something special. You can't afford the luxury of sitting around and dwelling on 'imaginary' mistakes – mistakes that can be mined for the truth about yourself that needs confronting and changing.

Living Authentically

You see someone being arrogant or self-righteous, and it triggers some negative emotional state in you. Look for the areas in your own life where you have portrayed those same behaviours. *Continually take ownership of the traits you despise.* This practice will not only humble you but will cause these negative aspects of your own character to wane and eventually disappear.

Jealousy. Should you experience jealousy, it is your emotions trying to teach you to learn about detachment. If it is directed toward a person, stop taking ownership of that person and recognise that people are only ever faithful to themselves. When we pull away from someone, they unconsciously drawback toward us – an important lesson to become aware of. If the jealousy is toward something you want that someone else has and you don't, stop wasting energy on that! Look at what they have or what they've accomplished as inspiration, knowing that whatever that is – and more – is also possible for you! Further, if you investigate, you may just discover that what you wish for you already have in a different form; if it is wealth, it may be in the contacts or in the idea you are about to deliver. Then move forward and pay the price to make it happen.

Fear. If you experience fear over a real threat, this is natural, and you should respond by moving yourself to safety. However, 99% of the fear we experience is a false alarm. A great example of this is public speaking – the number one phobia in the world. With the majority of people, the body responds as if they are under threat. The easiest way to deal with this emotion is to change your interpretation. By doing so, your brain starts to encode it differently. Tell yourself that what you're feeling is excitement, and pivot whatever fearful thoughts that were appearing into the image of success.

These are examples of how you listen and communicate your emotions honestly, from your heart to yourself, being truthful about what is going on without catastrophising. When we speak honestly from the heart, not only to ourselves but to others, it resonates as truth. Our truth.

Why does this matter? Because you cannot speak truth to others – as great leaders do – *until you can listen and speak the truth to yourself.*

This is just one way to lead yourself that allows you to then lead by example. When you allow your own light, your own truth, to shine, you permit others to do the same. Then, and only then, do you become the person that others want more than anything to learn from, to emulate, and to follow.

Just like the great leaders of the past whose exemplary light and truth continue to shine for us today, the light of your own truth becomes timeless, continuing to shine in the hearts and minds of generations to come.

The Power of the Intellect

While leaders continually strive to learn and improve, they do not equate the mere accumulation of facts and figures (intelligence) with intellect (critical thinking) – the ability to use the mind – which is something altogether different.

Have you ever wondered what the difference is between a doctor graduating from medical school and the one-in-a-million doctor who discovers a breakthrough cure? Or between the architect who designs cheap housing and the architect the likes of Henry Young Darracott Scott, who designed the Royal Albert Hall?

The distinct difference is not in the information they gather and learn. It is in the development of the mind. Intellect is developed by asking questions, meditating on answers, exploring truth, evaluating and reasoning. Intellect is the ability to create something original without attempting to be original.

Intellect is where ideas and opportunities for outstanding achievements come from, and the subsequent ability to lead others becomes a by-product of those achievements.

Moreover, just like you cannot become a great athlete without developing and strengthening the necessary muscles, you cannot make use of the power of your intellect without exercising it. The mind is a muscle, you see, and just like other muscles in the body, it is only developed and strengthened with use.

All too often, we are impressed by credentials. Nevertheless, it is the results – *real-life results* – that count. This is the truth that is often missed: *results are always the reward of thinking.*

It was July 2002, the Royal Albert Hall; I had briefly met Dana White in the UFC's Octagon after their first historic UK event. We had shared some pleasantries and had a brief word or two about matchmaking. I was writing for *Combat* magazine at the time. Dana had recently orchestrated a deal that had two friends purchase a year earlier the failing company the UFC for only $2 million pocket change for any entrepreneur. Dana became the CEO and took full charge, resulting in building the fastest-growing sport in the world, and in 2016 having grown into a juggernaut, was instrumental in selling the company for $4.6 billion. Come 2020 a pandemic could not stop this man's vision; with professional sports in lockdown White marched forward and did the unthinkable. The intent was not only a platform for his staff and employees, but it was also a symbol of hope when the world had plummeted into the depths of hell.

Dana was not an anointed leader rallying for support; he was and is his own support setting a current which the world of sport now follows.

Dana by no means is on this planet to win a popularity contest; further, he was just your everyday boxing fan and, at best, a mediocre promoter, yet this diamond in the rough created the unthinkable; it's time to take some lessons.

Observing Dana White over the years, I noticed in his interviews White spoke about capitalising on something apparent. The raw material of the UFC was a competitive arena where two gladiators go head-to-head, it struck something innate in the human psyche; there was something there that just needed to be packaged in a way that would have the masses hooked. White also revered the business acumen of the likes of Vince McMahon, CEO of WWE, a titan in his respective industry; there is plenty to learn from his meteoric rise to the top. White needed a degree in economics or marketing; what he had was far more valuable, and that was a vision. White had an immersion in the world of sports, a robust idea of how things should be done and the willingness to test; with no predetermined roadmap to go by, White was forced to draw the map and lay down a blueprint for creating something out of nothing! Authenticity exudes from his very presence he is not a showman, just an American dream speaking his truth as the legions of fans and the world of sport follow his lead

If anything, his provocative style and straightforward cut to the chase manner has created many haters. However, what White illustrates clearly is that the entity the business being built cannot have emotional attachments; rather the end goal needs to be viewed as such without attachment to persons or bias for even personal gain. This is about legacy, and legacy takes no prisoners on the path to victory.

Not only did White reconstruct and build a fallen company into a household name, not even a global pandemic had the might to stop his momentum. White single-handled created record-breaking shows when the world had ground to a halt, illustrating how one person's vision can triumph over any odds, obliterate any probability and slay any statistics.

Use Intellect

The person exercising intellect is the one who thinks independently, like the soldier in Nazi Germany who said, "No, this is wrong," and walked away. Or Rosa Parks, one of the pioneers in the civil rights movement. Or Giordano Bruno, who championed the Copernican system of astronomy, which placed the sun – not the earth – at the centre of the solar system. He opposed the stultifying authority of the Church and his country in order to choose the truth. Though he was burned at the stake, the truth he revealed and his essence has echoed through history; he is one of the rare few who are immortal.

The Power of Habit

Typically, when we think of habits, we think of behaviour. However, habitual behaviour is nothing more than the fruit of habitual *thinking*. Negative habit patterns of thinking are the root cause of negative behaviour patterns that keep you stuck in your current reality or whatever issue you are struggling with.

To continually improve and grow yourself into the influential leader you were destined to be, you must be able to get unstuck, to create changes in your own life. And to move from whatever your less desirable, current reality is to your new, more desirable reality, you have to cross the bridge that lies between them.

Simply stated, the 'bridge' takes you from what you currently believe to be true about you and about your world (negative habit patterns of thinking) to a new set of beliefs that will, in turn, create the new reality you seek. And the way you cross the bridge is by using your *intellect* to discover, evaluate, challenge and change your current limiting beliefs.

As an emerging leader, a fine mental exercise to develop your intellect would be to consider the questions you are already asking yourself and how they may be working against you.

Questions like…

"Why can't I ever lose weight?"

"Why do I always blow up a potentially healthy relationship?"

Or, "Why have I not achieved the level of success I am after?"

Stop and think for a moment. Evaluate how these types of questions would keep you stuck in a current reality that you don't want… preventing you from moving toward a more positive reality, one that you *do* want.

Once you raise the question in your mind, your subconscious immediately goes to work to answer it and then affirm and fulfil that reality. So the logical, rational way to get unstuck would be to create new questions that would then prompt your subconscious mind to get to work affirming and fulfilling a new reality.

And here's where emotional signals will come to your aid.

If you find yourself down and discouraged, lacking energy and motivation to move in the direction of your new reality, employ the use of your intellect to explore what you're *thinking* in the present moment (awareness) that would cause such negative, disempowering emotions.

That's step one.

Then step two is to *change the questions you're asking yourself 180 degrees*. Turn whatever negative thought you're telling yourself... or the negative, debilitating question you're asking yourself... into its mirror opposite.

So, instead, you might ask yourself:

Why is it so easy for me to lose weight and get in shape?

Why do healthy, positive relationships come naturally to me?

Why do I always have more money than I need?

And remember, the goal is not to come up with an answer. The magic behind this method is that you're directing your mind to think *differently* about your situation.

At first glance, you may think you are lying to yourself. In fact, not only are you stating the truth (all that you have said is an absolute possibility), you are forcing your mind to come up with creative solutions and justify why you believe it is true. As you remember from earlier chapters, belief lights up the entire brain, allowing you greater access to latent abilities.

Millions of individuals, as well as organisations, spend billions of dollars each year on traditional 'how to succeed' methods, with very little change to show for it. That's because you can't fix whatever current reality you are stuck in with 'why-to's'.

If you are serious about change, then focus on asking the right *why* questions – those that cause your subconscious to begin working to transform your new reality. Embrace the possibilities, and then systematically start replacing unproductive behaviours with new, more productive ones.

Exercise the muscles of your intellect to start digging up your subconscious 'why not-to's' and replace them with 'why-to's'... and you'll be crossing that bridge to your new reality in no time.

The Power of Your Story

Do you know why I share so many stories of EndGamers in this book?

Because stories are powerful; they are inspirational, engender hope and inspire. The right story at the right time can even change your life. Hearing how someone else overcame similar challenges, solved the same problem or improved a shared situation illustrates clearly the potential for change.

It stands to reason then that one of the most powerful tools a leader can use to influence others is the story of his or her own personal journey of transformation. In fact, the story of your own transformation may be the most impactful influencing method of all.

This is another reason you must first lead yourself before you can lead others. Without your own story of struggle and triumph, what proof do you have to show that you can lead someone else out of their darkness to the light of their own truth?

Stages of Leadership

One of the most exciting – and humbling – aspects of allowing the leader in you to emerge is the people you can begin to help by simply being your authentic self, embracing opportunities and living out the truth of who you are.

There are various perspectives of leadership: those who seem to lead naturally, those who develop into notable influencers, leading by example, and those who are appointed to leadership positions as a function of their job or career.

Unfortunately, many in the latter category have not earned the right to lead. Moreover, when that happens, people only follow if they think they have to. This is, of course, not a level of leadership to strive toward.

However, once you learn to lead yourself, you'll notice that others are naturally attracted to you because of your own transformation experience, and they will *want* to follow you. This is the beginning of your opportunity to influence by example, establishing a trust-based relationship and mutual respect.

Then as you continue to grow and your own leadership qualities mature, you may find more and more opportunities opening up, allowing you to influence a greater number of people on a larger scale. You begin to acquire a reputation for being a person of stature and positive change.

Once this level has been achieved, the possibilities and the potential for influencing others are virtually unlimited. You can choose to handpick people to develop deeper mentoring relationships with. You can begin developing other leaders by recreating your journey in process form.

Leaders at this level bear greater responsibility, of course, but they can also be major change agents for the greater good.

Just remember, to lead well you must embrace your own need for continual improvement. Because, if you recall, one trait of great leaders is a continual striving to improve.

And, of course, it goes without saying that everything you do must be done in the spirit of service and with the utmost attention to quality. Your reputation is on the line; never allow it to be compromised with anything less than your best.

Experiencing the Flow

As a leader pushing toward mastery, at some point you may find yourself experiencing an optimal state of consciousness, characterised by increased mental clarity and a peak level of performance. In this state, commonly known as 'the flow', ideas, insights and creativity come much more quickly, without the typical inhibitions or internal resistance.

This phenomenon is the result of neurobiological and neurochemical activity in the brain incited in times of intense focus and intent, and the naturally occurring neurochemicals supporting this state of being are among some of the most addictive drugs known. The more you become aware of this state, the more regular it will appear. These power states, once re-lived or recalled, help the body once again create those same feelings. Much like when you remember a happy memory or daydream about something you are looking forward to, the body begins naturally to trigger those feelings once again.

One of the greatest illustrations of being in 'the flow' occurred at the 1980 Winter Olympic Games and involved the US Hockey Team and their coach, Herb Brooks. And it also ranks as one of the greatest examples of leadership genius in recorded history.

Here's the backstory

The Soviet Hockey Team was a force to be reckoned with. They had won every gold medal in hockey since the 1960 games. In international meets, they had outscored opponents 175–44. They destroyed the National Hockey League All-Star team 6–0 in 1979, with a backup goalie. The term 'unrivalled' comes to mind, and for a good reason. They trained year-round, practising three times a day, and most of them had been playing together for ten years or longer.

The US team, on the other hand, was put together less than a year before the 1980 Games, mostly a collection of college kids from the University of Minnesota and the University of Boston (two programs that historically hated each other).

They essentially had a half-year to train and then a gruelling 60-exhibition-game schedule leading up to the Olympics.

Their challenge was unprecedented. So, Herb employed a unique set of strategies and some rather questionable tactics to get them ready. In short, he pushed them to the brink.

Tensions ran high. Players were at odds. Fights broke out on more than one occasion.

But Herb didn't get off course. He stuck to his original vision and followed through with the strategic plan he had put in place.

And then, lo and behold, there came a turning point... and from that moment forward, there was nothing Herb could do to break them. In a word, they gelled.

To such a degree, in fact, that after travelling through a massive blizzard to play an exhibition game in Minnesota, their plane clipped a pole on take-off, requiring the pilot to land at the end of the runway. As the plan couldn't back up on its own, all the players got off the plane and physically pushed it back to the start of the runway.

With very little time to prepare, this team effort forced all the players to dig deep and discover a side of themselves that they had never known.

In all positions of leadership – be it in sports, business or even war – you find that the troops are always a reflection and expression of the man or woman at the top.

The game had already been won in the minds of Herb and the players before they even stepped foot on the ice. Herb led himself to believe in victory and infused that conviction into every player. They took themselves to a place where the battle was not against the Soviets; it was against their own limiting ideas of what was possible.

When the Games opened, the odds of the US team winning gold were 1000 to 1.

Still... they won.

And they did it by getting in 'the flow'.

To this day, every player admits there's no way they could have ever beaten the Soviets and won the gold without Herb.

Herb was a real leader and a real-life example of what is possible for a leader to accomplish.

Right here... right now... you have no idea what you can accomplish. But it's time you accept the challenge and find out.

Lead yourself.

And then lead others in your world on to the greatest victory of their lives.

CHAPTER TEN

Thought Creates Legacy

Starting from something smaller than an atom, inflation can create an infinite space inside of it, containing infinitely many galaxies, without affecting the exterior space. – Max Tegmark

Author of *Our Mathematical Universe* and professor of physics at MIT, Max Tegmark expounds ideas about quantum theory and cosmology. I mention this here because I think it beneficial to expand your thinking and consider things that, at a glance, may seem unlikely. If infinite space can be created inside something as small as an atom, what do you think might be contained within your idea?

Suppose the initial component that set the universe in motion was smaller than an atom yet contained infinite space and an eternity of possibilities. In that case, we can surmise that whatever power was inherent at that moment is still inside of you, as you are part of that universe.

In the Presence of a Master

"Dominic: update me, what you are doing, what is your endgame and why aren't you there yet?"

I had just arrived at one of the most exclusive nightclubs in Mayfair. It was a little past 3 a.m. on an early Friday morning.

The bartender slid me a Don Julio 1942 – my drink of choice and I tuned in for a brief moment to experience its crispy agave nectar and a hint of citrus.

I headed toward the smoke-filled Green Room, a private section of the club. The music reverberated to my core. I felt a tap on my shoulder, and, looking around, I was greeted by Jason McNab, an extraordinarily successful but very private London hedge fund manager. He is also heavily involved in film and working with Hollywood's elite.

A tall, rugged, strong-featured man sporting shoulder-length hair and a biker jacket, McNab's presence itself is magnetising. He has navigated life by relying on his internal instincts, mapping out his journey to the shores of paradise by the signs and signals he perceives in life itself. Instead of getting direction through formulas, experts and books, as I have, McNab writes his own recipe based on keen observation and personal life experience. While others focus on the media attention of the masses, he has no interest, staying private and caring about the respect and love of his family, peers and those at the very pinnacle of industry who share his morality.

I have never met a better example of one who honours their own truth as the highest ideal, unfazed by the opinions of others – that Friday at 3 a.m. I found myself with a master, and by the time we parted, I felt as if I were Luke Skywalker in the presence of Yoda himself.

Getting back to our conversation, he asked me: "What is your edge? What are you doing right now to reverse engineer what you want to achieve?"

His provocative questions caught me off guard. I attempted to answer, but I realised my words had no substance. I found myself regurgitating someone else's truth instead of my own, a mere intellectual in the presence of an Intellect.

McNab listened, waited. Then, over the next half hour, he became one of the key figures who changed my life. He broke down my background, personality and life experience, the direction I was heading and his wisdom and intuition were beyond uncanny. After all, I had only met him socially amongst friends on a couple of occasions.

My training is in the sciences, but there are many moments in life that cannot be explained in terms of plausible science. Could telepathy be accurate, or is there another way to tap into the billions of bits of information travelling through our senses in every moment? Freud once said, "We leak the truth." Could one interpret this as a statement more spiritual than scientific?

That morning I learned that whatever the explanation when you take time to observe someone without bias, judgement or preconceived ideas, you can see and understand a great deal about them. With Jason McNab, there was nothing to hide behind. The protective veneer I routinely wore for the rest of the world became tiny as a freckle on my cheek. I could see how Jason McNab was instrumental in wielding billion-dollar accounts, strategically guiding the best of the best within both the entertainment and financial industries and how he had now become this avatar of success in the secret world of the elite.

One of the many things I find so fascinating about McNab is how he evaluates a business idea. He takes the potential product and looks at it from three angles. First: he sees the external design of a thing, observing its aesthetics objectively. Next: he looks at it through the lens of human psychology; how people will emotionally respond and react to it. Finally: once the idea is implemented, he evaluates the metrics as they come in – because numbers never lie.

McNab explained how integrity is sacred and that if you act with absolute long-term genuine loyalty and credibility, you will always defeat those short-term 'traders'. They survive on angles and a zero-sum game. He continued to explain that you must honestly know your edge and 'laser-beam' your focus on it. Have clarity in your Endgame, and then you can reverse engineer it move-by-move.

If you think of yourself as your product, applying sufficient and thoughtful execution, any idea you put forth has the potential to produce the result you are after. If you begin with the end in mind, you can choose the means to create. You can systematically map the necessary steps back to achieve that Endgame.

As Jason McNab did with me, I want to challenge you. It's time you recognise your own worth! Put yourself in the position to be who you want to be and orchestrate the life you want to lead. Take the required steps to get there. The consistent and mindful effort serves to make you stronger and is a necessary component of your journey. As much as we like to speculate about luck, no one truly gets lucky. One cannot fake strength of character or tenacity. Those are things you learn by doing and by being.

A couple of days after my conversation with McNab, I became aware of the riches on a project I had been holding back on for some time. Within this particular plan lay an untapped treasure – a source of income that I had overlooked and would exceed my greatest financial expectations. It seemed that somehow the universe had organised itself on my behalf to deliver the wealth I was seeking in the most unexpected way.

When I look back at that period of time now, I can see where passing comments from friends, other indicators and subtle signs had been nudging me in that direction all along. You don't need to know what this hidden asset was for me as your acres of diamonds will be different from mine, but one thing is for sure: they will always be situated directly under your feet. My encounter with McNab simply woke me to the power of what was already present in my world.

Yesterday You Said Tomorrow

Nike get it right: they understand that people are crying out for something in which to believe. Companies with a rich heritage stand the test of time because they possess the secret ingredient of belief; they inspire in you the idea that you, too, have the potential to make your mark on the planet. Nike's legacy is demonstrated in a simple swoosh mark that carries the positive challenge to us all: *Just do it!*

Phil Knight was your average mid-distance runner: on the track team, an observant student, looking for an advantage in speed, thinking that everything serves a purpose.

Knight noticed that his track coach at the University of Oregon, Bill Bowerman, modified running shoes. These modifications resulted in an immediate improvement in the athlete who wore them. Over the ensuing years, Knight travelled back and forth from Japan to the United States and studied business – cut-throat, first hand. Back in his home town obstacles appeared in his path, threatening to stifle the growth of this sleeping giant.

For the first 18 years after the company's conception, Knight was nearly always in debt. He maintained a philosophy that one incorrect move could bankrupt the company. Knight stared failure in the face almost every day from his company's creation in the early 60s, right up to the 1980s. Low on funds, they hired a student, paying them $35 to develop the company logo. A swoosh, a tick; Nike was born.

There was a period of time where other sports companies, threatened by the momentum of Nike, dug up rare taxation and pushed it forward as a strategic move to collapse the emerging giant. Faced with a tax bill that would cripple the company and put it out permanently, Nike had to find a way out or crumble. In this dark hour, they conceived an unconventional way out.

Nike had a factory in Exeter, NH, making 15,000 pairs a month. In a stroke of equal parts madness and genius, they asked themselves, "What if we created a second line? Knocked off ourselves, selling to discount retailers at a very low but marginally profitable price. No one could copy us closer than we could copy ourselves." When this first came up in a brainstorming session, everybody laughed at its absurdity… but the whole law was absurd. And it eventually evolved into, "Let's try it." Thus, the One Line was born, which sold a couple of thousand pairs in the following couple of years and reduced the increase in duties by two-thirds. This helped the company stay afloat long enough to breathe and create a way out of the dilemma.

The pressure of the competitors brought out the ingenuity necessary not only to survive but to thrive – an embodiment of Nike's own brand and beliefs.

Both support and challenge are necessary for the success of your objectives. You may discover that challenges inspire even greater outcomes, as the hero is determined by the size of his opponent. Resistance assists you in your endeavours by signifying that you are on to something and are on the right track.

Nike is one of those internationally recognised brands with a heritage to be proud of, one which hails back to Steve Prefontaine, a now-deceased runner, whose passion for better equipment inspired co-founder Bill Bowerman and CEO Phil Knight to create the Nike empire.

Today Nike actively recognises their legacy of extraordinary people working in collaboration as an intrinsic part of their culture. Like all great stories, they inspire and motivate, encouraging others to do the same.

If you analyse any successful company, you always find that each one eases and improves the condition of human life and elicits feelings of progress; a better life, a better world. Success comes to companies who provide the very things we all want.

What You Say on the Inside Echos on the Outside

It's never too late, to be the person you might have been. – George Eliot.

As you well know by our thorough discussion of this topic in earlier chapters, your inner dialogue has the potential to either create your reality or destroy it. Let's look at its power from a couple of different angles.

When you see someone with a tranquil and fulfilling life, you can be sure their inner monologue is also quiet. Someone who lives in a chaotic external world is simply mirroring the chaos going on inside their minds. Never, ever underestimate the power of the words inside your head. Develop an inner dialogue that works to build you up and support your dream.

Politicians are often condemned for saying one thing in order to gain the most votes from their constituency, but once voted into office perform in an altogether contradictory fashion. However before you criticise the guilty politician, you may want to ensure that you live mindfully and consistent with what you say, not only to the outside world but also to yourself. As you allow your intention and words to harmonise, you will recognise the difficulty and challenges. In doing this, you will naturally become less judgmental of others, increasing your own sense of positivity. It is cyclical. Like begets like.

When you see two athletes about to compete, if you have competed in the past you will observe a greater level of respect in yourself. You know that they truly know what a monumental task is to put oneself on the front line. It is like this when one has done the work to specify one's inner dialogue. When you meet someone who is consistent in the way they reflect their perceptions of others and their own goals and achievements, you will recognise a likeness.

We can tell ourselves we believe in our dream, but nothing changes until our internal belief genuinely matches what we say. The language we use to speak with ourselves, if positive, increases our chances of making intention and belief match. This is why what you say to yourself is infinitely more powerful than what you say to others. Accurate results begin to take place when the inner and outer dialogue align. That's the point at which magic happens.

Mahatma Gandhi said, "Be the change that you wish to see in the world." We have all heard this quote before, but I would like to offer an application of it that works for me. It is a matter of moving from consumer to creator – from follower to leader.

Learn to follow your own commands. Lead yourself first, and you will naturally begin to lead others.

Reflect on the fact that you have been with yourself longer than anyone else. You are the only one fully aware of all the skeletons in your closet, and all the lightbulbs in there waiting to illuminate. Determine what aspects of your character need addressing. Bring those out of the closet and work to change them. Become aware and the whole world becomes your school.

Constructing a Monopoly

Sam Walton: American businessman best known for founding Walmart and Sam's Club.

A couple of Brazilian men interested in launching a supermarket franchise similar to Walmart in their own country secured a meeting with Walton, who at that point was already a billionaire many times over. However, they realised during the interview that Walton was actually using the conversation to learn from them – in the event that he could discover additional areas in his own empire that he could improve on.

Like Walton, observe and learn from those things which you encounter every day. Stop pulling the wool over your eyes. Learn to sieve through your own noise, pain, prejudice, bias and excuses. Reach beyond the surface of your life to mine the gold in the person you are, because your quest for the truth of who you are and why you are here is the highest ideal.

All the while, endeavour to keep everything in balance. Understand both sides – the pros and the cons – of whatever you explore. The mark of a wise and educated person is one who considers all possibilities without bias. It is one who deciphers the noblest hypothesis from there without fear, limitations or imaginary, self-imposed boundaries.

Earlier in this book, we alluded to the idea of healthy competition, as it forces us to grow and get the best out of ourselves when the ego is out of the equation. Competition is only dangerous if it is ego-based and exaggerated – like when companies or individuals compete on price until what they are selling becomes obsolete, as no further profits can be made. In this scenario, the vendors completely lose sight of the customer. Instead of becoming more innovative, they get stuck in gridlock over price. The only outcome one can expect in a war over price is that there will be no survivors.

However, a superior application of competition does exist, which leads to growth for all and ultimately legacy for each. Though many see it as controversial, it is even more potent than competition itself.

Here I refer to monopoly.

I'm referring to a monopoly in the sense that you create something so outstanding that it is in a league of its own. Here the marketplace is dominated, or monopolised, by the sheer brilliance of your creation. By no means do I condone holding the marketplace ransom. From what I am describing, if it is achieved, nothing will come close to comparing to what you have created. This level of excellence can only be harnessed through creativity and authenticity. If you look at your vision from all possible angles, develop flexibility in thought, behaviour and action, and create without any desire or intent to mimic, you can construct your future as you wish. I have just described something that is only achievable with the hardest and most challenging work there is: thinking.

Thinking

It is no coincidence that the information age was ushered in so rapidly, as the catalyst was none other than learning to think in a way where you aren't bound to the ideas of the past or held captive to an authority bias.

Engaging in observing, reflecting and thinking without bias propels us forward into the future. Following something without stubbornly sticking to preconceived ideas and structures is what leads to discovering new truths.

Take the quantum theory, for example. Using this theory as a starting point, the quantum field theory of electrodynamics (or QED) emerged and resulted in the internet, GPS, laser beams, computers and broadband, just to name a few. The QED is considered to be one of the most accurate theories constructed to date. You might assume a theory would be congruently logical and intuitive; however, QED is not. It is a bizarre theory that reduces everything to probability, like the probability of two electrons being in different places at the same time. Believe it or not, in spite, or perhaps because, of this the QED provides an equation for that probability.

The reason I even mention it is to help open your eyes to the pure potential of the universe, a place full of possibilities. I want you to get to the place in your own mind where you are open to all possibilities yet attached to none. All EndGamers realise this. If any of the great minds in history had limited their thinking to their own previous and biographical narrative, as the potential for their destiny, very little progress would have ever been achieved.

Remember, authority is not truth. Truth should be viewed as the only real authority. To progress forward at the speed of thought, one must learn to detach from structural and imposed authorities.

Faith must always be seeking the truth, and that means your own truth. Whether your beliefs are based on a monotheistic religion or not, your ability to comprehend and decipher your own truth is what leads to growth and understanding. Never forget that contributions have been made in our world from people of all faiths, and even those with no religious faith. Whether or not religion provides you with a sense of morality, you are still responsible for your own faith in yourself, your own actions, and ultimately your own creations.

By definition, you own the monopoly on your own brand. Because if your pursuits are truly an outgrowth of who you are, then no one else can do what you do as well as you can. Your brand is distinctively your own. That fact, in essence, eliminates competition.

The key to success in business is to identify the market your brand best serves, and then begin to show up in that market. Begin small, monopolise your identified market, and grow from there organically by great design.

As a prime example, consider Steve Jobs' approach to monopolising the mobile device and personal computer market. A great deal of thought went into Apple's carefully designed product to ensure it had an irresistible appeal. Sleek, minimalist design, charismatic marketing and a fascinating user experience took their market by storm.

What makes Apple so successful? It can be found in this mix of discovering what people want and then creating a suite of proprietary systems that undergird everything they do. The unique qualities of the Apple brand provide the monopoly they have on the market. And that uniqueness comes through driving ideas (thinking) and pursuing with fervour an unparalleled level of excellence in the values of the simplicity of design and ease of use.

In light of his success, I reference Jobs' biography. Early on in life Jobs was intrigued with the birth of the PC. About that same time, he also became interested in the teachings of Yogi Paramahansa Yogananda, leading to a passionate pursuit of Eastern spirituality that influenced much of his life. Those closest to him believe some of the keys to Jobs' phenomenal successes were tied to his spiritual practices, like discovering that intuition (his own truth) was his greatest creative gift.

With that in mind, it is interesting to note that mp3 players, personal computers and even tablets existed in the market before Apple. However, Apple took a long hard look at what each one was supposed to be and then reinvented it into something of far greater value to the consumer. In other words, Apple took the essence (idea prototype) of each one and built that into an ultra-functional, magnificent creation that was irresistibly attractive to their market.

Legacies grow out of the ability to add value to people's lives through generations and even aeons of time. As you build up who you are, what you do and what you contribute, your vision moves from local survival to local contribution, progressing nationally, internationally, globally and finally astronomically. By reaching the league of visionaries like Richard Branson, Jeff Bezos and Elon Musk, you too may find yourself engaged in a race heading toward the direction of the stars.

These legacies are not superhuman. They are people who began with the premise that nothing is impossible and then, with self-reliance, marched forward, clothing the substance of their very thoughts for everyone to see. Permit yourself to do extraordinary things. If you are disciplined, reliant and committed to your dream, you can wake up your own leader, your own legacy.

This legacy must be your own. It is to be authentically yours and sprout from your own truth, using your own intuition, observation and brainstorming (thought). If you lack internal motivation, the most likely culprit is energy wasted on shame and guilt from the past. If that's the case, find a way to let go of your shame and guilt. Free up your energy. Liberate yourself, so you can recognise your inner genius to create something standalone.

Assessing patterns of behaviour will be a continual part of your journey, as both conscious and subconscious actions give clues to what is going on inside of you. Where are you investing your time, your predominant thoughts, your energies and your money right now? We invest in what we value. And with some investigation, you may discover that your value system is faulty and in need of repair.

You are the only one who can unlock the door to these discoveries. Change might be gradual, cataclysmic, or by design. The steps I am about to describe to you have the potential to change your destiny forever, as long as you want it enough and are willing to do what is necessary to get it.

Awareness

Awareness of potential puts you in touch with dormant powers. It instils within you the confidence to pursue and create what you want, rests the awareness on the first principle; or put another way, the essence of the prototype, this way remaining an original thinker.

If you are alert and perceive those subtle signals and respond accordingly, you will find they lead you down a path in which you can only ever win. It is the journey towards what you want. It is the thing that will allow you to transcend where you are or where you have been to become so much more than you could have ever wished for or even imagined. And it is simply a matter of being open and receptive to the signs the universe gives you and the legacy laid down right in front of your very eyes.

The more awareness you practise, the greater your concentration. And the greater the concentration, the more power you self-generate that can be utilised to reach your goal.

Take the example of sleep. If you become aware that you are dreaming, what happens? You begin to exercise more control in determining the content of your dreams; in other words, you achieve lucidity: a clear understanding, an awareness and the ability to control your surroundings. Simply by practising awareness of a thing you gain more control over thought, rather than thought controlling your awareness of that thing.

I often hear stories of people who experience a turning point in their lives, moments that are typically accompanied by pain or heartache. What does that moment do? It simply awakens one to the recognition that they really are the only one with the power to turn everything around.

As the universe continues expanding, maybe everything is eternally continuing forward and we are in a position to choose what we contribute to this incredible cosmic progress. Thinkers, creators, inventors and the like rule the world, for our thought processes enable us to expand beyond the known to discover the unknown.

From architecture to zoology, progress doesn't happen with memorising facts but from taking what is already known and questioning it and extrapolating it into new ideas. The flexibility to change and the bravery to challenge a tradition if you discover a better way show that you are faithful to the truth.

We typically default to following whatever pattern of thought and behaviour we saw modelled in childhood. The idea that "Everyone is doing it this way so it must be right." But when circumstances don't work in our favour, we tend to blame our parents, society, government, race, religion, social status or some other flawed imaginary limitation in the feeble attempt to relinquish our own power and divert responsibility.

It is only by realising there is no cavalry coming to your rescue, that you alone are the creator of your circumstances and condition, that you can begin to take responsibility for change. And if everything that has transpired in your life to this point was the result of your thought and behaviour patterns (that is, you had the power to create problems), then you have the creative power in yourself to solve those same problems. There is no in without an out. A negative cannot exist without a positive. Everything has its complementary opposite.

Honest self-reflection is essential to taking ownership of traits that I have built upon during this book – traits that lead you to own yourself and live your own truth. These contain the key to your success.

As simple as this sounds: improving how you think is the foundation that will make anything you could ever want, work.

Say you learn to play soccer and, as it turns out, you are as gifted as Pele, the Brazilian soccer player considered to be the greatest of all time. However, without adequate and regular training in your reflexes, intent, timing, coordination, endurance and all the other attributes needed to be a world-class athlete, you will fail. You have no more than someone with no abilities at all. Because it is the superior mix of natural talent and honed skill that creates EndGamers.

This program has been specifically designed to work on building and establishing that groundwork for you, the foundation necessary for you to then be able to execute the plans for whatever goal or target you set. There's no magic here. Learning and understanding principles of success only serve to educate you. Much like watching a movie may inspire you, nothing will change unless you take action on what you have learned. The world is full of spectators. Only a minuscule fraction of the population are performers, and an even smaller number are world-class performers. I choose to believe that the reason you picked up this book is that you want to be an EndGamer. And by developing the qualities found here, you can be.

Products that run Through Time

Nearly all great industries begin in markets small enough to dominate, as it is a rare occasion when one can break through the existing competition to create something extraordinary and capture market share immediately.

One such example is Charles Harrod, the founder of the iconic department store Harrods. Charles began by taking over his father's grocery store on Brompton Road in Knightsbridge. Charles planned to focus on personalised service by identifying the needs and wants of each prospective customer, a practice that was largely unknown at the time. Interestingly, this is the same approach used by Amazon. They consider your buying behaviours and consumer inclinations and then personalise their marketing based on those findings. This explains why Amazon's market domination is no accident. Success leaves massive clues that are often disregarded because they are so obvious to begin with.

Louis Vuitton began by creating a novel square trunk, quite different from the common round ones of the day. His thinking was that square trunks could more easily be stacked on top of one another. This distinction was enough to separate Louis Vuitton from the otherwise crowded market.

Google, Apple, Microsoft... these are not just random successes. They each provide alternate solutions to common needs. They represent services, products and technologies that are now in great demand, though initially they only existed as ideas in the minds of their creators.

Study any great product, brand or entrepreneur and you'll find that they succeeded by becoming world-class at one thing first. Then, and only then, did they expand into other markets, products and/or services.

You, too, could focus on finding the solution to one particular problem or need. Today, science shows us that we fail miserably at multitasking, take on too many things and literally scramble the brain. It's like opening too many programs at once on your computer: the system will end up crashing. Think through your new idea from multiple angles and then bring it to market with sufficient creativity, focus and persistent determination. Those who create a legacy begin by taking small steps toward organic growth. This leads to bigger and greater ideas in time, which brings us back to the importance of authenticity: owning who you are and establishing a legacy from the inside out.

Leverage From Universal Resources

Envy is ignorance, imitation is suicide. – Ralph Waldo Emerson

I believe this quote by Emerson is one of the most powerful quotes ever. Remember: you are only ever competing with yourself, and your challenge is only about being better today than you were yesterday.

Imagine there are no obstacles to your plan. Then put together the ideas around what you want and need and figure out a way to make it happen. EndGamers are fully integrated in their business or industry. They know their market and their product inside out. They are aware of their own personal strengths and limitations, and they build a support network around them that bridges their weaknesses by leveraging off the strengths of others.

Computer calculations would be used to determine the potential quantities of diamonds that rain on Saturn during a storm. A quantum computer would be utilised to perform a complex operation that contains near infinite variables. So why not employ the help of a person or machine who does what you need better than you? Delegating is an essential element to success; when one gives another permission to utilise their strength on a project it frees you up to focus on what you do best.

Your imagination is essential at this stage. Learn to use your imagination to animate your dream. Begin to court the invisible, creatively and strategically attracting each component necessary for its creation. Expect to run into obstacles; no great achievement comes without obstacles. With effort, focus, dedication and time, you begin to morph your dream into existence, and those obstacles become part of the history of your success; each atom of the universe has its own unique story to tell.

At this point it begins to take shape, and even greater exertion is necessary. Adjustments and collective effort are both required to ensure the idea is not stillborn. Once it comes to life, great care and attention are needed to nurture its growth and prosperity.

The act of creation is an act of love. When you fall in love with someone, they consume your every thought, every waking hour. Thoughts of them might even keep you awake at night. Bringing life to your idea follows a near enough identical pattern. So consider what market you could penetrate, become the thought leader, create momentum for and love your dream into existence.

EndGamers, the Architects of the World

You should well see by now that you can't sit around waiting for some random act of evolution to propel you forward to your destiny. Change doesn't happen without a catalyst, and you are that catalyst.

Do not try to reinvent the wheel. But when you observe a system and think it works 'well enough', many people believe there is no need to expand upon it, experiment with it and test its limits. An EndGamer sees 'good enough' as already broken. In other words, that is just the point at which an EndGamer comes in and says, "Let's tear this down and reconstruct it into a masterpiece."

To do so, EndGamers develop a keen insight to see fundamental flaws in existing operations. They observe something that works and then take it apart to recreate something truly great. If something is fast, they look at making it faster. If something performs okay, they look at making it perform more efficiently. The ethos of a true EndGamer is quality, progress and excellence.

Whatever one's field, be it sports, science, religion, technology – the masses are led into a habit of following a certain rule or understanding in a dogmatic way that solidifies itself into a near impossible to break ritual. On the other hand, the EndGamer in you questions everything without bias or emotional attachment, taking at times a clinical view of what needs to be done without nostalgia. This doesn't mean not respecting and adhering to traditional values, but the respect displayed is a conscious choice, not an emotional attachment.

As you pursue your vision, don't be surprised if some close to you attempt to pull you down. The old saying is true: misery likes company. That said, most of the time it is subconscious and rarely deliberate when one goes to keep misery company. If you have a partner who attempts to sabotage your progress, two things will help remedy the situation. First, communicate your dreams and plans to them in a way that demonstrates how what you are doing directly supports them in their highest values. Secondly, find a way to bring them along so they feel they are also contributing to the vision, and they will begin to be inspired. You will find that they soon will be the very people that get behind you, that follow you. Never sacrifice your vision for others; rather, inspire them to greatness no matter who it is.

The reason people rally behind certain sports teams, pop stars or products like Nike is because they want to identify themselves with that movement. They want to be part of that message. Determine your own message and lead from there.

As EndGamers create jobs, build industries, design new technologies and systems, a butterfly effect occurs. Everything affects everything else that happens in the cosmos. So, as we become more concerned with developing a better planet, many of the issues that were once battled out between sexes, races, nations and religions will begin to diminish as a natural by-product of creating a better world.

We no longer live in an 'either/or' world. If given the option between two things, you no longer have to choose, because now there is a third option: to take both.

Seven Steps to Building Your Legacy

These seven qualities are present in every legacy builder. They allow *EndGamers* to shift their financial destiny while simultaneously impacting the world.

1. Long-term thinking
Thought leaders who dream big also think long term. They are not short-sighted. Sure, we all tend to focus on what's right in front of us. We want everything now – success, money, happiness, fulfilment.

But legacies aren't built overnight. Consider the difference between a stately oak and a brilliantly coloured mushroom: though they are both a thing of beauty, one results from a maturing process that takes years, while the other springs up overnight. The mushroom will be gone tomorrow, but the oak will be there for generations to come.

This simple illustration aptly describes the difference between short-term and long-term thinking. If you truly want to build a legacy, you must play the long game. You must begin with the end in mind, knowing that the investment you make in your legacy will be your life, and the returns will last for generations.

2. Faith

Spirit without matter is expressionless and matter without spirit is motionless. – Dr John Demartini

One must possess both spirit (passion) and matter (action) to build a legacy. Your inspiration should come from a cause that serves the needs of humanity. True visionaries believe in something far more significant than themselves and commit to a cause much higher than their own selfish needs and desires.

Expand the time and space horizons in your mind. Start to see yourself beyond your own life, for you are an immortal soul. See yourself as a contribution to humanity, destined to serve vast amounts of people, and then take the necessary steps to bring your vision into reality.

3. Authenticity

Subordinating to other people's values leads to regression. Life isn't static. It doesn't standstill. You are either moving forward or you're deteriorating.

Never be afraid to live your own journey. Raise your standards and exemplify what is possible. By doing so, you cause a chain reaction in the culture around you that will begin to establish you as a leader in your own right.

My contempt for authority made me one. – Einstein

4. Positive relationship with money

Understand that money has no moral quality attached to it. In other words, it is, by nature, neither good nor bad. Rather, it is simply a means of fair exchange of value for the distribution of goods and services.

So, if you either harbour resentment toward wealth or are obsessed with an infatuation for it, you will repel it. Money has a personality of its own, and by attributing certain attitudes or feelings toward it, the resulting positive or negative magnetising charge will cause you to either attract or repel it.

5. Highest of standards

Live at the highest standards life has to offer. By investing in the highest standards, those around you will do the same. Remember to attain high standards, you must be a person worthy of receiving that.

This is the difference between the uninspired employee paid to flip hamburgers and the one who has taken years to master the craft of cooking, earning seven Michelin star. If we invest in people who are masters at their craft, we permit people to move up in all standards of life. By investing in inspiration, we inadvertently help rescue those in desperation, we move our culture forward instead of holding it back.

6. A cause

Start with the problem you want to solve in the world. – Mark Zuckerberg

Your cause must be more significant than wealth, but understand that cause cannot be fulfilled without wealth! Take Mother Teresa, for example. Tens of millions of dollars were raised and distributed as a result of the cause she represented.

All progress has a value component attached to it, whether it be healing people, entertaining them or making life easier for them. The more successful you are at fulfilling your cause, or your mission in life, the more successful you will be at building sustainable wealth.

7. Discovery

You are on a journey of discovery to unearth the concealed secrets of the universe. If your journey is to be a successful one, then you must become adept at two tasks.

The first is being observant enough to figure out what is going on around you, in the planet and the cosmos. The second is deciphering what is already in existence around you. Consider the examples of Uber, Airbnb, or even Facebook. These are all ideas and resources that were already in existence in seed form, developing and evolving, when the catalyst idea to create something far superior came about.

Greatness by Biological Design

The number one reason people don't live authentically is their willingness to subordinate to outside influence and authorities that they willingly give their power to. However, when you take this route, you end up minimising yourself, as a subordinate is less than a superior by definition.

You were not created to live in the shadows of anyone. You were born to be great. By design, you have a purpose to fulfil. Never stop pursuing until you find that purpose. And if you're struggling to see the forest for the trees when it comes to your goal, the best way to discover your path is to identify problems you are passionate about solving and then go solve them. In a nutshell, that's really what wealth building is about.

Legacies and their subsequent wealth are built on service. Successful, sustainable businesses serve ever-increasing numbers of people. It is a fantasy to think you can be wealthy without providing a valuable service to society. Believe you are capable of doing it and begin to do it.

A French mathematician says it this way: "The entire universe is designed to assist all biological organisms to grow most efficiently." Anytime we abide by this universal law, that same universe rewards us.

So learn to value yourself, and the whole world will begin to value you as well. Leaders who serve others with confidence and certainty in their cause are those who achieve wealth. It does not matter what the outside world does; do not allow yourself to be influenced and distracted from your own journey. Receive direction from inside, from your own value system about money and about life, because you will only act on what you value. You can only be motivated by what matters to you. In fact, we are biologically engineered by the glial cells in our brain to act on what we intrinsically value.

So, discover the service you want to bring to the world. And if you help people get what they want, you will get what you want.

Foolproof Success

Let's look at what you can do to help ensure the highest percentage of success in any new venture. You're no doubt familiar with the statement "The bigger the risk, the greater the reward." While that is true in most cases, you never want to set yourself up for failure. You can take calculated risks while at the same time ensuring every component and contingency that you can foresee is planned for.

Suppose you're truly serious about creating a legacy, something that lasts for generations to come. In that case, it's wise to borrow the concept I mentioned earlier from the engineering world called the margin of safety. The margin, or factor of safety, is the measured ability of a structure to carry a weight capacity that goes well beyond the anticipated or actual load. In other words, it means the structure is exponentially stronger than it needs to be for its intended purpose.

So, when architects create the design for a bridge across a body of water, for example, they build sufficient support to hold multiple times the weight that would ever be on that bridge at any given time. This ensures the safety of its users.

The wise EndGamer will practise a similar idea when designing their future. Build sufficient support to carry you through the lean times and secure enough savings and investments to ensure the ability to grow and sustain your legacy for generations to come. Investment is not only financial; it's investing in creating friendships and relationships where everyone benefits and grows.

One of the most critical elements for foolproof success is a clear vision of where you're going and what you want to accomplish. Forward thinkers clarify their end goal and intricately design the steps to get there. This approach allows you to see potential obstacles and take action necessary to resolve them even before they appear. This is precisely what Tesla was doing inside his mind before bringing his creations to life.

I applied this same principle whenever I was preparing to compete in an upcoming martial arts match. If the rounds were scheduled for five minutes, I prepared for a 15 to 20-minute round to ensure that I would feel like I was doing nothing in the ring unless I were pushing the pace. My training partners were almost always bigger, faster and stronger. I ran with ankle weights, up gradients and in higher altitudes. My training was geared towards pushing the limits of what was possible, so much so that the actual fight ended up being the easy part.

You don't need complex formulas or PhD-level training to build a legacy. Look at the great investor Warren Buffett's company Berkshire Hathaway. At the outset, Buffett knew what he wanted. He mapped out a strategy that was sound and virtually foolproof. It was also simple. But with the addition of time, patience and integrity, one single share of Berkshire Hathaway is now worth well over $250,000 (at the time of this writing, that is). A clear vision coupled with simplicity of design, integrity and patience to persist were primary ingredients in Buffett's success.

A good friend of mine and one of the UK's leading experts of constructing a legacy Dillon Dhanecha, once compared financial success to getting in shape. Getting in shape is simple: eat healthy, nutritious food, remove refined sugar from your diet except for special occasions and cheat meals, do a few push-ups, and run for 20 minutes every day. But if you did this consistently for a year, imagine how different you would look. It's so simple anybody can do it, but very few people actually follow through with it.

In the same way, compounding your wealth and building your legacy is not a complex process, but it requires a clear vision of your end goal detailing each step in between, and patience, to get there.

If you're ready, begin by looking deep inside your soul to find your dream. Discover your passion. Design a strategy. Map out a definitive, clear plan. Use your own intelligence to make it happen, instead of relying on the opinions of others, as that one thing gets people side-tracked and pulls them back more than anything else. Learn to figure out for yourself, and you'll never look back.

Championship Legacy

Some are born great, some achieve greatness, and some have greatness thrust upon them. – Twelfth Night, William Shakespeare

While running regular family errands in Westfield Mall one Saturday afternoon, I was surprised to see among the crowd the famous Brazilian Jiu-Jitsu champion Roger Gracie, only a short distance from me holding his son's hand.

After a second glance, I paused, and in an instant my mind was thrown back through generations. This is history standing in front of me... legacy... royalty. Many consider Roger to be the greatest Jiu-Jitsu fighter of all time, having won ten gold medals. And I certainly wouldn't disagree. In addition, he's a member of the family responsible for the climactic overthrow of so many superstitious and dogmatic ideas surrounding martial arts. By abolishing outdated norms and old customs, Gracie Jiu-Jitsu became legendary in the world of unarmed combat. As a result, the Gracie family brought discipline, structure and intelligence to an immeasurable number of people, not to mention self-preservation and protection.

In order to better understand the legacy of the Gracie family, we need to turn back the clock to 1914 when judo expert and prize-fighter Mitsuyo Maeda was given the opportunity to travel to Brazil with a large Japanese immigration colony. (In time, Maeda would single-handedly bring judo to Brazil and the United Kingdom, as well as several other countries.)

While there, an influential Brazilian businessman named Gastão Gracie helped Maeda get established. To show his gratitude, Maeda offered to teach traditional Japanese Jiu-Jitsu to Gastão's oldest son, Carlos Gracie. Carlos was a star student, and in turn passed his knowledge down to his younger brothers.

Helio Gracie, Gastão's youngest son, had always been a physically frail child. As a result, most of the techniques of his older brother Carlos were too difficult for him to execute. Eager to learn Jiu-Jitsu for himself, the brothers began modifying the traditional moves to accommodate any visible weakness by focusing on leverage and timing over strength and speed. In time, the brothers modified virtually all the techniques and Gracie-Brazilian Jiu-Jitsu was born.

Fast forward to 1993, when the Gracies promoted the first-ever Ultimate Fighting Championship event. Not since the days of the gladiators in Rome would there be such a challenge to test every area of unarmed combat in order to see truth prevail... and it did! Other than the late Bruce Lee's influence, there had not been such a resurgence in martial arts as this, and one family's lineage was responsible: the Gracies.

Continuous refinement and improvement whilst maintaining exacting fundamental principles allowed the art to evolve, the family created a legacy by unconsciously seeking the truth, and in essence illustrating how the world rewards us for improvement and penalises us for ignorance and stagnation.

No business or industry ever fail. People do, and quite simply they fail by a lack of improvement. Let's look at it this way: the industry evolves. From the earliest professions in the world, you will still see the essence of them existing, just in a different form.

From information being stored in cave paintings to now, information is recorded and stored on quantum computers; entertainment, music, travel transport have always been there, since antiquity. A master will be observant of this and have the flexibility to adapt by thought and what is it other than the ability to observe change without being tied to the past.

Roger's father Mauricio Gomes, one of only a few masters in the world to have been awarded a red belt, brought Jiu-Jitsu to the United Kingdom in 1998. In the absence of any other clubs and only a couple of practitioners in the entire country, Mauricio along with his son Roger, began to teach and in doing so produced a number of World Champions and legions of competent practitioners, once again building something from nothing. In doing so every lesson and every moment added to the equity of experience and understanding of execution of these two masters and undoubtedly the physical practice accompanied by teaching served to reinforce their own understanding. Learning without application is useless and application without learning only serves in the creation of an automaton. Yet when one teaches and practises simultaneously you have evolution.

Capitalising on such a rare opportunity, I walked over to Roger and introduced myself. Roger introduced his son Tristan establishing the unspoken respect of fathers. "I have a son as well, and would be honoured if he could train with you."

"Of course!" Roger smiled. "Bring him down to the academy..."

Indeed the desire to pick up fighting once again reappeared but in the most unexpected form; nature has a strange way of continuing what we start. Sometimes the desires we have are played out through our very offspring or even future generations; only 18 months after I took my son to the academy, he entered the European Championships and walked out with Gold.

Conclusion

It was 1942: the Venezuelan, Rafael Solano, washed out and in despair says to his comrades "I can't do this anymore, there's no use going on any longer. See this stone? It makes 999,999 I've picked up and not a diamond so far. If I pick up another, it will make a million – but what's the use? I'm quitting." It had been months sieving through hundreds of thousands of worthless rocks. On the brink of despair, Solano said, "I'm through." One of the men bellowed, "Pick up another, make it a million." "I will do it," Solano said, grabbing a pile of stones, he pulled one out. It was almost the size of a cricket ball. "It's here," he declared, "the last one." For that millionth stone, Harry Winston, the New York jeweller, paid Rafael Solano $200,000. Named 'The Liberator', it was the largest diamond ever found, and many attribute Harry Winston the coining the phrase, one in a million.

December 2020 New Year's Eve: the timing couldn't be better as I wound down my writing, concluding this final chapter. I walked into Winston's jewellers on New Bond Street to procure the teardrop diamond I had chosen for the proposal to my one in a million, Liana.

You now have in your possession a blueprint on how to exercise, control and direct your thinking processes in order to diligently pursue and create your dreams. At the same time, we've demonstrated the importance of maintaining the flexibility of thought to accept new ideas for continuous improvement by breaking free of any dogmatic chains of thought. But perhaps your most important discovery in this final chapter will be to realise that the lessons you have been learning are about taking inspired action, becoming self-reliant and awakening to the truth that you are the catalyst that creates the change you want to see in the world.

The genie in the bottle is you.

I am now passing the baton to you. As an Architect of Destiny, your future is right before your eyes, and you are the only one responsible for writing it the way you want it to read. The conclusion of this book is not the end, it's only the beginning...

Acknowledgments

Liana Somkhshvili, Nina S, Tamaz S, George S, Alice S,
David Shalolashvili, Lili, Levani S, Lena, Anastasia, Krill, Dan, Alina,
Sofi W, Alkan & Moubetjel Volkan, Alkan R V, Yasemin V, David Hess,
Nevzat & Miko families, Dr Marie McGrath, Dr Massimo Stocchi Fontana,
Ornella, Carlo F, Simon A Ong, Gaven Orlando, Marc J Burton,
Dillon Dhanecha, Ravi Chopra, Mellissa Laycy, Marc Tidd, Ahmet Mustafa,
Hattie, Mustafa, Aynur, Patrick Drake, Kylie Flavell, E Emin, Lazo Freeman,
Carlos Espinal, Vedat, Sibel, Labinot Kransiqi, Marijana Jakupi, Debora
Krasniqi, Alex B, Ari, Gia, Adam & Melody Grant, Daniel Priestly,
Boris Kofman, Alain Dona, Seng Khou, Tom Errington, Lewis Goodsell,
Filipe Dantas, Ascher Grant, Sergey Men, Shaka, Shane McPherson,
Jamie Lisa, Salim, Ed Buckley, Daniel Francis, Enes Azemi, Thiago,
Pritan A, Kem, Antonio, Maurice Marshall, Sam K, Angelika,
Piers Dunhill, Laurent De Brabandt, David De Min, Bilge Kacmaz,
Viktor J, Vasily, Aya, Jessica Patterson, Adam Cumberland, James Taylor,
Fadi Samhoun, Milly Elvis, Andrew Smith, Charles Negromonte,
Charles Priebatsch, Mauricio Gomes, Roger Gracie, Kywan Gracie,
Vik Hothi, Junio, J W Demile, R Bustillo, Richard Osterfield,
Charli Fisher, Zak Johnson, Hugo Martini, Eloise C, Victoria Alexis,
Tom Eulenberg, Rebecca Riofrio, Saylan, Sedat, Richard Marshall,
Antonia & Con Hatz, Natalia K, Naomi Buff, Brian Would, King Ahmed,
Reuel Sing, John Laithwaite, Michelle Kleanthous, Matthew Roberts,
Peter McKenzie, Muladi Badibengi, Robert Nova, George Barbor, Suraj,
Ravi and Victoria Sharma, Emperor A. L, Labinot Zequiri, Vlera Potera,
Danio, Colin Turner, Owen Fitzpatrick, Brian Tracy, Dr J DeMartini,
Dr Bandler & McKenna, Derek Mills, Andrew Masanto, Katherine Jegede,
Tarun Ghulati, Preeti Rana, Colin Rose, Emma Griffths Chris G,
Tony Selemi, Dan Fleyshman, Carmen Reed, Nolla, Emma Radin,
Chelsea Green, Natasha Kotlyarova, Brydie Taylor, Charles Oakley,
Alla, Viktoria, Lydia, Suza, Goda, Sophie Churchill, Cece, Oona, Kush,

Derya, Luke, Ombeline, Micheal James, Aimee D, Stefani, Liz Dring, YR,
Sofia B, Hana, Pakiza, Jake, Bianca, Nadine, Ali Karakas, Carol Stone,
Ekatarina, Zola, Simone, B Andrews, Carlo Viva, Jack Toner, Jayraj,
Kai Duggal, Shaub Miah, Charles K, Anthony Wade, Laurie Wang,
Lorna D, Jade, Anna Franco, Samar, Yasmin M, Rehan Jelali, Natalia D'S,
Katya Boirand, Eleney, Natalie Smyth, Ozlem, Harold, Sakina, Jay Bajaj,
Charles Ngo, Johnny Cassell, Mark Stratum, Martin Bugaj, Kunal Tulsiani,
Mahesh T, Kavita T, Cevat, Jason McNab, Pola P, Hari, Nick Jovanovic,
Giuseppe Rodio, Risha P, Elinga, Peng, Susan Ruth, Pete Salmon,
Gareth Howard, David Cenicola, Ian Howe, De Brabandt Foundation,
RSPCA, Mental Health Foundation & Plan International.

Lightning Source UK Ltd.
Milton Keynes UK
UKHW040636020323
417918UK00004B/164